CYMBELINE

The RSC Shakespeare

Edited by Jonathan Bate and Eric Rasmussen

Chief Associate Editors: Jan Sewell and Will Sharpe

Associate Editors: Trey Jansen, Eleanor Lowe, Lucy Munro,
Dee Anna Phares, Héloïse Sénéchal

CYMBELINE

Textual editing: Eric Rasmussen and Will Sharpe

Introduction: Jonathan Bate and Will Sharpe

Shakespeare's Career in the Theatre: Jonathan Bate

Commentary: Will Sharpe and Héloïse Sénéchal

Scene-by-Scene Analysis: Will Sharpe

In Performance: Penelope Freedman (RSC stagings)
and Will Sharpe (overview)

The Director's Cut (interviews by Will Sharpe and Kevin Wright):
Dominic Cooke and Emma Rice

The RSC Shakespeare

WILLIAM SHAKESPEARE

CYMBELINE

Edited by
Jonathan Bate, Eric Rasmussen and Will Sharpe

Introduced by Jonathan Bate and Will Sharpe

Macmillan

Published by arrangement with Modern Library, an imprint of The Random House Publishing Group, a division of Random House, Inc.

Published 2011 by
MACMILLAN PUBLISHERS LTD
registered in England, company number 785998, of 4 Crinan Street, London N1 9XW.
Companies and representatives throughout the world

ISBN-13 978–0–230–30090–3 paperback

CONTENTS

INTRODUCTION

'AND VIEWED HER IN HER BED'

Many commentators have observed how fitting it is that *The Tempest* is printed at the beginning of the First Folio of Shakespeare's plays. Its reflections on art, together with the resemblance of Prospero to a dramatist and his island to a theatre, where a play is staged within the play by actors who are spirits, make it seem like a Shakespearean showpiece, a summation of his art. Far fewer commentators have considered how equally appropriate it is that *Cymbeline* is printed at the end of the First Folio. Though entitled *The Tragedy of Cymbeline*, it ends not with multiple deaths but with family reunion and political reconciliation. 'Pardon's the word to all' as revelations pile in upon one another, each of them 'a mark of wonder', while a nation is restored to peace: the play could equally well have been classed as a comedy or a British history. The stylistic experimentation almost serves as an ironic epilogue to the Folio's tripartite division into comedies, histories and tragedies: tragical-comical-historical-pastoral, *Cymbeline* would have been Polonius' favourite work in the canon. Furthermore, in a manner analogous to the wittily extreme variations on classical motifs in Baroque art, both the narrative arc and the characterization revisit and revise, in a highly self-conscious manner, an array of favourite Shakespearean motifs: the cross-dressed heroine, the move from court to country, obsessive sexual jealousy, malicious machiavellian plotting, the interrogation of Roman values.

For Shakespeare, the material provided the opportunity to reach back to some of his earliest work. As in *Titus Andronicus*, a copy of Ovid's *Metamorphoses* is brought on stage as a prop. It is Innogen's bedtime reading: 'She hath been reading late, / The tale of Tereus. Here the leaf's turned down / Where Philomel gave up'. The allusion marks the moment at which Innogen is betrayed. An eyewitness account of a performance of the play in 1611 makes much of this scene, in which the machiavellian Iachimo emerges from a trunk. Watching for the plot, what Dr Simon Forman seems to have remembered most vividly was Innogen's bedchamber:

> Remember also the story of Cymbeline king of England, in Lucius' time, how Lucius came from Octavius Caesar for tribute, and being denied, after sent Lucius with a great army of soldiers who landed at Milford Haven, and after were vanquished by Cymbeline, and Lucius taken prisoner, and all by means of 3 outlaws, of the which 2 of them were the sons of Cymbeline, stolen from him when they were but 2 years old by an old man whom Cymbeline banished, and he kept them as his own sons 20 years with him in a cave. And how [one] of them slew Cloten, that was the queen's son, going to Milford Haven to seek the love of Innogen the king's daughter, whom he had banished also for loving his daughter, and how the Italian that came from her love conveyed himself into a chest, and said it was a chest of plate sent from her love and others, to be presented to the king. And in the deepest of the night, she being asleep, he opened the chest, and came forth of it, and viewed her in her bed, and the marks of her body, and took away her bracelet, and after accused her of adultery to her love, etc. And in the end how he came with the Romans into England and was taken prisoner, and after revealed to Innogen, who had turned herself into man's apparel and fled to meet her love at Milford Haven, and chanced to fall on the cave in the woods where her 2 brothers were, and how by eating a sleeping dram they thought she had been dead, and laid her in the woods, and the body of Cloten by her, in her love's apparel that he left behind him, and how she was found by Lucius, etc.

'*Viewed* her in her bed . . . and after accused her': whereas in *Titus* Lavinia's quoting of Philomel's tragic tale is the means to the revelation of her own rape, Iachimo can destroy Innogen's reputation simply by looking at her. His removal of the bracelet from her arm is a symbolic violation of her chastity. In Shakespeare's other rape story, the poem of *Lucrece*, Tarquin presses violently down on his victim's breasts, but here Iachimo merely watches and reports, noting in particular an identifying mole on her left breast. It is the eyes of a spectator that do the undressing here, not the tearing hands of a Tarquin. When Iachimo himself alludes to the rapacious emperor – 'Our' Tarquin, a fellow-Roman – he rewrites the night scene of *Lucrece* in a lyrical mode: 'Our Tarquin thus / Did softly press the rushes, ere he wakened / The chastity he wounded'. The sibilance seems tender rather than sinister: 'Softly press' suggests not only stealth, but also a lover's touch. And 'wounded' grossly understates the severity of Tarquin's deed. This has the effect of sublimating the image of rape – Philomel gives up as in a dream, not in brutal reality as on the stage of *Titus*, thus making it easier for the audience to put itself in the position of Iachimo. To note and to wonder at the beauty of the sleeping Innogen does not seem to do any harm. Yet 'yellow Iachimo' does work harm, and it takes all the play's twists and turns, including an apparent death and an actual physical violation when Posthumus strikes Fidele/Innogen, to undo that harm.

The audience, then, is forced to confront its own complicity in Iachimo's deed. His gaze is ours. Shakespeare makes the point by means of the chimney-piece in the bedroom. While in the room, Iachimo records 'the contents o'th'story'. In his subsequent narration to Posthumus he reveals them:

> The chimney
> Is south the chamber, and the chimney-piece
> Chaste Dian bathing: never saw I figures
> So likely to report themselves; the cutter
> Was as another nature dumb, outwent her,
> Motion and breath left out.

The gaze is fixed on the naked Diana bathing: Iachimo and with him the audience stand in the position occupied in Ovidian mythology by the hunter Actaeon, who is metamorphosed into a stag and torn to pieces by his own hounds as punishment for his desiring gaze upon the goddess of chastity. Shakespeare uses this reference to introduce the motif of auto-destructive sexual desire. The poetry almost makes us forget that we never saw the chimney-piece: what we witnessed was the sleeping figure of Innogen, as mediated through the language of Iachimo's gorgeous but prurient soliloquy.

The art of the chimney-piece, like that of Hermione's statue in *The Winter's Tale*, is said to have outdone nature. A few lines earlier, Iachimo has reported that the tapestry in the chamber told the story of Mark Antony meeting Cleopatra at Cydnus; here Shakespeare echoes back his own recent play in which Enobarbus describes Cleopatra at Cydnus as being so desirable that 'but for vacancy' the air would have joined the people of the city in going to gaze on her. The fictive chimney-piece recapitulates and goes beyond this: the artist's figures seem on the verge of speech and movement, they are 'likely to report themselves' and though they are 'dumb' they seem to make nature seem dumber. The air has vacated nature and entered the artwork. When we associate Diana with Innogen, the goddess seems to step down from the chimney-piece and become embodied on stage in the form of a lovely boy-actor. The image effects in the audience's mind what *The Winter's Tale* feigns to deliver in performance: the metamorphosis of art into life. This is late Shakespeare at his most sophisticated and self-consciously inventive.

Simon Forman's report reveals how much detail an attentive spectator could grasp in a complex Shakespearean drama – though he does seem to have momentarily muddled Cloten and Posthumus, just as Innogen/Fidele does. The account also suggests that Shakespearean playgoers worried little about the plot's dependence on frequent coincidences. Strikingly, though, this spectator's enthusiasm peters out towards the end: the closing reunions and the descent of Jupiter in Posthumus' dream do not merit a mention. The long and outlandish final scene is extremely difficult to stage effectively: it has sometimes been played as parody, is often heavily cut, and has even been comprehensively rewritten (by George Bernard Shaw).

In the movement of the action from court to country, *Cymbeline* has a similar structure to the more popular and better-known *Winter's Tale*. The two plays were probably written within a year of each other. The similarities are abundant. A man is falsely led to believe in his wife's infidelity, with the result that his powers of reasoning are distorted and his language collapses into crabbed, dense invective against female wiles:

> Is there no way for men to be, but women
> Must be half-workers? We are all bastards,
> And that most venerable man, which I
> Did call my father, was I know not where
> When I was stamped. Some coiner with his tools
> Made me a counterfeit . . .
> . . .
> . . . for there's no motion
> That tends to vice in man, but I affirm
> It is the woman's part: be it lying, note it,
> The woman's: flattering, hers: deceiving, hers:
> Lust and rank thoughts, hers, hers: revenges, hers:
> Ambitions, covetings, change of prides, disdain,
> Nice longing, slanders, mutability,
> All faults that may be named, nay, that hell knows,
> Why, hers, in part or all . . .

In fact, throughout Shakespeare's works, most of these vices and faults are to be found in the men's parts, not the women's. It is the woman – Marina, Perdita, Innogen – who restores harmony.

In *Cymbeline*, as in *The Winter's Tale*, she does so in combination with the forces of nature. The febrile air of court intrigue is cleared when we move outdoors and encounter princes disguised as shepherds. It is perhaps in *Cymbeline* that Shakespeare's art of natural observation is at its most acute. The supposedly dead Fidele is apostrophized with the phrase 'The azured harebell, like thy veins'. The colour and structure of the harebell does precisely resemble those of human veins. Then there is Belarius speaking of how his two adopted sons show princely natures even as they are dressed as shepherds:

> O thou goddess,
> Thou divine Nature, thou thyself thou blazon'st
> In these two princely boys! They are as gentle
> As zephyrs blowing below the violet,
> Not wagging his sweet head; and yet as rough,
> Their royal blood enchafed, as the rud'st wind,
> That by the top doth take the mountain pine,
> And make him stoop to th'vale . . .

The wind has the capacity not to move a violet but to flatten a mountain pine: Shakespeare likes that paradox.

The association of Innogen with nature goes back to the bedroom scene. The key token of recognition, the mole on her breast, is 'cinque-spotted, like the crimson drops / I'th'bottom of a cowslip'. Is there any other English poet save the country labourer John Clare who could have created such a simile, who has such an eye as acute as Shakespeare's for the intricacies of natural history and the apt metaphorical application of them to human encounters?

THE CRITICS DEBATE

Perhaps more than any other Shakespearean play, *Cymbeline* has polarized critics and audiences in their judgements on its quality as a work of art. Yet despite an uneven critical heritage, the twentieth century going into the early twenty-first has seen a massive resurgence in its popularity on both page and stage, and recent criticism now widely accepts it as a masterwork that no longer needs to be explained away or apologized for.

Historically, critics have been divided over the play's mixed genre, improbable plot, characterization, moral texture, difficult language, bifurcated political position and contrived ending. Dr Johnson's view, in his 1765 edition of Shakespeare, is typical:

> This play has many just sentiments, some natural dialogues and some pleasing scenes, but they are obtained at the expense of much incongruity. To remark the folly of the fiction, the absurdity of the conduct, the confusion of the names and manners of different times, and the impossibility of the events in any system of life, were to waste criticism upon unresisting imbecility, upon faults too evident for detection, and too gross for aggravation.[1]

George Bernard Shaw was even more dismissive:

> I do not defend *Cymbeline*. It is for the most part stagey trash of the lowest melodramatic order, in parts abominably written, throughout intellectually vulgar, and judged in point of thought

by modern intellectual standards, vulgar, foolish, offensive, indecent, and exasperating beyond all tolerance.[2]

But the play has always had its defenders. The early nineteenth-century essayist William Hazlitt thought that:

Cymbeline is one of the most delightful of Shakespear's [sic] historical plays. It may be considered as a dramatic romance ... The reading of this play is like going on a journey with some uncertain object at the end of it, and in which the suspense is kept up and heightened by the long intervals between each action. Though the events are scattered over such an extent of surface, and relate to such a variety of characters, yet the links which bind the different interests of the story together are never entirely broken. The most straggling and seemingly casual incidents are contrived in such a manner as to lead at last to the most complete development of the catastrophe. The ease and conscious unconcern with which this is effected only makes the skill more wonderful.[3]

The last act, in which all the plot threads reconvene in a series of almost comically improbable revelations has, like the play as a whole, been for a long time the object of critical scorn before more recently finding a reacceptance, especially in performance. Critics are now in fairly unanimous agreement on its dizzying, strange brilliance: 'The finale is an intricate, beautiful machine in which an astonishing number of disguises are removed, misunderstandings swept away and reunions accomplished.'[4]

Traditionally, the play's three main plots have been identified as the marriage/wager plot (involving Innogen's marriage to Posthumus, his resultant banishment, Cloten's attempted 'revenge', and the wager Posthumus makes with Iachimo over Innogen's fidelity), the dynastic plot (involving the return of Guiderius and Arviragus, Cymbeline's long-lost sons, and, unbeknownst to them, the future rulers of Britain), and the nations plot (involving the Roman invasion of Britain over Cymbeline's refusal to pay the required tribute, and the eventual reunion of the two powers). Critical concerns have recently engaged with each of these elements and debated the politics of the play in terms of gender and state and the interplay between them.

THE WAGER PLOT

The wager story had its roots in popular folklore, narrated many times in the medieval period, though Shakespeare seems to have based his plot on a version in Boccaccio's *Decameron* (Day 2, Novella 9), in which:

> The villain, Ambrogiuolo, gets into Ginevra's bedchamber in a chest and steals a ring, a purse, a girdle and a gown. Bernabò, the husband, is convinced, not by these, but by the description of a mole with golden hairs under his wife's left breast. He orders a servant to kill Ginevra, but the servant helps her to escape in male clothes.[5]

Many nineteenth- and early twentieth-century critics chose to take sides over the wager plot, and to make moral judgements upon the action. For a long time Innogen was seen as an ideal portrait of womanhood and wifely virtue:

> in Imogen we have an embodiment of the highest possible characteristics of womanhood – untainted health of soul, unshaken fortitude, constancy that withstands all trials, inexhaustible forbearance, unclouded intelligence, love that never wavers, and unquenchable radiance of spirit.[6]

Unsurprisingly, many critics denounced Posthumus:

> The wrong of Posthumus is the commonest of moral perversions, the false sense of honour that dares not refuse a challenge, whatever the moral cost implied in its acceptance, it is the perversion which is the product of social narrowness and artificiality; the duellist dreads the sentiment immediately surrounding him in the coterie that has dubbed itself 'men of honour', and forgets the great world with its balanced judgements and eternal principles of right.[7]

More recently, masculine anxieties and a male-driven culture of commodity have also been seen as driving the wager. Twentieth-century feminist criticism was especially interested in the socially constructed 'virgin/whore' binary that women are fetishistically bracketed into by men, and the wager plot can be seen as a literal playing out of this, with the two men betting over Innogen's chastity. Her sexual purity has been interpreted as prudery, and, paradoxically, the very thing that makes her an object of sexual desire. Rather than the moral touchstone or untouchable object of desire that towers above the other characters in the play, Innogen has also been seen as marginal to the male relationships in the play, subjugated by a domineering, insecure and oppressive patriarchy: 'Innogen begins the play as its primary defining figure, defining herself, her husband, and the dramatic focus of the audience; by the end, she has learnt her place.'[8] In psychoanalytic critic Janet Adelman's formulation, the play's 'happy ending' is seen as 'radically contingent' on Innogen's 'self-loss, on the ascendancy of male authority and the circumscription of the female ... the unmaking of female authority, the curtailing of female pride, as much for Imogen as for the wicked queen'.[9]

Although we know Iachimo is lying about sleeping with Innogen, critics have argued for a kind of sexual conquest in the 'trunk' scene and this violation has also been seen as a metaphorical playing out of one of the play's other plots:

> In this context, Giacomo's [modernized spelling of *Iachimo's*] intrusion into Innogen's bedroom becomes itself a tale of a British 'haven' infiltrated by scurrilous foreign forces. His secret incursion becomes an enemy 'voyage upon her', its invasive metaphors speak of assaulting the 'walls' of Innogen's honour, the 'temples' of her mind.[10]

THE DYNASTIC PLOT AND THE PASTORAL MODE

Although the figures of Cymbeline's sons, Guiderius and Arviragus, came from Holinshed's *Chronicles*, Shakespeare's source for the play's quasi-historical narrative, the Wales plot has its roots in romances and folk stories. This part of the drama has frequently been seen to share in the conventions of pastoral: 'In common with a number of his other plays from *As You Like It*, via *King Lear* to *The Tempest*, Shakespeare's *Cymbeline* uses an excursion to a wilderness setting so that characters can return to their normal lives and roles, refreshed and, to an extent, sorted.'[11] The pastoral environment has been seen as shaping the princes, and providing them with an earthy, simple model of morality they can apply to courtly life on their return:

> The fine young men, schooled to endurance by their teacher and their habitat, take their places among the other courtiers naturally enough, their youthful discipline offering the promise that Cymbeline's kingdom will be reorganized on new and different moral lines. Nature has raised these boys so that they can return to a birthright compromised in their absence and purify it by the simple strengths of their natural characters.[12]

A more recent critic has argued conversely that:

> *Cymbeline* is innovative because it dares to follow the characters home and suggests that their moral transformation may not last ... What marks the boys' nobility out as far as Belarius is concerned is their ability to imagine themselves into his heroic stories, to occupy another world that they have never personally known. Ironically, however, this imaginative understanding of the 'other' is merely a restitution of the unexamined heroic but also brutal values that caused Belarius to flee in the first place.[13]

The culmination of the fictitious pastoral and the play's move back into history, where the princes can become kings, as well as the mixing of plots and genres, has been brilliantly described by the critic Robert Henke:

> Belarius recognizes that the arrival and killing of Cloten spell the beginning and the end of his protected, pastoral theatre and initiates the move back into history ... The killing of Cloten initiates a more active interplay between pastoral and history than that effected by Belarius's cave stories. Violence inappropriate to

the pastoral decorum invades its boundaries – although the displacement of violence offstage adjusts the levels of violence in a manner appropriate to a tragicomic decorum. And Belarius realizes that as an uncanny messenger, Cloten is an earnest of further negotiations with the court. As 'pastoral-historical', *Cymbeline* aims to join the 'lopp'd branches' to the 'old stock' of the 'stately cedar': to graft the pastoral denizens Guiderius and Belarius back onto the British dynastic tree.[14]

KING OF BRITAIN

A number of critics have emphasized the play's roots in fairytale. Northrop Frye, one of the most influential critics of the twentieth century, saw the play as unhistorical, and its fairytale elements as defining:

> *Cymbeline* is not, to put it mildly, a historical play: it is pure folk tale, featuring a cruel stepmother with her loutish son, a calumniated maiden, lost princes brought up in a cave by a foster father, a ring of recognition that works in reverse, villains displaying false trophies of adultery and faithful servants displaying equally false trophies of murder, along with a great firework display of dreams, prophecies, signs, portents, and wonders.[15]

Much recent criticism, however, has focused on the play's politics in the widest sense, on the play's treatment of Rome as well as its evocation of British nationhood. J. P. Brockbank adjudged the accounts of Holinshed to be 'consonant' with the adventures of Brute, founder of the British nation according to Geoffrey of Monmouth, and noted that Shakespeare's dovetailing of sources creates a magical, principally theatrical, yet brilliantly researched historical narrative:

> Shakespeare's reading offers a paradigm for an action which makes the reconciliation with Rome a high event in the magical movement of British history from the vision of Brute to the golden prospect of the vision of Cadwallader ... but he had scope still to exercise his imagination on other elements in the chronicle. In pursuit of that 'odd and distinctive music' he chose

to modulate from the Brutan into the Roman key and from the Roman into the Renaissance Italian.[16]

Earlier in the twentieth century, G. Wilson Knight had seen the play as dramatizing the passing of the baton from Rome to what would become England, which could be read in terms of the neoclassical world of the Renaissance taking up – in no small part through Shakespeare's art – the torch of the classical world:

> Certainly we are to feel the Roman power vanishing into the golden skies of a Britain destined to prove worthy of her Roman tutelage. Jupiter's blessing on Posthumus' marriage and the soothsayer's vision thus make similar statements. Both symbolise a certain transference of virtue from Rome to Britain. Shakespeare's two national faiths are here married; his creative faith in ancient Rome, felt in the dramas from *Titus Andronicus* to *Coriolanus*, and his faith in England.[17]

Other critics felt the union between the two nations, based on mutual respect, rather than the supersession of one over the other, was key:

> I find it difficult to accept [G. Wilson] Knight's idea of Britain taking over from Rome. Iachimo is a corrupt Roman and he repents. Cloten is a villainous Briton and he is killed. Although there can be no doubt that some in the Jacobean audience would indeed see themselves as the successors of Rome, the play is not talking about the succession of empires but about the only true form of empire, which is when vassalage is removed, and union is a contract freely entered into.[18]

Gendering has also been identified as central to the Roman thread of the play, leading to the banishment of the Queen – who stands in defiant vocal opposition to Rome – from the final act: 'powerful and rebellious females in native historiography threatened the establishment of a stable, masculine identity for the early modern state'.[19] This gendering of nations has had a powerful hold on recent interpretations, including application of a 'parthenogenesis' theory, which argued for *Cymbeline*'s desire to expunge the female from his world; not only his wife, the wicked Queen, but also the memory of the mother of his sons, and ultimately find union with the male world of Rome (also used to explain the play's perceived structural problems):

> In *Cymbeline*, a plot ostensibly about the recovery of trust in woman and the renewal of marriage is circumscribed by a plot in which distrust of women is the great lesson to be learned and in which male autonomy depends upon the dissolution of marriage. Moreover, the effect of the Imogen-Posthumus plot is everywhere qualified by the effect of the Cymbeline plot, and the two plots seem to be emotionally at cross-purposes: if one moves toward the resumption of heterosexual bonds in marriage, the other moves toward the renewed formation of male bonds as Cymbeline regains both his sons and his earlier alliance with an all-male Rome, the alliance functionally disrupted by his wife. Hence the emotional incoherence of the last scene: the resolution of each plot interrupts the other, leaving neither satisfactorily resolved.[20]

The scholar Robert S. Miola has argued that the play's treatment of Rome veers in and out of, and ultimately rejects, the social and behavioural codes Shakespeare had worked so carefully to delineate in his previous, less fantastical, Roman plays:

> *Cymbeline*'s loose aggregation of miniatures combines to portray a Rome that gradually yields to Britain. The chaste Roman matron Lucrece finally gives way to Imogen, the British maiden for whom honour and reputation are idle impositions, oft lost without deserving. Comic flexibility, evident in Posthumus as well as in Imogen, succeeds tragic constancy as austere *Romanitas* dissolves into historical-pastoral romance.[21]

Politically self-conscious critic Terence Hawkes, meanwhile, focuses on the significance of Wales in the play's various articulations of nationhood:

> After all, any future 'mixing' of Roman and British ways of life is surely implicitly to be modelled on and judged by the success or

otherwise of the prior mixing of the cultures of Wales and England. This, evidently, is the point the Welsh setting seeks to affirm. And that raises a major difficulty in *Cymbeline*. Assertions of an achieved Britishness certainly abound ... But where are the Welsh? Even though two-thirds of the play is set in Wales, we meet no native-born Welsh people there – unless we count the two 'beggars' of whom Innogen asks directions [3.6.8–9]. Their status may be significant.[22]

There has also been an interest in seeing the play as a Jacobean panegyric, and many commentators have felt that it is utterly confusing until placed in the context of the historical circumstances of James I's reign:

Cymbeline (in Shakespeare, though not in Holinshed) has one daughter and two sons; so did James I. James's elder son, Henry, was created Prince of Wales in 1610, and some editors point to 1610 as a likely date for *Cymbeline*; and in connexion with the stress on peace with which the play closes, it is perhaps of interest that 1610 was the only year, of this period, in which all the European states were at peace. Lastly, *Cymbeline*'s final submission to Rome, even after he has won the war against the Romans, might have had some topical value in view of James's efforts to enter into friendly negotiations with Papal Rome ... the audience must have made a complex identification: the peace is both the peace of the world at the time of Christ's birth, in which Britain participates, and also its attempted re-creation at the very time of the play's performance, with Jacobus Pacificus – who was a figure of Augustus – on the throne.[23]

In the politically devolved Britain of the twenty-first century, G. Wilson Knight's slippage, in the passage quoted earlier, from 'England' to 'Britain' looks sloppy. And it certainly would not have made sense to Shakespeare and his original audiences, for whom 1603 was a turning point, as Queen Elizabeth of England was succeeded by King James VI of Scotland and I of England, with his project to unite the two nations into a new 'Britain'.

ABOUT THE TEXT

Shakespeare endures through history. He illuminates later times as well as his own. He helps us to understand the human condition. But he cannot do this without a good text of the plays. Without editions there would be no Shakespeare. That is why every twenty years or so throughout the last three centuries there has been a major new edition of his complete works. One aspect of editing is the process of keeping the texts up to date – modernizing the spelling, punctuation and typography (though not, of course, the actual words), providing explanatory notes in the light of changing educational practices (a generation ago, most of Shakespeare's classical and biblical allusions could be assumed to be generally understood, but now they can't).

Because Shakespeare did not personally oversee the publication of his plays, with some plays there are major editorial difficulties. Decisions have to be made as to the relative authority of the early printed editions, the pocket format 'Quartos' published in Shakespeare's lifetime and the elaborately produced 'First Folio' text of 1623, the original 'Complete Works' prepared for the press after his death by Shakespeare's fellow-actors, the people who knew the plays better than anyone else. *Cymbeline* exists only in a Folio text that is reasonably well printed, with few errors, and showing signs – especially in its heavy punctuation – of being set from copy prepared by a scribe, who was probably Ralph Crane. The following notes highlight various aspects of the editorial process and indicate conventions used in the text of this edition:

Lists of Parts are supplied in the First Folio for only six plays, not including *Cymbeline*, so the list here is editorially supplied. Capitals indicate that part of the name used for speech headings in the script (thus 'POSTHUMUS Leonatus, husband to Innogen').

Locations are provided by the Folio for only two plays, of which *Cymbeline* is not one. Eighteenth-century editors, working in an age of elaborately realistic stage sets, were the first to provide detailed locations ('*another room in the palace*'). Given that Shakespeare wrote for a bare stage and often an imprecise sense of place, we have relegated locations to the explanatory notes at the foot of the page, where they are given at the beginning of each scene where the imaginary location is different from the one before. In the case of *Cymbeline* the action moves between ancient Britain and Rome.

Act and Scene Divisions were provided in Folio in a much more thoroughgoing way than in the Quartos. Sometimes, however, they were erroneous or omitted; corrections and additions supplied by editorial tradition are indicated by square brackets. Five-act division is based on a classical model, and act breaks provided the opportunity to replace the candles in the indoor Blackfriars playhouse which the King's Men used after 1608, but Shakespeare did not necessarily think in terms of a five-part structure of dramatic composition. The Folio convention is that a scene ends when the stage is empty. Nowadays, partly under the influence of film, we tend to consider a scene to be a dramatic unit that ends with either a change of imaginary location or a significant passage of time within the narrative. Shakespeare's fluidity of composition accords well with this convention, so in addition to act and scene numbers we provide a *running scene* count in the right margin at the beginning of each new scene, in the typeface used for editorial directions. Where there is a scene break caused by a momentary bare stage, but the location does not change and extra time does not pass, we use the convention *running scene continues*. There is inevitably a degree of editorial judgement in making such calls, but the system is very valuable in suggesting the pace of the plays.

Speakers' Names are often inconsistent in Folio. We have regularized speech headings, but retained an element of deliberate inconsistency in entry directions, in order to give the flavour of Folio.

court to country, and elements of masque-form. Some scholars, however, propose that *Cymbeline* influenced *Philaster* rather than vice versa.

TEXT: First Folio of 1623 is the only text. Probably set from a transcript by Ralph Crane, scribe to the King's Men. Fairly well-printed text, though some correction required, especially in those parts of the play that were typeset by 'Compositor E', the least competent man in the printing house. The heroine is called 'Innogen' in both Holinshed's *Chronicles* and Simon Forman's notes on seeing the play; this name also appears in *Much Ado about Nothing* (as well as in works by contemporaries such as Thomas Heywood and Michael Drayton). 'Imogen' did not exist as a name at this time and, besides, the heroines of Shakespeare's late plays are given symbolic names (Marina = from the sea; Perdita = the lost one; Miranda = cause for admiration; hence Innogen = innocent one). All this very strongly suggests that Folio's 'Imogen' was a minim scribal or compositorial error for 'Innogen', so we have corrected accordingly.

THE TRAGEDY OF CYMBELINE

CYMBELINE, King of Britain

INNOGEN, his daughter by a
former queen, later disguised
as Fidele

QUEEN, his second wife

CLOTEN, her son, Cymbeline's
stepson

POSTHUMUS Leonatus, husband to
Innogen

PISANIO, his servant

CORNELIUS, a doctor

LADY attendant on Innogen, named
Helen

Two LORDS attendant on Cloten

Two GENTLEMEN

Two British CAPTAINS

Two JAILERS

BELARIUS, a banished lord, living in
Wales under the name Morgan

GUIDERIUS ⎫ Cymbeline's sons,
ARVIRAGUS ⎭ known as sons of
Belarius called
Polydore and Cadwal

PHILARIO, an Italian, Posthumus'
host in Rome

IACHIMO, an Italian nobleman,
friend to Philario

A FRENCHMAN

A Dutchman

A Spaniard

Caius LUCIUS, general of the
Roman army

SOOTHSAYER, named
Philharmonus

Two Roman SENATORS

A Roman TRIBUNE

A Roman CAPTAIN

JUPITER

Ghost of SICILIUS LEONATUS,
Posthumus' father

Ghost of Posthumus' MOTHER

Ghosts of Posthumus' two
BROTHERS

Lords, Attendants, Messengers,
Musicians, Roman Tribunes, British
and Roman Captains, Soldiers

Act 1 Scene 1   *running scene 1*

Enter two Gentlemen

FIRST GENTLEMAN You do not meet a man but frowns.
    Our bloods
    No more obey the heavens than our courtiers
    Still seem as does the king.
SECOND GENTLEMAN But what's the matter?
5 FIRST GENTLEMAN His daughter, and the heir of's
    kingdom, whom
    He purposed to his wife's sole son — a widow
    That late he married — hath referred herself
    Unto a poor but worthy gentleman. She's wedded,
    Her husband banished, she imprisoned, all
10 Is outward sorrow, though I think the king
    Be touched at very heart.
SECOND GENTLEMAN None but the king?
FIRST GENTLEMAN He that hath lost her too: so is the
    queen,
    That most desired the match. But not a courtier,
15 Although they wear their faces to the bent
    Of the king's looks, hath a heart that is not
    Glad at the thing they scowl at.
SECOND GENTLEMAN And why so?
FIRST GENTLEMAN He that hath missed the princess is a
    thing
20 Too bad for bad report: and he that hath her —
    I mean, that married her, alack, good man,
    And therefore banished — is a creature such
    As, to seek through the regions of the earth
    For one his like, there would be something failing
25 In him that should compare. I do not think
    So fair an outward and such stuff within
    Endows a man but he.
SECOND GENTLEMAN You speak him far.

1.1 *Location: the British royal court (the play moves between ancient Britain and Rome)* **1 but frowns** who does not frown **1 bloods** dispositions, temperaments **3 Still . . . king** mimic the king's emotions; **seem** suggests a lack of sincerity **6 purposed to** intended for, i.e. to marry **7 late** recently **referred . . . Unto** given herself to/chosen **9 all . . . heart** i.e. Cymbeline is deeply wounded whereas the courtiers' **outward sorrow** is false **13 He . . . her** i.e. Cloten **15 bent** inclination **19 missed** failed to win; also suggests Innogen's lucky escape **thing** contemptuous being, beneath humanity **22 creature** living being, suggesting he is beyond common humanity **24 his like** like him **something . . . compare** anyone chosen for comparison would have some fault to distinguish them **26 outward** physical appearance **stuff** substance, quality **27 Endows . . . he** so enriches/is to be found in any other **28 speak him far** speak highly of him

Than to be sure they do — for certainties
Either are past remedies, or, timely knowing,
The remedy then born — discover to me
What both you spur and stop.
115 IACHIMO Had I this cheek
To bathe my lips upon: this hand, whose touch,
Whose every touch, would force the feeler's soul
To th'oath of loyalty: this object, which
Takes prisoner the wild motion of mine eye,
120 Firing it only here: should I, damned then,
Slaver with lips as common as the stairs
That mount the Capitol: join grips with hands
Made hard with hourly falsehood — falsehood, as
With labour — then by-peeping in an eye
125 Base and illustrous as the smoky light
That's fed with stinking tallow: it were fit
That all the plagues of hell should at one time
Encounter such revolt.
INNOGEN My lord, I fear,
130 Has forgot Britain.
IACHIMO And himself. Not I
Inclined to this intelligence pronounce
The beggary of his change: but 'tis your graces
That from my mutest conscience to my tongue
135 Charms this report out.
INNOGEN Let me hear no more.
IACHIMO O dearest soul: your cause doth strike my heart
With pity that doth make me sick. A lady
So fair, and fastened to an empery
140 Would make the great'st king double, to be partnered
With tomboys hired with that self-exhibition
Which your own coffers yield: with diseased ventures
That play with all infirmities for gold

---

112 **timely knowing** learning in time   113 **born** found   **discover . . . stop** reveal to me what makes your speech start and **stop** (the image is from horse-riding)   115 **Had I** if I had   117 **feeler's** i.e. the person who felt the touch (of Innogen's hand)   118 **this object** Innogen herself/her eye   119 **Takes . . . motion** transfixes the restless gaze   120 **Firing** setting it aflame (with desire)   121 **Slaver** flatter/wet with saliva   **common . . . Capitol** i.e. used by everyone   **Capitol** the national temple of Rome dedicated to Jupiter   123 **falsehood . . . labour** i.e. just as manual labour hardens the hands, habitual falsehood hardens the heart   124 **by-peeping** glancing sideways   125 **illustrous** lacklustre, dull   126 **fed with** produced by   **tallow** animal fat, used to make candles   **fit** right, appropriate   128 **Encounter such revolt** punish such a transgression   131 **Not . . . pronounce** it gives me no pleasure to reveal this news   139 **empery** empire   140 **Would . . . double** which would double the power of even the greatest king   **partnered** equated, considered alongside   141 **tomboys** prostitutes   **self-exhibition** same allowance of money   142 **ventures** hazards/prostitutes   143 **play** gamble   **infirmities** diseases

Which rottenness can lend nature: such boiled stuff
145   As well might poison poison. Be revenged,
Or she that bore you was no queen, and you
Recoil from your great stock.

INNOGEN Revenged?
How should I be revenged? If this be true —
150   As I have such a heart that both mine ears
Must not in haste abuse — if it be true,
How should I be revenged?

IACHIMO Should he make me
Live like Diana's priest, betwixt cold sheets,
155   Whiles he is vaulting variable ramps,
In your despite, upon your purse — revenge it.
I dedicate myself to your sweet pleasure,
More noble than that runagate to your bed,
And will continue fast to your affection,
160   Still close as sure.

INNOGEN What ho, Pisanio!   *Calls*

IACHIMO Let me my service tender on your lips.

INNOGEN Away, I do condemn mine ears that have
So long attended thee. If thou wert honourable
165   Thou wouldst have told this tale for virtue, not
For such an end thou seek'st, as base as strange.
Thou wrong'st a gentleman who is as far
From thy report as thou from honour, and
Solicit'st here a lady that disdains
170   Thee and the devil alike.— What ho, Pisanio!
The king my father shall be made acquainted
Of thy assault: if he shall think it fit,
A saucy stranger in his court to mart
As in a Romish stew, and to expound
175   His beastly mind to us, he hath a court
He little cares for, and a daughter who
He not respects at all.— What ho, Pisanio!

IACHIMO O happy Leonatus I may say,
The credit that thy lady hath of thee

---

144 **boiled stuff** women who have been made to sweat in steam-rooms: a treatment for venereal
disease   147 **Recoil…stock** degenerate from your royal lineage   154 **Diana's priest** Diana was the
goddess of chastity, whose female priests were virgins   **cold** chaste, sexless   155 **vaulting** to mount
sexually   **variable ramps** various prostitutes   **ramp** a bold, vulgar woman   156 **In your despite** in
contempt, scorn of you   **upon your purse** at your expense   158 **runagate** runaway, vagabond   159 **fast**
constant, firm   162 **Let…lips** allow me to kiss you   164 **attended** listened, paid attention to   **thee** less
polite than **you** as a term of address, used to inferiors but also to intimates   173 **saucy** impudent, insolent
mart do business; literally 'market-place'   174 **Romish stew** Roman brothel   175 **us** the royal plural
pronoun   179 **credit** trust, belief, good reputation, plays on economic sense

180   Deserves thy trust, and thy most perfect goodness
       Her assured credit. Blessèd live you long,
       A lady to the worthiest sir that ever
       Country called his; and you his mistress, only
       For the most worthiest fit. Give me your pardon.
185   I have spoke this to know if your affiance
       Were deeply rooted, and shall make your lord
       That which he is new o'er: and he is one
       The truest mannered, such a holy witch
       That he enchants societies into him:
190   Half all men's hearts are his.

INNOGEN You make amends.

IACHIMO He sits 'mongst men like a descended god;
       He hath a kind of honour sets him off
       More than a mortal seeming. Be not angry,
195   Most mighty princess, that I have adventured
       To try your taking of a false report, which hath
       Honoured with confirmation your great judgement
       In the election of a sir so rare,
       Which you know cannot err. The love I bear him
200   Made me to fan you thus, but the gods made you,
       Unlike all others, chaffless. Pray your pardon.

INNOGEN All's well, sir: take my power i'th'court for
       yours.

IACHIMO My humble thanks. I had almost forgot
       T'entreat your grace but in a small request,
205   And yet of moment too, for it concerns
       Your lord: myself and other noble friends
       Are partners in the business.

INNOGEN Pray what is't?

IACHIMO Some dozen Romans of us and your lord —
210   The best feather of our wing — have mingled sums
       To buy a present for the emperor:
       Which I, the factor for the rest, have done
       In France: 'tis plate of rare device, and jewels
       Of rich and exquisite form, their value's great,
215   And I am something curious, being strange,

---

185 affiance troth-plight, marriage promise   **187 new o'er** all over again   **188 truest mannered** most honestly given, most faithful   **holy witch** i.e. good wizard who uses holy magic   **196 try your taking** test how you would take   **198 In … rare** in choosing such an exceptional husband   **200 fan** winnow; blow air through grain to separate the wheat from the chaff or husks   **201 chaffless** without chaff or refuse   **204 but** only   **205 moment** importance, significance   **210 best … wing** best among our group of friends   **mingled sums** all contributed money   **212 factor** agent   **213 plate** gold or silver utensils/ tableware   **rare device** exceptional craftwork, carving   **215 something curious** somewhat anxious   **strange** a stranger, foreigner

To have them in safe stowage: may it please you
To take them in protection?

INNOGEN Willingly:
And pawn mine honour for their safety, since
220   My lord hath interest in them. I will keep them
In my bedchamber.

IACHIMO They are in a trunk
Attended by my men: I will make bold
To send them to you, only for this night:
225   I must aboard tomorrow.

INNOGEN O, no, no.

IACHIMO Yes, I beseech: or I shall short my word
By length'ning my return. From Gallia
I crossed the seas on purpose and on promise
230   To see your grace.

INNOGEN I thank you for your pains:
But not away tomorrow.

IACHIMO O, I must, madam.
Therefore I shall beseech you, if you please
235   To greet your lord with writing, do't tonight.
I have outstood my time, which is material
To th'tender of our present.

INNOGEN I will write:
Send your trunk to me, it shall safe be kept,
240   And truly yielded you. You're very welcome.

Exeunt

Act 2 Scene 1   *running scene 4*

Enter Cloten and the two Lords

CLOTEN Was there ever man had such luck? When I
kissed the jack upon an upcast, to be hit away! I had
a hundred pound on't: and then a whoreson
jackanapes must take me up for swearing, as if I
5   borrowed mine oaths of him, and might not spend
them at my pleasure.

FIRST LORD What got he by that? You have broke his
pate with your bowl.

---

219 **pawn** lay down   220 **interest** a stake, a share   227 **short** fall short of, not live up to   228 **Gallia**
France   236 **outstood** outstayed   **material** crucial   237 **tender** giving   2.1   1 **kissed the jack** bowling
term, i.e. Cloten's bowl touched the small target ball   2 **upon an upcast** meaning uncertain: by accident/
tossing a throw up/on the last shot (as in upshot)   4 **jackanapes** upstart/impertinent fellow   **take me up**
rebuke me   5 **oaths** swearwords   **of** from   **spend…pleasure** utter them when I please   8 **pate** head

| | SECOND LORD If his wit had been like him that broke it, | *Aside* |

10   it would have run all out.

      CLOTEN When a gentleman is disposed to swear, it is not
        for any standers-by to curtail his oaths. Ha?

      SECOND LORD No my lord.— Nor crop the ears of them.   *Aside*

      CLOTEN Whoreson dog! I give him satisfaction? Would

15   he had been one of my rank.

      SECOND LORD To have smelled like a fool.   *Aside*

      CLOTEN I am not vexed more at anything in th'earth:
        a pox on't! I had rather not be so noble as I am: they
        dare not fight with me, because of the queen my

20   mother: every jack-slave hath his bellyful of fighting,
        and I must go up and down like a cock that nobody
        can match.

      SECOND LORD You are cock and capon too, and you   *Aside*
        crow, cock, with your comb on.

25   CLOTEN Sayest thou?

      SECOND LORD It is not fit your lordship should undertake
        every companion that you give offence to.

      CLOTEN No, I know that: but it is fit I should commit
        offence to my inferiors.

30   SECOND LORD Ay, it is fit for your lordship only.

      CLOTEN Why, so I say.

      FIRST LORD Did you hear of a stranger that's come to
        court tonight?

      CLOTEN A stranger, and I not know on't?

35   SECOND LORD He's a strange fellow himself, and knows   *Aside*
        it not.

      FIRST LORD There's an Italian come, and 'tis thought
        one of Leonatus' friends.

      CLOTEN Leonatus? A banished rascal; and he's another,

40   whatsoever he be. Who told you of this stranger?

      FIRST LORD One of your lordship's pages.

      CLOTEN Is it fit I went to look upon him? Is there no
        derogation in't?

      SECOND LORD You cannot derogate, my lord.

---

9 If . . . out i.e. Cloten's brain is thin, poor stuff   **11 gentleman** i.e. a nobleman   **12 curtail** cut short
15 rank status, plays on secondary sense of 'smell'   **18 a pox on't** expression of anger   **pox** any disease
characterized by pustules/venereal disease   **so** as   **20 jack-slave** low-born person   **21 cock** cockerel,
plays on sense of 'penis'   **23 capon** castrated cockerel/idiot   **24 comb** i.e. like a fool; **cock** and **comb**
together make 'cockscomb' a jester's cap/fool   **25 Sayest thou?** What did you say?   **26 undertake** take
on, fight   **27 companion** fellow   **28 commit offence** take on in fight/be offensive to   **30 fit . . . only** i.e.
only you would show such ill breeding (although on the surface the First Lord means 'it is your right
alone')   **40 whatsoever** whoever   **43 derogation** disgrace, loss of dignity   **44 You cannot derogate** i.e.
because you have no dignity to lose in the first place

45   **CLOTEN** Not easily, I think.

SECOND LORD You are a fool granted, therefore your   *Aside*
        issues, being foolish, do not derogate.

CLOTEN Come, I'll go see this Italian: what I have lost
        today at bowls I'll win tonight of him. Come, go.

50   **SECOND LORD** I'll attend your lordship.—

                              Exeunt [Cloten and First Lord]

        That such a crafty devil as is his mother
        Should yield the world this ass: a woman that
        Bears all down with her brain, and this her son
        Cannot take two from twenty, for his heart,

55   And leave eighteen. Alas, poor princess,
        Thou divine Innogen, what thou endur'st,
        Betwixt a father by thy stepdame governed,
        A mother hourly coining plots, a wooer
        More hateful than the foul expulsion is

60   Of thy dear husband, than that horrid act
        Of the divorce he'd make! The heavens hold firm
        The walls of thy dear honour, keep unshaked
        That temple, thy fair mind, that thou mayst stand,
        T'enjoy thy banished lord and this great land.

                                                    Exit

Act 2 Scene 2   *running scene 5*

Enter Innogen in her bed, and a Lady   *A trunk is brought in*

INNOGEN Who's there? My woman Helen?

LADY Please you, madam.

INNOGEN What hour is it?

LADY Almost midnight, madam.

5   **INNOGEN** I have read three hours then: mine eyes are
        weak.
        Fold down the leaf where I have left: to bed.   *Gives her the book*
        Take not away the taper, leave it burning:
        And if thou canst awake by four o'th'clock,
        I prithee call me.— Sleep hath seized me wholly.

                                            [Exit Lady]

10   To your protection I commend me, gods,

---

47 **issues** deeds, puns on 'children'   53 **Bears all down** crushes everything that stands in her way   54 **for his heart** for the life of him   57 **Betwixt** between   58 **mother** i.e. stepmother   **coining** devising, creating   59 **expulsion** banishment   61 **he'd make** i.e. which he would make happen, in order to marry her himself   **2.2**   5 **weak** tired   6 **leaf** page   **left** left off   7 **taper** candle

To feed again, though full. You do remember
This stain upon her?

POSTHUMUS Ay, and it doth confirm
175   Another stain, as big as hell can hold,
Were there no more but it.

IACHIMO Will you hear more?

POSTHUMUS Spare your arithmetic, never count the
    turns:
Once, and a million!

180 **IACHIMO** I'll be sworn.

POSTHUMUS No swearing.
If you will swear you have not done't, you lie,
And I will kill thee if thou dost deny
Thou'st made me cuckold.

185 **IACHIMO** I'll deny nothing.

POSTHUMUS O, that I had her here, to tear her limb-
    meal!
I will go there and do't, i'th'court, before
Her father. I'll do something.   *Exit*

PHILARIO Quite besides
190   The government of patience. You have won:
Let's follow him and pervert the present wrath
He hath against himself.

IACHIMO With all my heart.   *Exeunt*
Enter Posthumus

POSTHUMUS Is there no way for men to be, but women
195   Must be half-workers? We are all bastards,
And that most venerable man, which I
Did call my father, was I know not where
When I was stamped. Some coiner with his tools
Made me a counterfeit: yet my mother seemed
200   The Dian of that time: so doth my wife
The nonpareil of this. O, vengeance, vengeance!
Me of my lawful pleasure she restrained,
And prayed me oft forbearance: did it with
A pudency so rosy, the sweet view on't

---

173 stain mark (the mole); Posthumus shifts sense to 'moral blot'   **178 turns** i.e. the number of times you
had sex   **179 Once . . . million** i.e. if you've had her once, you may as well have had her a million times
184 Thou'st thou hast (you have)   **cuckold** a husband whose wife was unfaithful   **186 limb-meal** limb
from limb   **189 besides** beyond, outside of   **190 government** control, management   **191 pervert** avert,
turn aside   **195 half-workers** co-workers, i.e. is there no way for men to live without women?
We . . . bastards i.e. because there are no faithful women in the world   **196 venerable** old and worthy of
respect   **198 stamped** made, conceived   **coiner** counterfeit coin-maker   **201 nonpareil** unrivalled
person   **202 lawful pleasure** i.e. marital sex   **203 prayed . . . forbearance** often entreated me to restrain
my desire   **204 pudency** modesty   **rosy** presumably referring to her blushes   **view on't** sight of it

205 Might well have warmed old Saturn, that I thought
       her
     As chaste as unsunned snow. O, all the devils!
     This yellow Iachimo in an hour — wast not? —
     Or less — at first? Perchance he spoke not, but
     Like a full-acorned boar, a German one,
210 Cried 'O!' and mounted; found no opposition
     But what he looked for should oppose, and she
     Should from encounter guard. Could I find out
     The woman's part in me — for there's no motion
     That tends to vice in man, but I affirm
215 It is the woman's part: be it lying, note it,
     The woman's: flattering, hers: deceiving, hers:
     Lust and rank thoughts, hers, hers: revenges, hers:
     Ambitions, covetings, change of prides, disdain,
     Nice longing, slanders, mutability,
220 All faults that may be named, nay, that hell knows,
     Why, hers, in part or all: but rather all,
     For even to vice
     They are not constant, but are changing still
     One vice, but of a minute old, for one
225 Not half so old as that. I'll write against them,
     Detest them, curse them: yet 'tis greater skill
     In a true hate, to pray they have their will:
     The very devils cannot plague them better.   *Exit*

Act 3 Scene 1   *running scene 7*

*Enter in state Cymbeline, Queen, Cloten and Lords at one
door, and at another, Caius Lucius and Attendants*

CYMBELINE Now say, what would Augustus Caesar
      with us?
LUCIUS When Julius Caesar — whose remembrance yet
      Lives in men's eyes and will to ears and tongues
      Be theme and hearing ever — was in this Britain
5   And conquered it, Cassibelan, thine uncle —

205 **Saturn** Roman god associated with melancholy and coldness   207 **yellow** sallow, i.e. dark-complexioned   208 **at first** straight away   209 **full-acorned boar** well-fed male pig   **German** i.e. fierce and fat   211 **looked for** anticipated   212 **encounter** sexual encounter   213 **woman's part** fault specific to women; plays on sense of 'vagina'   **motion** impulse   217 **rank** lascivious   218 **covetings** desires for material objects   **change of prides** continually changing (or variety of) excesses   219 **Nice longing** wanton desires   **mutability** changeableness, inconsistency   223 **still** always, constantly   224 **but of** only   225 **so** as   226 **skill** wisdom   227 **have their will** get their way, have their sexual desires fulfilled   **3.1** *Location: Britain, the royal court*   2 **remembrance** memory   **yet** still   4 **theme** topic of discussion

Famous in Caesar's praises no whit less
Than in his feats deserving it — for him,
And his succession, granted Rome a tribute,
Yearly three thousand pounds, which by thee lately
10   Is left untendered.

QUEEN And to kill the marvel,
Shall be so ever.

CLOTEN There be many Caesars
Ere such another Julius: Britain's
15   A world by itself, and we will nothing pay
For wearing our own noses.

QUEEN That opportunity
Which then they had to take from's, to resume
We have again. Remember, sir, my liege,
20   The kings your ancestors, together with
The natural bravery of your isle, which stands
As Neptune's park, ribbed and paled in
With oaks unscalable and roaring waters,
With sands that will not bear your enemies' boats,
25   But suck them up to th'topmast. A kind of conquest
Caesar made here, but made not here his brag
Of 'came, and saw, and overcame': with shame —
The first that ever touched him — he was carried
From off our coast, twice beaten: and his shipping —
30   Poor ignorant baubles — on our terrible seas
Like eggshells moved upon their surges, cracked
As easily gainst our rocks. For joy whereof
The famed Cassibelan, who was once at point —
O giglot fortune! — to master Caesar's sword,
35   Made Lud's town with rejoicing fires bright,
And Britons strut with courage.

---

6 Famous . . . **it** famous because Caesar praised him, but equally for the feats he performed to earn that praise   **7 for** . . . **succession** on behalf of himself and his successors, i.e. future British kings   **9 pounds** i.e. pounds weight   **10 untendered** unpaid   **11 kill the marvel** put an end to the surprise   **13 be** may/will be   **18 from's** from us   **resume** . . . **again** we have to take back again   **19 liege** lord, used to a feudal superior owed duty and allegiance   **21 bravery** . . . **isle** beauty of the land/courage of the inhabitants   **22 Neptune's** of Neptune, Roman god of the sea   **park** tract of land held by royal grant used for hunting; also used for an enclosed body of water in which oysters or fish are bred   **paled in** fenced with pales (long, vertical stakes); the coastline was densely forested with trees which formed a sort of **unscalable** (hard to climb) perimeter fence   **24 bear** support   **25 suck** . . . **th'topmast** i.e. like quicksand they will suck the ships under until only the **topmast** (formerly the uppermost mast) is visible   **27 'came** . . . **overcame'** Caesar reported his victory at the battle of Zela in 47 BC with this phrase in Latin: *veni, vidi, vici*   **30 ignorant baubles** foolish, inexperienced toys   **33 at point** ready, just about   **34 giglot** whore (i.e. fickle, disloyal)   **master** overcome, defeat   **35 Lud's town** i.e. London, after King Lud, Cymbeline's grandfather

CLOTEN Come, there's no more tribute to be paid: our
kingdom is stronger than it was at that time, and, as
I said, there is no more such Caesars. Other of them
40   may have crooked noses, but to owe such straight
arms, none.

CYMBELINE Son, let your mother end.

CLOTEN We have yet many among us can grip as hard
as Cassibelan: I do not say I am one, but I have a
45   hand. Why tribute? Why should we pay tribute? If
Caesar can hide the sun from us with a blanket, or
put the moon in his pocket, we will pay him tribute
for light: else, sir, no more tribute, pray you now.

CYMBELINE You must know,   *To Lucius*
50   Till the injurious Romans did extort
This tribute from us, we were free. Caesar's ambition,
Which swelled so much that it did almost stretch
The sides o'th'world, against all colour here
Did put the yoke upon's; which to shake off
55   Becomes a warlike people, whom we reckon
Ourselves to be. We do say then to Caesar,
Our ancestor was that Mulmutius which
Ordained our laws, whose use the sword of Caesar
Hath too much mangled, whose repair and franchise
60   Shall, by the power we hold, be our good deed,
Though Rome be therefore angry. Mulmutius made
our laws
Who was the first of Britain which did put
His brows within a golden crown and called
Himself a king.

65   LUCIUS I am sorry, Cymbeline,
That I am to pronounce Augustus Caesar —
Caesar, that hath more kings his servants than
Thyself domestic officers — thine enemy:
Receive it from me, then. War and confusion
70   In Caesar's name pronounce I gainst thee: look
For fury not to be resisted. Thus defied,
I thank thee for myself.

---

40 **crooked** i.e. hooked, Roman   **owe** own   **straight** powerful, forceful   43 **grip** i.e. the handle of a
sword   48 **else** otherwise   50 **injurious** insulting/malicious   53 **against all colour** without any pretext;
perhaps playing on 'collar' in conjunction with **yoke** in the next line meaning 'wooden collar fastened to a
pair of animals and attached to a plough or cart'   55 **Becomes** is appropriate for   57 **Mulmutius**
supposedly the first British king (from fourth century BC)   **which** who   58 **use** application, practice (of the
laws)   59 **repair** restoration   **franchise** enfranchisement   69 **confusion** destruction   70 **pronounce**
proclaim   71 **Thus defied** i.e. now that I have issued this declaration

CYMBELINE Thou art welcome, Caius.
Thy Caesar knighted me; my youth I spent
75   Much under him: of him I gathered honour,
Which he to seek of me again, perforce,
Behoves me keep at utterance. I am perfect
That the Pannonians and Dalmatians for
Their liberties are now in arms, a precedent
80   Which not to read would show the Britons cold:
So Caesar shall not find them.

LUCIUS Let proof speak.

CLOTEN His majesty bids you welcome. Make pastime
with us a day or two, or longer: if you seek us
85   afterwards in other terms, you shall find us in our
saltwater girdle: if you beat us out of it, it is yours: if
you fall in the adventure, our crows shall fare the
better for you: and there's an end.

LUCIUS So, sir.

90 CYMBELINE I know your master's pleasure, and he mine:
All the remain is 'Welcome'.   *Exeunt*

Act 3 Scene 2   *running scene 7 continues*

Enter Pisanio, reading of a letter

PISANIO How? Of adultery? Wherefore write you not
What monster's her accuser? Leonatus,
O master, what a strange infection
Is fall'n into thy ear! What false Italian,
5   As poisonous-tongued as handed, hath prevailed
On thy too ready hearing? Disloyal? No.
She's punished for her truth, and undergoes,
More goddess-like than wife-like, such assaults
As would take in some virtue. O my master,
10   Thy mind to her is now as low as were
Thy fortunes. How? That I should murder her,
Upon the love and truth and vows which I
Have made to thy command? I, her? Her blood?

---

76 **perforce** by necessity   77 **Behoves…utterance** obliges me to defend it to the death   **perfect** well
aware/reliably informed   78 **Pannonians and Dalmatians** ancient inhabitants of what are now Hungary
and the Balkans   79 **precedent** example   80 **read** interpret   **cold** lacking spirit   82 **Let proof speak** let
the outcome of the battle/the battle itself do the talking   83 **Make pastime** stay   86 **saltwater girdle** the
sea   87 **adventure** attempt   **crows** birds which feed on carrion, i.e. dead flesh   89 **So** so be it
90 **pleasure** desire, aim   91 **the remain** that remains (to say)   3.2 1 **How?** What?   **Wherefore** why
5 **As…handed** as capable a poisoner by word as by hand   7 **truth** loyalty   **undergoes** endures
9 **take in** defeat, conquer   **some virtue** some people's virtue   12 **Upon** because of

If it be so to do good service, never
15   Let me be counted serviceable. How look I,
That I should seem to lack humanity
So much as this fact comes to? 'Do't: the letter   *Reads*
That I have sent her, by her own command
Shall give thee opportunity.' O damned paper,
20   Black as the ink that's on thee! Senseless bauble,
Art thou a fedary for this act, and look'st
So virgin-like without? Lo, here she comes.
Enter Innogen
I am ignorant in what I am commanded.
INNOGEN How now, Pisanio?
25   **PISANIO** Madam, here is a letter from my lord.
INNOGEN Who, thy lord? That is my lord, Leonatus!
O, learned indeed were that astronomer
That knew the stars as I his characters —
He'd lay the future open. You good gods,
30   Let what is here contained relish of love,
Of my lord's health, of his content: yet not
That we two are asunder, let that grieve him;
Some griefs are med'cinable, that is one of them,
For it doth physic love: of his content,
35   All but in that. Good wax, thy leave: blest be   *Opens the seal*
You bees that make these locks of counsel! Lovers
And men in dangerous bonds pray not alike:
Though forfeiters you cast in prison, yet
You clasp young Cupid's tables. Good news, gods!
40   'Justice and your father's wrath, should he take me   *Reads*
in his dominion, could not be so cruel to me, as you,
O the dearest of creatures, would even renew me
with your eyes. Take notice that I am in Cambria, at
Milford Haven: what your own love will out of this
45   advise you, follow. So he wishes you all happiness,
that remains loyal to his vow, and your increasing in
love, Leonatus Posthumus.'

---

17 **fact** deed   20 **Senseless bauble** unfeeling, worthless thing   21 **fedary** confederate, accomplice
23 **ignorant in** to pretend to be ignorant of   27 **astronomer** includes sense of an 'astrologer'
28 **characters** handwriting   30 **relish** taste   31 **not** i.e. not his content   33 **med'cinable** restorative,
able to heal   34 **physic love** i.e. being apart makes love healthier, stronger   35 **wax** i.e. used to seal the
letter   **thy leave** by thy leave; Innogen is asking its permission for her to break it and read the letter
36 **locks of counsel** seals to secrecy, private matters   38 **forfeiters** defaulters of contracts   39 **Cupid's** of
Cupid, Roman god of love   **tables** writing tablets   42 **even renew** could not restore   43 **Cambria** Wales
44 **Milford Haven** most south-westerly Welsh port

O, for a horse with wings! Hear'st thou, Pisanio?
He is at Milford Haven: read, and tell me
50   How far 'tis thither. If one of mean affairs
May plod it in a week, why may not I
Glide thither in a day? Then, true Pisanio,
Who long'st like me to see thy lord; who long'st —
O, let me bate — but not like me: yet long'st
55   But in a fainter kind. O, not like me,
For mine's beyond, beyond: say, and speak thick —
Love's counsellor should fill the bores of hearing,
To th'smothering of the sense — how far it is
To this same blessèd Milford. And by th'way
60   Tell me how Wales was made so happy as
T'inherit such a haven. But first of all,
How we may steal from hence: and for the gap
That we shall make in time, from our hence-going
And our return, to excuse: but first, how get hence.
65   Why should excuse be born or e'er begot?
We'll talk of that hereafter. Prithee, speak,
How many score of miles may we well ride
'Twixt hour and hour?
   PISANIO One score 'twixt sun and sun,
70   Madam, 's enough for you: and too much too.
   INNOGEN Why, one that rode to's execution, man,
    Could never go so slow: I have heard of riding
      wagers,
    Where horses have been nimbler than the sands
    That run i'th'clock's behalf. But this is foolery:
75   Go, bid my woman feign a sickness, say
    She'll home to her father; and provide me presently
    A riding-suit, no costlier than would fit
    A franklin's housewife.
   PISANIO Madam, you're best consider.

---

50 mean affairs trivial business   **54 bate** abate, i.e. qualify what I have just said   **55 fainter kind** more moderate fashion   **56 mine** my longing (to see Posthumus)   **thick** fast, the words crammed together **57 bores of hearing** i.e. ears   **58 smothering** overwhelming   **59 by th'way** on the way   **62 steal** creep away, surreptitiously go   **64 to excuse** i.e. how to explain our absence   **how get hence** how to get away   **65 Why … begot?** i.e. why should an excuse be made before the act which needs excusing has been performed   **67 score** twenty   **well** possibly/comfortably   **68 'Twixt … hour** i.e. in an hour   **69 'twixt … sun** i.e. in a day   **72 riding wagers** horse races with bets on them   **74 i'th'clock's behalf** in place of a clock, i.e. an hourglass   **75 feign** pretend to be affected by   **76 home** go home   **presently** immediately **77 fit** be suitable for   **78 franklin** small landowner, below the rank of a gentleman   **79 you're best** you had better

80   **INNOGEN** I see before me, man: nor here, nor here,
        Nor what ensues, but have a fog in them
        That I cannot look through. Away, I prithee,
        Do as I bid thee: there's no more to say:
        Accessible is none but Milford way.   *Exeunt*

Act 3 Scene 3

running scene 8

Enter Belarius, Guiderius and Arviragus   *From their cave*

  BELARIUS A goodly day not to keep house with such
        Whose roof's as low as ours. Stoop, boys: this gate
        Instructs you how t'adore the heavens, and bows
          you
        To a morning's holy office. The gates of monarchs
5   Are arched so high that giants may jet through
        And keep their impious turbans on, without
        Good morrow to the sun. Hail, thou fair heaven!
        We house i'th'rock, yet use thee not so hardly
        As prouder livers do.
10   **GUIDERIUS** Hail, heaven!
  ARVIRAGUS Hail, heaven!
  BELARIUS Now for our mountain sport. Up to yond hill,
        Your legs are young: I'll tread these flats. Consider,
        When you above perceive me like a crow,
15   That it is place which lessens and sets off,
        And you may then revolve what tales I have told you
        Of courts, of princes, of the tricks in war.
        This service is not service, so being done,
        But being so allowed. To apprehend thus
20   Draws us a profit from all things we see:
        And often, to our comfort, shall we find
        The sharded beetle in a safer hold
        Than is the full-winged eagle. O, this life
        Is nobler than attending for a check,
25   Richer than doing nothing for a robe,

---

80 before me what's in front of me   **nor** neither   **81 what ensues** what will happen   **but** but that they **84 none** no route   **3.3** *Location: Wales, outside Belarius' cave*   **1 keep house** stay inside   **with such** among those   **2 gate** entrance   **3 Instructs . . . heavens** i.e. by forcing you to bow   **4 office** divine service   **5 jet** strut   **6 impious turbans** i.e. non-Christian (**giants** were frequently imaged as Saracens in Romance literature)   **8 use** treat   **hardly** badly   **9 prouder livers** those who live more ostentatiously **13 these flats** this plain   **15 place** physical position/social rank   **lessens . . . off** diminishes and enhances   **16 revolve** consider/turn over in the mind   **17 tricks** accidents   **19 so allowed** acknowledged as such   **apprehend thus** look at things this way   **22 sharded** living in dung/with scaly wings **hold** stronghold, refuge   **24 attending** serving/awaiting   **for** in exchange for   **check** rebuke **25 robe** i.e. robe of office

Prouder than rustling in unpaid-for silk:
Such gain the cap of him that makes 'em fine,
Yet keeps his book uncrossed: no life to ours.

GUIDERIUS Out of your proof you speak: we poor
     unfledged
30   Have never winged from view o'th'nest, nor know
     not
What air's from home. Haply this life is best,
If quiet life be best: sweeter to you
That have a sharper known, well corresponding
With your stiff age; but unto us it is
35   A cell of ignorance, travelling abed,
A prison for a debtor that not dares
To stride a limit.

ARVIRAGUS What should we speak of
When we are old as you? When we shall hear
40   The rain and wind beat dark December, how,
In this our pinching cave, shall we discourse
The freezing hours away? We have seen nothing:
We are beastly: subtle as the fox for prey,
Like warlike as the wolf for what we eat:
45   Our valour is to chase what flies: our cage
We make a choir, as doth the prisoned bird,
And sing our bondage freely.

BELARIUS How you speak!
Did you but know the city's usuries,
50   And felt them knowingly: the art o'th'court,
As hard to leave as keep, whose top to climb
Is certain falling, or so slipp'ry that
The fear's as bad as falling: the toil o'th'war,
A pain that only seems to seek out danger
55   I'th'name of fame and honour, which dies
     i'th'search,
And hath as oft a sland'rous epitaph
As record of fair act. Nay, many times

---

27 Such those who do so   **gain . . . fine** gain the respect (by doffing the cap) of the tailor that provides their fine clothes   **28 Yet . . . uncrossed** i.e. the debts in his account book never get crossed off   **to** compared to   **29 proof** experience   **unfledged** young things; literally of young birds 'not yet covered with feathers'   **31 air's from home** the air is like away from home   **Haply** perhaps   **34 stiff** rigid, not flexible or pliant   **35 travelling abed** i.e. in the imagination, dreaming of going places   **37 stride a limit** step over the threshold, go out   **41 pinching** bitingly cold/narrowly restricting   **43 beastly** beastlike   **44 Like** as   **45 what flies** what runs away, i.e. food or prey (as opposed to men who would stand and fight)   **49 usuries** corrupt financial practices   **50 knowingly** i.e. from experience   **art** artifice/artfulness   **51 keep** stay in   **54 pain** labour, effort   **56 oft** often   **57 record . . . act** i.e. report of good deeds

Doth ill deserve by doing well: what's worse,
Must curtsy at the censure. O boys, this story
60 The world may read in me: my body's marked
With Roman swords, and my report was once
First with the best of note. Cymbeline loved me,
And when a soldier was the theme, my name
Was not far off: then was I as a tree
65 Whose boughs did bend with fruit. But in one night,
A storm, or robbery — call it what you will —
Shook down my mellow hangings, nay, my leaves,
And left me bare to weather.
GUIDERIUS Uncertain favour!
70 **BELARIUS** My fault being nothing — as I have told you
        oft —
But that two villains, whose false oaths prevailed
Before my perfect honour, swore to Cymbeline
I was confederate with the Romans: so
Followed my banishment, and this twenty years
75 This rock and these demesnes have been my world
Where I have lived at honest freedom, paid
More pious debts to heaven than in all
The fore-end of my time. But up to th'mountains!
This is not hunters' language. He that strikes
80 The venison first shall be the lord o'th'feast,
To him the other two shall minister,
And we will fear no poison, which attends
In place of greater state. I'll meet you in the valleys.
                              Exeunt [*Guid. and Arv.*]
How hard it is to hide the sparks of nature!
85 These boys know little they are sons to th'king,
Nor Cymbeline dreams that they are alive.
They think they are mine, and though trained up
        thus meanly
I'th'cave wherein they bow, their thoughts do hit
The roofs of palaces and nature prompts them
90 In simple and low things to prince it much

---

58 **Doth ill deserve** i.e. is ill rewarded   59 **curtsy…censure** bow at the (unjust) reproof   **61 report** reputation   **62 best of note** most renowned, distinguished   **63 theme** topic of discussion   **64 as** like   67 **mellow hangings** ripe fruit   **68 weather** bad weather i.e. ill fortune   **69 favour** good will, especially of a superior or multitude   **72 perfect** unblemished, true   **74 this** these   **75 demesnes** lands, domains   76 **at** in   **78 fore-end** early part   **time** life   **80 venison** deer   **81 minister** be servants   **82 attends…** **state** is an ever-present threat in places of greater status, pomp   **84 sparks of nature** signs of inherent qualities   **87 trained…meanly** brought up in such a humble way/in such lowly surroundings   **88 they** **bow** i.e. because the roof is so low   **hit** i.e. reach as high as   **90 prince it** behave like princes

Beyond the trick of others. This Polydore,
The heir of Cymbeline and Britain, who
The king his father called Guiderius — Jove!
When on my three-foot stool I sit, and tell
95   The warlike feats I have done, his spirits fly out
Into my story: say 'Thus mine enemy fell,
And thus I set my foot on's neck', even then
The princely blood flows in his cheek, he sweats,
Strains his young nerves, and puts himself in posture
100   That acts my words. The younger brother, Cadwal,
Once Arviragus, in as like a figure
Strikes life into my speech, and shows much more
His own conceiving. Hark, the game is roused!   *A horn sounds*
O Cymbeline, heaven and my conscience knows
105   Thou didst unjustly banish me: whereon,
At three and two years old, I stole these babes,
Thinking to bar thee of succession, as
Thou reft'st me of my lands. Euriphile,
Thou wast their nurse, they took thee for their
        mother,
110   And every day do honour to her grave:
Myself, Belarius, that am Morgan called,
They take for natural father. The game is up.   *Exit*

Act 3 Scene 4   *running scene 9*

Enter Pisanio and Innogen   *Innogen in a riding-suit*

INNOGEN Thou told'st me when we came from horse the
        place
Was near at hand: ne'er longed my mother so
To see me first as I have now. Pisanio, man,
Where is Posthumus? What is in thy mind
5   That makes thee stare thus? Wherefore breaks that
        sigh
From th'inward of thee? One but painted thus
Would be interpreted a thing perplexed

---

91 **trick** capacity, skill   94 **three-foot** i.e. having three legs (a modest item of furniture)   96 **say** when I
say   99 **nerves** sinews   101 **in . . . figure** in a similar fashion/posture   102 **much more** i.e. than
Guiderius   103 **conceiving** understanding (of the story)   **Hark . . . roused!** Listen, the quarry (the animal
being hunted) is driven from cover!   105 **whereon** for which reason   107 **bar** deprive   **succession**
successors (to the throne)   108 **reft'st** robbed   109 **nurse** wet nurse, i.e. a woman employed to suckle
another woman's children   110 **her** i.e. Euriphile's   3.4 *Location: near Milford Haven*   1 **came from
horse** dismounted   2 **ne'er . . . now** i.e. the longing I have now (to see Posthumus) exceeds my mother's
longing to see me for the first time   6 **but painted thus** i.e. who looked like that in a picture   7 **perplexed**
troubled, distressed/confused

Beyond self-explication. Put thyself
Into a 'haviour of less fear, ere wildness
10   Vanquish my staider senses. What's the matter?
Why tender'st thou that paper to me with
A look untender? If't be summer news,
Smile to't before: if winterly, thou need'st
But keep that count'nance still. My husband's hand?
15   That drug-damned Italy hath out-craftied him,
And he's at some hard point. Speak, man, thy tongue
May take off some extremity, which to read
Would be even mortal to me.

PISANIO Please you read,
20   And you shall find me, wretched man, a thing
The most disdained of fortune.

INNOGEN *Reads* 'Thy mistress, Pisanio, hath played the
strumpet in my bed: the testimonies whereof lies
bleeding in me. I speak not out of weak surmises, but
25   from proof as strong as my grief, and as certain as I
expect my revenge. That part thou, Pisanio, must act
for me, if thy faith be not tainted with the breach of
hers; let thine own hands take away her life: I shall
give thee opportunity at Milford Haven. She hath my
30   letter for the purpose: where, if thou fear to strike,
and to make me certain it is done, thou art the
pander to her dishonour, and equally to me disloyal.'

PISANIO What shall I need to draw my sword? The paper   *Aside*
Hath cut her throat already. No, 'tis slander,
35   Whose edge is sharper than the sword, whose tongue
Outvenoms all the worms of Nile, whose breath
Rides on the posting winds, and doth belie
All corners of the world. Kings, queens and states,
Maids, matrons, nay, the secrets of the grave
40   This viperous slander enters. What cheer, madam?

---

8 self-explication the ability to explain themselves   **Put . . . fear** i.e. don't act in such a frightening way
9 ere before   **10 staider** calmer, more settled   **11 tender'st thou** do you offer   **paper** letter
12 summer i.e. good   **13 to't before** i.e. before giving it to me/in accordance with it (the good news)
winterly i.e. bad   **14 But** only   **hand** handwriting   **15 drug-damned Italy** Italians had a reputation for
knowledge of poisons and other substances   **out-craftied** outwitted through guile   **16 hard point** tight
spot, difficult situation   **tongue . . . extremity** i.e. telling me what's in it may help me bear the worst
18 mortal fatal   **23 testimonies** evidence   **lies . . . me** i.e. has cut me to the quick   **25 grief** injury/
anguish   **27 tainted** contaminated   **32 pander** procurer, pimp   **33 What** why, for what purpose
36 Outvenoms is more poisonous than   **worms of Nile** serpents of the Nile; the allusion is to the asp,
which Cleopatra used to kill herself   **37 posting winds** i.e. speeding, like a post-horse, the winds carry the
slanderous news far and wide   **belie** deceive, spread lies over   **38 states** people of high rank, statesmen/
countries

INNOGEN False to his bed? What is it to be false?
    To lie in watch there, and to think on him?
    To weep 'twixt clock and clock? If sleep charge
       nature,
    To break it with a fearful dream of him,
45   And cry myself awake? That's false to's bed, is it?
PISANIO Alas, good lady.
INNOGEN I false? Thy conscience witness: Iachimo,
    Thou didst accuse him of incontinency.
    Thou then looked'st like a villain: now methinks
50   Thy favour's good enough. Some jay of Italy,
    Whose mother was her painting, hath betrayed him:
    Poor I am stale, a garment out of fashion,
    And for I am richer than to hang by th'walls,
    I must be ripped: to pieces with me! O,
55   Men's vows are women's traitors. All good seeming,
    By thy revolt, O husband, shall be thought
    Put on for villainy; not born where't grows,
    But worn a bait for ladies.
PISANIO Good madam, hear me.
60 INNOGEN True honest men being heard like false Aeneas
    Were in his time thought false: and Sinon's weeping
    Did scandal many a holy tear, took pity
    From most true wretchedness. So thou, Posthumus,
    Wilt lay the leaven on all proper men;
65   Goodly and gallant shall be false and perjured
    From thy great fail.— Come, fellow, be thou honest,   *To Pisanio*
    Do thou thy master's bidding. When thou see'st him,
    A little witness my obedience. Look,
    I draw the sword myself: take it, and hit   *Draws sword and*
70   The innocent mansion of my love, my heart.   *gives it to Pisanio*
    Fear not, 'tis empty of all things but grief:
    Thy master is not there, who was indeed
    The riches of it. Do his bidding, strike.

---

43 'twixt…clock from hour to hour **charge** overcomes, i.e. so that I go to sleep **47 Thy conscience witness** perhaps addressed to the absent Posthumus **48 incontinency** unchastity, lack of sexual self-control **50 favour's** appearance is **jay** whore, literally a brightly-coloured bird **51 painting** use of cosmetics **52 stale** out of date/a lover made the object of ridicule for a rival's amusement **53 richer… th'walls** too valuable to just hang on a wall (like an old coat) **54 ripped** torn up for reusing/violently destroyed **55 seeming** outward show, appearance **56 revolt** reversal of ideas/betrayal **57 born where't grows** natural **58 worn** deliberately put on **bait** lure, temptation **60 being heard like** who were heard to speak like **Aeneas** hero of Virgil's *Aeneid*, who swore love to, and then deserted, Dido, who committed suicide as a result **61 Sinon** wept crocodile tears outside the walls of Troy to persuade the Trojans to admit the wooden horse containing the Greek warriors who destroyed the city **62 scandal** discredit, disgrace **took…wretchedness** prevented truly wretched cases from receiving any pity **64 leaven** agent for fermenting dough **66 fail** failure **68 witness** testify to **70 mansion** dwelling place

Thou mayst be valiant in a better cause,
75   But now thou seem'st a coward.
    PISANIO Hence, vile instrument,   *Throws away sword*
        Thou shalt not damn my hand!
    INNOGEN Why, I must die:
        And if I do not by thy hand, thou art
80   No servant of thy master's. Against self-slaughter
        There is a prohibition so divine
        That cravens my weak hand. Come, here's my heart:
        Something's afore't: soft, soft, we'll no defence,
        Obedient as the scabbard. What is here?   *Takes letters from*
85   The scriptures of the loyal Leonatus,   *her bosom*
        All turned to heresy? Away, away,   *Throws letters away*
        Corrupters of my faith, you shall no more
        Be stomachers to my heart! Thus may poor fools
        Believe false teachers: though those that are betrayed
90   Do feel the treason sharply, yet the traitor
        Stands in worse case of woe. And thou, Posthumus,
        That didst set up my disobedience gainst the king
        My father, and make me put into contempt the suits
        Of princely fellows, shalt hereafter find
95   It is no act of common passage, but
        A strain of rareness: and I grieve myself
        To think, when thou shalt be disedged by her
        That now thou tirest on, how thy memory
        Will then be panged by me. Prithee dispatch,
100   The lamb entreats the butcher. Where's thy knife?
        Thou art too slow to do thy master's bidding
        When I desire it too.
    PISANIO O gracious lady:
        Since I received command to do this business
105   I have not slept one wink.
    INNOGEN Do't, and to bed then.
    PISANIO I'll wake mine eyeballs out first.

---

76 vile instrument i.e. his sword   **80 self-slaughter** suicide   **82 cravens** makes a coward of   **83 afore't**
in front of it   **soft** not so fast, wait   **we'll no defence** I shan't defend myself   **84 Obedient ... scabbard**
i.e. as willing to receive the sword as the scabbard is   **85 scriptures ... heresy** Posthumus' letters are
likened to sacred writings, which, because of his breaking faith with love, are now heretical, sacrilegious
87 faith truth/honesty   **88 stomachers** decorative breast coverings   **91 Stands ... woe** is worse off
(because guilty)   **92 set up** initiate, instigate   **93 suits** love-suits, wooing   **94 princely** royal/fine
95 It ... rareness my love for you/my disobedience against my father was no ordinary thing, but one born of
exceptional qualities, circumstances   **97 disedged** dulled, blunted, plays on sexual sense   **98 tirest** feeds
(ravenously, like a bird of prey)   **99 panged** afflicted by pangs of conscience   **Prithee** please, literally 'I
pray thee'   **dispatch** hurry up/make an end (of me)   **107 wake ... first** stay awake until my eyeballs drop
out before I do that

INNOGEN Wherefore then
Didst undertake it? Why hast thou abused
110   So many miles with a pretence? This place?
Mine action and thine own? Our horses' labour?
The time inviting thee? The perturbed court
For my being absent, whereunto I never
Purpose return? Why hast thou gone so far
115   To be unbent when thou hast ta'en thy stand,
Th'elected deer before thee?
PISANIO But to win time
To lose so bad employment, in the which
I have considered of a course: good lady,
120   Hear me with patience.
INNOGEN Talk thy tongue weary, speak:
I have heard I am a strumpet, and mine ear,
Therein false struck, can take no greater wound,
Nor tent to bottom that. But speak.
125   **PISANIO** Then, madam,
I thought you would not back again.
INNOGEN Most like,
Bringing me here to kill me.
PISANIO Not so, neither:
130   But if I were as wise as honest, then
My purpose would prove well: it cannot be
But that my master is abused. Some villain,
Ay, and singular in his art, hath done you both
This cursèd injury.
135   **INNOGEN** Some Roman courtesan.
PISANIO No, on my life:
I'll give but notice you are dead, and send him
Some bloody sign of it, for 'tis commanded
I should do so: you shall be missed at court,
140   And that will well confirm it.
INNOGEN Why, good fellow,
What shall I do the while? Where bide? How live?

---

109 abused deceived/made bad use of   **112 inviting thee** i.e. by providing such a good opportunity
113 whereunto to which, where   **114 Purpose** intend to   **115 be unbent** change your mind; the image
is of the bent, drawn hunter's bow being unbent again without firing at the quarry   **stand** hidden shooting
position   **116 Th'elected** the chosen   **119 course** i.e. of action   **122 strumpet** prostitute   **123 Therein
false struck** in that matter falsely wounded   **take** receive   **124 tent** surgical probe to assess the depth of a
wound/roll of lint to clean a wound   **bottom** probe the depths/go deeper than   **126 back** go back
127 Most like that's very likely   **131 purpose would prove** plan would turn out   **132 abused**
deceived   **133 singular** unrivalled   **135 courtesan** one attached to a prince's court/prostitute   **142 bide**
abide, live

Or in my life what comfort, when I am
Dead to my husband?

145   **PISANIO** If you'll back to th'court—

INNOGEN No court, no father, nor no more ado
With that harsh, noble, simple nothing,
That Cloten, whose love-suit hath been to me
As fearful as a siege.

150   **PISANIO** If not at court,
Then not in Britain must you bide.

INNOGEN Where then?
Hath Britain all the sun that shines? Day? Night?
Are they not but in Britain? I'th'world's volume

155   Our Britain seems as of it, but not in't:
In a great pool a swan's nest. Prithee, think
There's livers out of Britain.

PISANIO I am most glad
You think of other place: th'ambassador,

160   Lucius the Roman, comes to Milford Haven
Tomorrow. Now, if you could wear a mind
Dark as your fortune is, and but disguise
That which, t'appear itself, must not yet be
But by self-danger, you should tread a course

165   Pretty and full of view: yea, haply, near
The residence of Posthumus; so nigh, at least,
That though his actions were not visible, yet
Report should render him hourly to your ear
As truly as he moves.

170   **INNOGEN** O, for such means,
Though peril to my modesty, not death on't,
I would adventure.

PISANIO Well then, here's the point:
You must forget to be a woman: change

175   Command into obedience, fear and niceness —
The handmaids of all women, or more truly
Woman it pretty self — into a waggish courage,
Ready in gibes, quick-answered, saucy and

---

154 **not but** only   **I'th'world's volume** in the book of the world; Britain is likened to a page torn out
of it   156 **swan's nest** i.e. built in the middle of a pool   157 **livers** people who live   161 **wear a mind**
entertain an idea/follow a course of action   163 **That** i.e. her female identity   164 **self-danger** bringing
danger upon yourself, i.e. as a woman alone   165 **view** prospects   **haply** perhaps   166 **nigh** near
168 **render** bring/describe   171 **modesty** chastity   **death on't** its loss   172 **adventure** take the risk
175 **Command into obedience** i.e. from a princess to a servant   **niceness** coyness/fastidiousness
176 **handmaids** i.e. qualities/attributes   177 **it** i.e. her   **waggish** roguish; 'wag' was a term for a saucy
boy, habitual joker   178 **Ready in gibes** ready to make mocking remarks   **quick-answered** quick in
reply

As quarrellous as the weasel: nay, you must
180 Forget that rarest treasure of your cheek,
Exposing it — but O, the harder heart!
Alack, no remedy — to the greedy touch
Of common-kissing Titan, and forget
Your laboursome and dainty trims, wherein
185 You made great Juno angry.

INNOGEN Nay, be brief.
I see into thy end, and am almost
A man already.

PISANIO First, make yourself but like one.
190 Forethinking this, I have already fit —   ⌊*Gives a bag of clothes*⌋
'Tis in my cloak-bag — doublet, hat, hose, all
That answer to them: would you in their serving,
And with what imitation you can borrow
From youth of such a season, 'fore noble Lucius
195 Present yourself, desire his service: tell him
Wherein you're happy — which will make him
      know,
If that his head have ear in music — doubtless
With joy he will embrace you, for he's honourable,
And, doubling that, most holy. Your means abroad:
200 You have me rich, and I will never fail
Beginning nor supplyment.

INNOGEN Thou art all the comfort
The gods will diet me with. Prithee away,
There's more to be considered: but we'll even
205 All that good time will give us. This attempt
I am soldier to, and will abide it with
A prince's courage. Away, I prithee.

PISANIO Well, madam, we must take a short farewell,
Lest being missed, I be suspected of
210 Your carriage from the court. My noble mistress,
Here is a box, I had it from the queen,
What's in't is precious: if you are sick at sea,

179 **quarrellous** quarrelsome   180 **Forget** neglect   **rarest...cheek** i.e. pale complexion, signifying her
social rank   183 **common-kissing Titan** the sun, who shines on everybody alike   184 **laboursome**...
trims beautifully-made and pretty clothes   185 **Juno** wife of the supreme Roman god Jupiter, was jealous of
her husband's attraction to beautiful mortals   187 **end** purpose, intention   190 **Forethinking** anticipat-
ing   **fit** ready   191 **doublet** close-fitting padded men's jacket   **hose** clothing for the legs   192 **answer to**
belong with, go with   **in their serving** with them serving you, i.e. using them as a disguise   194 **season**
age   195 **his service** to serve him   196 **Wherein you're happy** in what ways you are accomplished
make him know convince him   197 **If...music** if he has any appreciation for music at all   199 **means**
abroad resources away from home   201 **Beginning nor supplyment** i.e. beginning nor continuing to
supply you with money   203 **diet** feed, supply   204 **even** keep up with   206 **soldier to** willing to fight
for/bravely prepared for   **abide** endure   208 **short** brief, hurried   210 **Your carriage** taking you away

Or stomach-qualmed at land, a dram of this
Will drive away distemper. To some shade,
215   And fit you to your manhood: may the gods
Direct you to the best.
INNOGEN Amen: I thank thee.   *Exeunt*

Act 3 Scene 5   *running scene 10*

Enter Cymbeline, Queen, Cloten, Lucius and Lords

CYMBELINE Thus far, and so farewell.
LUCIUS Thanks, royal sir:
My emperor hath wrote, I must from hence,
And am right sorry that I must report ye
5   My master's enemy.
CYMBELINE Our subjects, sir,
Will not endure his yoke; and for ourself
To show less sovereignty than they, must needs
Appear unkinglike.
10   **LUCIUS** So, sir: I desire of you
A conduct over land, to Milford Haven.
Madam, all joy befall your grace, and you.
CYMBELINE My lords, you are appointed for that office:
The due of honour in no point omit.
15   So farewell, noble Lucius.
LUCIUS Your hand, my lord.
CLOTEN Receive it friendly: but from this time forth
I wear it as your enemy.
LUCIUS Sir, the event
20   Is yet to name the winner. Fare you well.
CYMBELINE Leave not the worthy Lucius, good my lords,
Till he have crossed the Severn. Happiness.
        Exeunt Lucius and others
QUEEN He goes hence frowning: but it honours us
That we have given him cause.
25   **CLOTEN** 'Tis all the better,
Your valiant Britons have their wishes in it.

---

214 **distemper** illness **shade** cover 215 **fit you** adapt, adjust yourself 3.5 *Location: Britain*
1 **Thus far** i.e. this is as far (as I will accompany you) 7 **ourself** myself using the royal plural pronoun
8 **must needs** can only 10 **So** very good, so be it 11 **conduct** safe conduct/escort 12 **befall** come to
13 **office** duty, task (i.e. accompanying Lucius) 14 **honour** i.e. the honour due to Lucius as an
ambassador **point** small way 19 **event** battle/outcome 22 **Severn** river bordering England and Wales
23 **it honours us** it does us credit (because we have been patriotic and defiant) 24 **cause** reason, grounds

CYMBELINE Lucius hath wrote already to the emperor
How it goes here. It fits us therefore ripely
Our chariots and our horsemen be in readiness:
30 The powers that he already hath in Gallia
Will soon be drawn to head, from whence he moves
His war for Britain.
QUEEN 'Tis not sleepy business,
But must be looked to speedily and strongly.
35 CYMBELINE Our expectation that it would be thus
Hath made us forward. But, my gentle queen,
Where is our daughter? She hath not appeared
Before the Roman, nor to us hath tendered
The duty of the day. She looks us like
40 A thing more made of malice than of duty,
We have noted it. Call her before us, for
We have been too slight in sufferance.

[Exit one or more]

QUEEN Royal sir,
Since the exile of Posthumus, most retired
45 Hath her life been: the cure whereof, my lord,
'Tis time must do. Beseech your majesty,
Forbear sharp speeches to her. She's a lady
So tender of rebukes that words are strokes,
And strokes death to her.

Enter a Messenger

50 CYMBELINE Where is she, sir? How
Can her contempt be answered?
MESSENGER Please you, sir,
Her chambers are all locked, and there's no answer
That will be given to th'loud'st of noise we make.
55 QUEEN My lord, when last I went to visit her,
She prayed me to excuse her keeping close,
Whereto constrained by her infirmity,
She should that duty leave unpaid to you
Which daily she was bound to proffer: this
60 She wished me to make known, but our great court
Made me to blame in memory.

---

28 **fits us** befits us, is appropriate that we   **ripely** immediately (because the time is ripe)   31 **drawn to head** brought to full strength   36 **forward** prepared   39 **duty . . . day** daily greeting she owes Cymbeline as her father and king   **looks us** appears to me (us)   42 **slight in sufferance** lax in allowing such behaviour   44 **retired** withdrawn, reclusive   47 **Forbear** hold back, refrain from   48 **tender of** sensitive to   51 **answered** accounted for, excused   56 **close** private, secluded   57 **Whereto . . . infirmity** to which she is compelled by her illness   59 **proffer** offer, present

CYMBELINE Her doors locked?
        Not seen of late? Grant heavens that which I fear
        Prove false.   *Exit*
65   QUEEN Son, I say, follow the king.
        CLOTEN That man of hers, Pisanio, her old servant
        I have not seen these two days.   *Exit*
        QUEEN Go, look after.—
        Pisanio, thou that stand'st so for Posthumus!
70   He hath a drug of mine: I pray his absence
        Proceed by swallowing that, for he believes
        It is a thing most precious. But for her,
        Where is she gone? Haply despair hath seized her:
        Or, winged with fervour of her love, she's flown
75   To her desired Posthumus: gone she is
        To death or to dishonour, and my end
        Can make good use of either. She being down,
        I have the placing of the British crown.—
Enter Cloten
        How now, my son?
80   CLOTEN 'Tis certain she is fled:
        Go in and cheer the king, he rages, none
        Dare come about him.
        QUEEN All the better: may   *Aside*
        This night forestall him of the coming day. *Exit Queen*
85   CLOTEN I love and hate her: for she's fair and royal,
        And that she hath all courtly parts more exquisite
        Than lady, ladies, woman — from every one
        The best she hath, and she, of all compounded,
        Outsells them all — I love her therefore: but
90   Disdaining me, and throwing favours on
        The low Posthumus, slanders so her judgement
        That what's else rare is choked: and in that point
        I will conclude to hate her, nay, indeed,
        To be revenged upon her. For when fools shall—
Enter Pisanio
95   Who is here?— What, are you packing, sirrah?
        Come hither: ah, you precious pander! Villain,

---

69 **stand'st so for** support/represent   71 **Proceed by** result from   73 **Haply** it may be, perhaps   76 **end** aim, design   78 **placing** arranging, disposal   84 **forestall…day** prevent him from seeing tomorrow   85 **her** Innogen   **for** because   86 **that** because   **parts** qualities   87 **from…hath** as though she has taken the best qualities from each and every woman   88 **compounded** made up   89 **Outsells** exceeds in value   91 **slanders** discredits   92 **rare** exceptional about her   95 **packing** plotting, scheming/running away, leaving   **sirrah** fellow (addressed to a social inferior)   96 **pander** bawd, sexual go-between

Where is thy lady? In a word, or else
Thou art straightway with the fiends.   *Threatens him*

PISANIO O, good my lord!

100   CLOTEN Where is thy lady? Or, by Jupiter,
I will not ask again. Close villain,
I'll have this secret from thy heart, or rip
Thy heart to find it. Is she with Posthumus,
From whose so many weights of baseness cannot

105   A dram of worth be drawn?

PISANIO Alas, my lord,
How can she be with him? When was she missed?
He is in Rome.

CLOTEN Where is she, sir? Come nearer:

110   No further halting: satisfy me home,
What is become of her?

PISANIO O my all-worthy lord!

CLOTEN All-worthy villain,
Discover where thy mistress is at once,

115   At the next word: no more of 'worthy lord!'
Speak, or thy silence on the instant is
Thy condemnation and thy death.

PISANIO Then, sir,
This paper is the history of my knowledge

120   Touching her flight.   *Shows a letter*

CLOTEN Let's see't: I will pursue her
Even to Augustus' throne.

PISANIO Or this, or perish.   *Aside*
She's far enough, and what he learns by this

125   May prove his travel, not her danger.

CLOTEN Hum!

PISANIO I'll write to my lord she's dead: O Innogen,   *Aside*
Safe mayst thou wander, safe return again!

CLOTEN Sirrah, is this letter true?

130   PISANIO Sir, as I think.

CLOTEN It is Posthumus' hand, I know't. Sirrah, if thou
wouldst not be a villain, but do me true service,
undergo those employments wherein I should have
cause to use thee with a serious industry, that is,

---

98 **Thou…fiends** i.e. I will instantly kill you, sending your soul to hell   101 **Close** secretive
104 **weights** i.e. weights and measures   105 **dram** a tiny measure   109 **Come nearer** get to the point/
come (physically) closer to me   110 **halting** hesitation   **home** completely   114 **Discover** reveal
120 **Touching** regarding   123 **Or…perish** i.e. either show him the letter or be killed   125 **travel** literally
'travelling'; plays on 'travail', meaning 'trouble'/'labour'   133 **undergo** undertake   **employments**
tasks   134 **serious** careful, meticulous   **industry** application, diligence

135   what villainy soe'er I bid thee do, to perform it
           directly and truly, I would think thee an honest man:
           thou shouldst neither want my means for thy relief,
           nor my voice for thy preferment.
        PISANIO Well, my good lord.
140   CLOTEN Wilt thou serve me? For since patiently and
           constantly thou hast stuck to the bare fortune of that
           beggar Posthumus, thou canst not in the course of
           gratitude but be a diligent follower of mine. Wilt thou
           serve me?
145   PISANIO Sir, I will.
        CLOTEN Give me thy hand, here's my purse. Hast any of
           thy late master's garments in thy possession?
        PISANIO I have, my lord, at my lodging, the same suit he
           wore when he took leave of my lady and mistress.
150   CLOTEN The first service thou dost me, fetch that suit
           hither: let it be thy first service, go.
        PISANIO I shall, my lord.   *Exit*
        CLOTEN Meet thee at Milford Haven! — I forgot to ask
           him one thing, I'll remember't anon. — Even there,
155   thou villain Posthumus, will I kill thee. I would these
           garments were come. She said upon a time — the
           bitterness of it I now belch from my heart — that she
           held the very garment of Posthumus in more respect
           than my noble and natural person, together with the
160   adornment of my qualities. With that suit upon my
           back will I ravish her: first kill him, and in her eyes;
           there shall she see my valour, which will then be a
           torment to her contempt. He on the ground, my
           speech of insultment ended on his dead body, and
165   when my lust hath dined — which, as I say, to vex
           her I will execute in the clothes that she so praised —
           to the court I'll knock her back, foot her home again.
           She hath despised me rejoicingly, and I'll be merry in
           my revenge.—
        Enter Pisanio   **With Posthumus' clothes**
170   Be those the garments?
        PISANIO Ay, my noble lord.
        CLOTEN How long is't since she went to Milford Haven?
        PISANIO She can scarce be there yet.

---

137 want lack   relief assistance   138 voice … preferment support for your promotion, advancement
142 course ordinary way   143 but other than   146 Hast do you have   147 late i.e. former   156 upon
a time once   161 her eyes i.e. in her sight   164 insultment scornful, contemptuous triumph   167 knock
beat   foot kick

CLOTEN Bring this apparel to my chamber. That is the
175   second thing that I have commanded thee. The third
is that thou wilt be a voluntary mute to my design.
Be but duteous, and true preferment shall tender
itself to thee. My revenge is now at Milford: would I
had wings to follow it. Come, and be true.   *Exit*
180 PISANIO Thou bid'st me to my loss: for true to thee
Were to prove false, which I will never be,
To him that is most true. To Milford go,
And find not her whom thou pursuest. Flow, flow,
You heavenly blessings, on her. This fool's speed
185   Be crossed with slowness; labour be his meed.   *Exit*

Act 3 Scene 6

running scene 11

Enter Innogen alone   *In boy's clothes*

INNOGEN I see a man's life is a tedious one:
I have tired myself, and for two nights together
Have made the ground my bed. I should be sick,
But that my resolution helps me. Milford,
5   When from the mountain-top Pisanio showed thee,
Thou wast within a ken. O Jove, I think
Foundations fly the wretched: such, I mean,
Where they should be relieved. Two beggars told me
I could not miss my way. Will poor folks lie,
10   That have afflictions on them, knowing 'tis
A punishment or trial? Yes; no wonder,
When rich ones scarce tell true. To lapse in fullness
Is sorer than to lie for need, and falsehood
Is worse in kings than beggars. My dear lord,
15   Thou art one o'th'false ones. Now I think on thee
My hunger's gone; but even before, I was
At point to sink for food. But what is this?
Here is a path to't: 'tis some savage hold:
I were best not call; I dare not call: yet famine,
20   Ere clean it o'erthrow nature, makes it valiant.

---

176 voluntary mute i.e. willingly silent; mutes were servants whose tongues were cut out to stop them
telling secrets   **177 tender** offer, present   **180 to my loss** i.e. to lose my honour   **182 him . . . true** i.e.
Posthumus   **185 crossed** hindered, thwarted   **meed** reward   **3.6** *Location: Wales, outside Belarius'*
cave   **2 tired** exhausted/dressed (attired)   **6 ken** sight   **7 Foundations . . . wretched** things recede as the
poor or desperate approach/charitable organizations fail those who need them most   **11 trial** test of their
moral character/endurance   **12 scarce** hardly ever   **lapse in fullness** do wrong when in a state of
prosperity   **13 sorer** worse   **15 on** of, about   **16 even before** only a moment ago   **17 At point** ready,
just about   **18 hold** stronghold, lair   **19 were best** had better   **20 Ere . . . nature** i.e. before it kills me
it nature

Plenty and peace breeds cowards: hardness ever
Of hardiness is mother. Ho! Who's here?
If anything that's civil, speak: if savage,
Take or lend. Ho! No answer? Then I'll enter.
25   Best draw my sword; and if mine enemy
But fear the sword like me, he'll scarcely look on't.   *Draws*
Such a foe, good heavens!   *Exit [into the cave]*
Enter Belarius, Guiderius and Arviragus
BELARIUS You, Polydore, have proved best woodman
      and
Are master of the feast: Cadwal and I
30   Will play the cook and servant: 'tis our match.
The sweat of industry would dry and die
But for the end it works to. Come, our stomachs
Will make what's homely savoury: weariness
Can snore upon the flint when resty sloth
35   Finds the down pillow hard. Now peace be here,
Poor house, that keep'st thyself.
GUIDERIUS I am throughly weary.
ARVIRAGUS I am weak with toil, yet strong in appetite.
GUIDERIUS There is cold meat i'th'cave, we'll browse on
      that
40   Whilst what we have killed be cooked.
BELARIUS Stay; come not in: *Looks into the cave*
But that it eats our victuals, I should think
Here were a fairy.
GUIDERIUS What's the matter, sir?
45   **BELARIUS** By Jupiter, an angel! Or if not,
An earthly paragon. Behold divineness
No elder than a boy.
Enter Innogen
INNOGEN Good masters, harm me not:
Before I entered here, I called, and thought
50   To have begged or bought what I have took: good
      troth,
I have stol'n nought, nor would not, though I had
      found

---

21 hardness...mother hardship always gives rise to (is the mother of) endurance   **24 Take or lend** take my life/money, or give me food, help me   **25 Best** I had better   **27 Such...heavens!** i.e. she begs the heavens to let it be a foe of that sort   **28 woodman** hunter   **30 match** bargain, agreement   **31 The...to** i.e. no one would work if it weren't for some purpose   **33 homely** plain   **34 flint** hard, stony ground   **resty sloth** well-rested laziness   **35 down** feather   **36 keep'st thyself** i.e. looks after itself, is uninhabited **37 throughly** thoroughly, utterly   **39 browse** nibble   **42 But that** if it weren't for the fact that   **victuals** food   **46 paragon** outstanding example   **50 good troth** in good truth   **51 nought** nothing

Gold strewed i'th'floor. Here's money for my meat: *Offers money*
I would have left it on the board so soon
As I had made my meal, and parted
55   With prayers for the provider.
GUIDERIUS Money, youth?
ARVIRAGUS All gold and silver rather turn to dirt,
As 'tis no better reckoned but of those
Who worship dirty gods.
60   **INNOGEN** I see you're angry:
Know, if you kill me for my fault, I should
Have died had I not made it.
BELARIUS Whither bound?
INNOGEN To Milford Haven.
65   **BELARIUS** What's your name?
INNOGEN Fidele, sir: I have a kinsman who
Is bound for Italy; he embarked at Milford,
To whom being going, almost spent with hunger,
I am fall'n in this offence.
70   **BELARIUS** Prithee, fair youth,
Think us no churls: nor measure our good minds
By this rude place we live in. Well encountered!
'Tis almost night: you shall have better cheer
Ere you depart, and thanks to stay and eat it.
75   Boys, bid him welcome.
GUIDERIUS Were you a woman, youth,
I should woo hard but be your groom in honesty:
Ay, bid for you as I'd buy.
ARVIRAGUS I'll make't my comfort
80   He is a man, I'll love him as my brother:
And such a welcome as I'd give to him
After long absence, such is yours. Most welcome!
Be sprightly, for you fall 'mongst friends.
INNOGEN 'Mongst friends
85   If brothers.— Would it had been so that they   *Aside*
Had been my father's sons, then had my prize

---

52 i'th'floor on the floor/in among the rushes on the floor   **53 board** table   **so** as   **54 parted** departed
58 reckoned valued, esteemed   **but of** except by   **61 should** would   **62 made** committed   **63 Whither
bound?** Where are you going?   **66 Fidele** means 'the faithful one' (Latin)   **68 spent** exhausted   **69 in**
into   **71 churls** impolite, mean-spirited people/peasants   **72 rude** uncivilized   **73 cheer** food/
entertainment   **74 thanks** our approval   **77 hard** vigorously, boldly   **but be** but to be/if I could not
otherwise be   **in honesty** your honest, loyal husband/by honourable means   **78 Ay . . . buy** i.e. woo you in
the same way as I would love you as your husband   **83 sprightly** cheerful   **84 'Mongst . . . brothers** I
must be amongst friends if I am amongst brothers   **86 prize . . . ballasting** value would be less since she
would no longer be next in line to the throne and thus more equal to Posthumus; puns on **prize** as 'cargo,
booty in a captured ship'

Been less, and so more equal ballasting
To thee, Posthumus.

BELARIUS He wrings at some distress.

90   **GUIDERIUS** Would I could free't.

ARVIRAGUS Or I, whate'er it be,
What pain it cost, what danger. Gods!

BELARIUS Hark, boys.   *They whisper aside*

INNOGEN Great men   *To herself*

95   That had a court no bigger than this cave,
That did attend themselves and had the virtue
Which their own conscience sealed them —
    laying by
That nothing-gift of differing multitudes —
Could not out-peer these twain. Pardon me, gods,

100   I'd change my sex to be companion with them,
Since Leonatus' false.

BELARIUS It shall be so:
Boys, we'll go dress our hunt. Fair youth, come in:
Discourse is heavy, fasting: when we have supped

105   We'll mannerly demand thee of thy story,
So far as thou wilt speak it.

GUIDERIUS Pray draw near.

ARVIRAGUS The night to th'owl and morn to th'lark less
    welcome.

INNOGEN Thanks, sir.

110   **ARVIRAGUS** I pray draw near.   *Exeunt*

Act 3 Scene 7   *running scene 12*

Enter two Roman Senators and Tribunes

FIRST SENATOR This is the tenor of the emperor's writ:
That since the common men are now in action
Gainst the Pannonians and Dalmatians,
And that the legions now in Gallia are

5   Full weak to undertake our wars against
The fall'n-off Britons, that we do incite

89 **wrings** writhes/wrings his hands   90 **free't** remove the trouble   96 **attend themselves** i.e. had no
servants   97 **sealed them** confirmed in them   **laying by** setting aside   98 **nothing-gift** worthless gift
(flattery, adulation)   **differing multitudes** fickle crowds   99 **out-peer** surpass   **twain** two
101 **Leonatus'** Leonatus is   103 **dress our hunt** i.e. prepare what we have caught for cooking
104 **Discourse . . . fasting** speech is tedious while hungry   105 **mannerly** politely   **demand** ask
108 **The . . . welcome** i.e. not even the night to the owl or the morning to the lark are as welcome to us
3.7 *Location: Rome*   1 **tenor** substance   **writ** order   2 **men** soldiers   3 **Pannonians and Dalmatians**
ancient inhabitants of what are now Hungary and the Balkans   5 **Full** very   6 **fall'n off** rebellious/
defaulting   **incite** summon/stir up

The gentry to this business. He creates
Lucius proconsul: and to you the tribunes,
For this immediate levy, he commands
10 His absolute commission. Long live Caesar!
TRIBUNE Is Lucius general of the forces?
SECOND SENATOR Ay.
TRIBUNE Remaining now in Gallia?
FIRST SENATOR With those legions
15 Which I have spoke of, whereunto your levy
Must be supplyant: the words of your commission
Will tie you to the numbers and the time
Of their dispatch.
TRIBUNE We will discharge our duty.   *Exeunt*

Act 4 Scene 1   *running scene 13*

Enter Cloten alone

CLOTEN I am near to th'place where they should meet, if
Pisanio have mapped it truly. How fit his garments
serve me! Why should his mistress, who was made by
him that made the tailor, not be fit too? The rather —
5 saving reverence of the word — for 'tis said a woman's
fitness comes by fits. Therein I must play the
workman. I dare speak it to myself, for it is not
vainglory for a man and his glass to confer in his own
chamber; I mean, the lines of my body are as well
10 drawn as his: no less young, more strong, not beneath
him in fortunes, beyond him in the advantage of the
time, above him in birth, alike conversant in general
services, and more remarkable in single oppositions;
yet this imperceiverant thing loves him in my despite.
15 What mortality is! Posthumus, thy head, which now
is growing upon thy shoulders, shall within this hour
be off, thy mistress enforced, thy garments cut to
pieces before thy face: and all this done, spurn her
home to her father, who may haply be a little angry

9 commands appoints   **10 absolute commission** complete authority   **16 supplyant** ready to supply
troops/supplementary   **4.1** *Location: Wales*   **2 fit** fittingly, perfectly   **4 fit** inclined, plays on sense of
'sexually compatible'   **5 saving ... word** standard apology for coarse language; in this case **fitness**, meaning
'sexual inclination'   **6 fits** fits and starts   **play the workman** use my skill like a craftsman   **8 vainglory**
idle boasting   **glass** mirror   **11 advantage ... time** i.e. current favourable circumstances   **12 alike**
conversant equally experienced   **general services** military operations serving alongside others, probably
with bawdy connotations   **13 single oppositions** individual combats   **14 imperceiverant** imperceptive
in my despite in spite of my qualities/to spite me   **15 mortality** mankind/existence/death   **17 enforced**
forced, constrained/raped   **18 spurn** kick   **19 haply** perhaps

20   for my so rough usage: but my mother, having power
         of his testiness, shall turn all into my commendations.
         My horse is tied up safe. Out, sword, and to a sore   *Draws*
         purpose! Fortune put them into my hand. This is the
         very description of their meeting-place, and the fellow
25   dares not deceive me.   *Exit*

Act 4 Scene 2   *running scene 14*

Enter Belarius, Guiderius, Arviragus and Innogen from the
cave   *Innogen disguised as Fidele*

BELARIUS You are not well: remain here in the cave,   *To Innogen*
      We'll come to you after hunting.
ARVIRAGUS Brother, stay here: *To Innogen*
      Are we not brothers?
5   **INNOGEN** So man and man should be,
      But clay and clay differs in dignity,
      Whose dust is both alike. I am very sick.
    GUIDERIUS Go you to hunting, I'll abide with him.
    INNOGEN So sick I am not, yet I am not well:
10   But not so citizen a wanton as
      To seem to die ere sick: so please you, leave me,
      Stick to your journal course: the breach of custom
      Is breach of all. I am ill, but your being by me
      Cannot amend me. Society is no comfort
15   To one not sociable: I am not very sick,
      Since I can reason of it: pray you trust me here,
      I'll rob none but myself, and let me die,
      Stealing so poorly.
    GUIDERIUS I love thee: I have spoke it,
20   How much the quantity, the weight as much,
      As I do love my father.
    BELARIUS What? How? How?
    ARVIRAGUS If it be sin to say so, sir, I yoke me
      In my good brother's fault: I know not why
25   I love this youth, and I have heard you say
      Love's reason's without reason. The bier at door,

20 **usage** treatment   **power of** control over   21 **testiness** short temper/rashness   **commendations**
credit, renown   22 **sore** grievous, violent; bawdy quibble on **sword** (penis) and **sore** (wound/vagina)
23 **Fortune** may Fortune   **4.2**   10 **citizen** city-bred   **wanton** weakling/spoiled child/unchaste, lewd
person   11 **ere** before   12 **journal** daily, usual routine   **breach of custom** disruption of usual habit
14 **amend me** make me better   **Society** company   16 **reason of** talk (lucidly) about   17 **none** no one
18 **Stealing so poorly** i.e. if I steal from those who have so little   20 **weight** intensity   23 **yoke me** am
joined, associated   26 **bier at door** if the coffin were at the door

And a demand who is't shall die, I'd say
'My father, not this youth.'

BELARIUS O noble strain!   *Aside*

30   O worthiness of nature, breed of greatness!
Cowards father cowards, and base things sire base:
Nature hath meal and bran, contempt and grace.
I'm not their father, yet who this should be
Doth miracle itself, loved before me.—

35   'Tis the ninth hour o'th'morn.   *Aloud*

ARVIRAGUS Brother, farewell.

INNOGEN I wish ye sport.

ARVIRAGUS You health.— So please you, sir.

INNOGEN These are kind creatures.   *Aside*

40   Gods, what lies I have heard!
Our courtiers say all's savage but at court;
Experience, O, thou disprov'st report!
Th'imperious seas breeds monsters; for the dish
Poor tributary rivers as sweet fish:

45   I am sick still, heart-sick. Pisanio,
I'll now taste of thy drug.   *Drinks*

GUIDERIUS I could not stir him:
He said he was gentle, but unfortunate;
Dishonestly afflicted, but yet honest.

50   **ARVIRAGUS** Thus did he answer me, yet said hereafter
I might know more.

BELARIUS To th'field, to th'field!
We'll leave you for this time, go in and rest.

ARVIRAGUS We'll not be long away.

55   **BELARIUS** Pray be not sick,
For you must be our housewife.

INNOGEN Well or ill,
I am bound to you.   *Exit [into the cave]*

BELARIUS And shalt be ever.

60   This youth, howe'er distressed, appears he hath had
Good ancestors.

ARVIRAGUS How angel-like he sings!

GUIDERIUS But his neat cookery! He cut our roots in
characters,

---

29 strain offspring, stock/inherited character/disposition   **30 breed** lineage, ancestry   **32 meal and bran**
grain and husks   **33 yet…me** it is a miracle that they should love this boy, whoever he is, more than
me   **38 So…sir** at your service, sir (to Belarius)   **41 but** except   **44 tributary** subsidiary   **47 stir** move,
persuade   **48 gentle** well-born   **49 Dishonestly afflicted** unjustly oppressed/troubled by others'
dishonesty   **52 To th'field** i.e. let's go hunting   **58 bound** tied, allied/indebted   **60 distressed** troubled,
afflicted   **63 roots** vegetables   **characters** shapes, especially letters

And sauced our broths as Juno had been sick
65   And he her dieter.
ARVIRAGUS Nobly he yokes
A smiling with a sigh, as if the sigh
Was that it was for not being such a smile:
The smile mocking the sigh, that it would fly
70   From so divine a temple, to commix
With winds that sailors rail at.
GUIDERIUS I do note
That grief and patience, rooted in him both,
Mingle their spurs together.
75 **ARVIRAGUS** Grow patience,
And let the stinking elder, grief, untwine
His perishing root with the increasing vine.
BELARIUS It is great morning. Come away.— Who's
    there?

Enter Cloten

CLOTEN I cannot find those runagates, that villain
80   Hath mocked me. I am faint.
BELARIUS 'Those runagates'?
Means he not us? I partly know him, 'tis
Cloten, the son o'th'queen. I fear some ambush.
I saw him not these many years, and yet
85   I know 'tis he. We are held as outlaws: hence!
GUIDERIUS He is but one: you and my brother search
What companies are near: pray you away,
Let me alone with him.

                        [Exeunt Belarius and Arviragus]

CLOTEN Soft, what are you
90   That fly me thus? Some villain mountaineers?
I have heard of such. What slave art thou?
GUIDERIUS A thing
More slavish did I ne'er than answering
A slave without a knock.
95 **CLOTEN** Thou art a robber,
A law-breaker, a villain: yield thee, thief.

---

64 **as** as though   **Juno** wife of Jupiter and queen of the gods   65 **dieter** one who regulates the diet/
feeder   66 **yokes** ties together, attaches   68 **that** what   70 **commix** mingle   71 **rail** utter abusive
language   74 **spurs** tree roots   75 **Grow . . . vine** the wish is that grief, like a **stinking elder** (which had an
evil reputation because of its pungent smell), will disentangle its deadly roots from those of the growing vine
(patience)   77 **with** from   78 **great morning** broad daylight   79 **runagates** runaways/rogues
80 **mocked** tricked, fooled   85 **held** regarded   86 **but** only   87 **companies** followers, others   89 **Soft**
not so fast   90 **fly** run away, flee from   94 **A . . . knock** I never did anything more slave-like than
responding to an insulting slave/someone calling me a slave without beating, hitting them

GUIDERIUS To who? To thee? What art thou? Have not I
        An arm as big as thine? A heart as big?
        Thy words I grant are bigger, for I wear not
100   My dagger in my mouth. Say what thou art,
        Why I should yield to thee?
CLOTEN Thou villain base,
        Know'st me not by my clothes?
GUIDERIUS No, nor thy tailor, rascal,
105   Who is thy grandfather: he made those clothes,
        Which, as it seems, make thee.
CLOTEN Thou precious varlet,
        My tailor made them not.
GUIDERIUS Hence, then, and thank
110   The man that gave them thee. Thou art some fool,
        I am loath to beat thee.
CLOTEN Thou injurious thief,
        Hear but my name, and tremble.
GUIDERIUS What's thy name?
115 **CLOTEN** Cloten, thou villain.
GUIDERIUS Cloten, thou double villain be thy name,
        I cannot tremble at it: were it toad, or adder, spider,
        'Twould move me sooner.
CLOTEN To thy further fear,
120   Nay, to thy mere confusion, thou shalt know
        I am son to th'queen.
GUIDERIUS I am sorry for't: not seeming
        So worthy as thy birth.
CLOTEN Art not afeard?
125 **GUIDERIUS** Those that I reverence, those I fear, the wise:
        At fools I laugh, not fear them.
CLOTEN Die the death:
        When I have slain thee with my proper hand,
        I'll follow those that even now fled hence,
130   And on the gates of Lud's town set your heads:
        Yield, rustic mountaineer.   *Fight and exeunt*
Enter Belarius and Arviragus
BELARIUS No company's abroad?

---

99 I . . . mouth i.e. I am not all talk when it comes to fighting   103 clothes i.e. courtly clothes, showing
rank   107 varlet scoundrel   111 loath reluctant   112 injurious insulting   120 mere confusion
absolute destruction/agitation of the mind   122 not seeming since you don't seem   123 So as
128 proper own   130 on . . . heads the heads of traitors were fixed on poles at the gateway to London
Bridge   132 abroad around, about

ARVIRAGUS None in the world: you did mistake him, sure.

BELARIUS I cannot tell: long is it since I saw him,

135   But time hath nothing blurred those lines of favour
Which then he wore: the snatches in his voice
And burst of speaking were as his: I am absolute
'Twas very Cloten.

ARVIRAGUS In this place we left them.

140   I wish my brother make good time with him,
You say he is so fell.

BELARIUS Being scarce made up,
I mean to man, he had not apprehension
Of roaring terrors: for defect of judgement

145   Is oft the cause of fear.

Enter Guiderius   *With Cloten's head*

But see thy brother.

GUIDERIUS This Cloten was a fool, an empty purse,
There was no money in't: not Hercules
Could have knocked out his brains, for he had none:

150   Yet I not doing this, the fool had borne
My head, as I do his.

BELARIUS What hast thou done?

GUIDERIUS I am perfect what: cut off one Cloten's head,
Son to the queen, after his own report,

155   Who called me traitor, mountaineer, and swore
With his own single hand he'd take us in,
Displace our heads where — thank the gods — they
grow,
And set them on Lud's town.

BELARIUS We are all undone.

160   **GUIDERIUS** Why, worthy father, what have we to lose
But that he swore to take, our lives? The law
Protects not us, then why should we be tender
To let an arrogant piece of flesh threat us,
Play judge and executioner all himself,

165   For we do fear the law? What company
Discover you abroad?

---

133 **sure** clearly   135 **lines of favour** facial lines, lineaments   136 **snatches** catches, hesitancy
137 **absolute** certain   138 **very** indeed   140 **make...with** to do well against   141 **fell** fierce
142 **Being... man** being intellectually defective/barely come to manhood   143 **apprehension** perception,
understanding   144 **judgement** reason, i.e. the rational mind   148 **Hercules** classical hero, who wielded a
club, and performed a series of impossible tasks   150 **I...this** if I hadn't done this   153 **perfect** well aware
154 **after** according to   156 **take us in** capture us   161 **The...us** i.e. because they are banished
162 **tender** meek/submissive   163 **threat** threaten   165 **For** because

BELARIUS No single soul
Can we set eye on, but in all safe reason
He must have some attendants. Though his humour
170 Was nothing but mutation, ay, and that
From one bad thing to worse, not frenzy,
Not absolute madness could so far have raved
To bring him here alone: although perhaps
It may be heard at court that such as we
175 Cave here, hunt here, are outlaws, and in time
May make some stronger head, the which he
    hearing —
As it is like him — might break out and swear
He'd fetch us in, yet is't not probable
To come alone, either he so undertaking,
180 Or they so suffering: then on good ground we fear,
If we do fear this body hath a tail
More perilous than the head.

ARVIRAGUS Let ord'nance
Come as the gods foresay it: howsoe'er,
185 My brother hath done well.

BELARIUS I had no mind
To hunt this day: the boy Fidele's sickness
Did make my way long forth.

GUIDERIUS With his own sword,
190 Which he did wave against my throat, I have ta'en
His head from him: I'll throw't into the creek
Behind our rock, and let it to the sea
And tell the fishes he's the queen's son, Cloten:
That's all I reck.   *Exit*

195 **BELARIUS** I fear 'twill be revenged:
Would, Polydore, thou hadst not done't, though
    valour
Becomes thee well enough.

ARVIRAGUS Would I had done't,
So the revenge alone pursued me! Polydore,
200 I love thee brotherly, but envy much
Thou hast robbed me of this deed: I would revenges

---

168 safe sane, sound   **169 humour** disposition, frame of mind   **170 mutation** changeableness (of mood)
175 Cave dwell in caves   **176 make … head** assemble a stronger force   **177 like him** just like him, in his
nature   **might break out** he might burst out   **178 fetch us in** capture us and bring us before the court
179 To come that he would come   **180 suffering** allowing   **181 tail** i.e. a group coming after him
183 ord'nance what is ordained   **184 foresay** predict/determine   **howsoe'er** however it may turn out/
nevertheless   **186 mind** inclination   **188 way long forth** way forward seem long   **192 to** i.e. flow to
194 reck care   **199 So** so that   **201 I would** I wish that (all the)

That possible strength might meet would seek us
　　through
And put us to our answer.

BELARIUS Well, 'tis done:

205 We'll hunt no more today, nor seek for danger
Where there's no profit. I prithee, to our rock,
You and Fidele play the cooks: I'll stay
Till hasty Polydore return, and bring him
To dinner presently.

210 **ARVIRAGUS** Poor sick Fidele!
I'll willingly to him: to gain his colour
I'd let a parish of such Clotens' blood,
And praise myself for charity.　　　*Exit [into the cave]*

BELARIUS O thou goddess,

215 Thou divine Nature, thou thyself thou blazon'st
In these two princely boys! They are as gentle
As zephyrs blowing below the violet,
Not wagging his sweet head; and yet as rough,
Their royal blood enchafed, as the rud'st wind,

220 That by the top doth take the mountain pine,
And make him stoop to th'vale. 'Tis wonder
That an invisible instinct should frame them
To royalty unlearned, honour untaught,
Civility not seen from other, valour

225 That wildly grows in them, but yields a crop
As if it had been sowed. Yet still it's strange
What Cloten's being here to us portends,
Or what his death will bring us.

Enter Guiderius

GUIDERIUS Where's my brother?

230 I have sent Cloten's clotpoll down the stream
In embassy to his mother; his body's hostage
For his return.　　　　　　　　*Solemn music*

BELARIUS My ingenious instrument!
Hark, Polydore, it sounds: but what occasion

235 Hath Cadwal now to give it motion? Hark!

---

202 **possible strength** power we might muster　**meet** i.e. in battle　203 **put . . . answer** force us to
answer them in battle/cause us to show them what we're made of　208 **hasty** rash, impetuous　211 **gain**
restore　212 **let . . . blood** blood letting or bleeding a patient was a common medical procedure; Arviragus is
proposing a different kind of bloodletting here, shedding the blood of (killing) a parish full of Clotens to make
Innogen well　215 **blazon'st** are depicted　217 **zephyrs** soft winds, breezes; the **zephyr** is the west wind
218 **wagging** moving/disturbing　219 **enchafed** heated, aroused　**rud'st** roughest (rudest)　222 **frame**
train, direct/fit, suit　224 **seen from other** not learned from others　225 **wildly** naturally, without being
cultivated　230 **clotpoll** blockhead　233 **ingenious** skilfully constructed　234 **occasion** reason
235 **give it motion** i.e. play it

GUIDERIUS Is he at home?

BELARIUS He went hence even now.

GUIDERIUS What does he mean? Since death of my
      dear'st mother
It did not speak before. All solemn things
240   Should answer solemn accidents. The matter?
Triumphs for nothing and lamenting toys
Is jollity for apes and grief for boys.
Is Cadwal mad?

Enter Arviragus, with Innogen dead, bearing her in his arms

BELARIUS Look, here he comes,
245   And brings the dire occasion in his arms
Of what we blame him for.

ARVIRAGUS The bird is dead
That we have made so much on. I had rather
Have skipped from sixteen years of age to sixty,
250   To have turned my leaping time into a crutch,
Than have seen this.

GUIDERIUS O sweetest, fairest lily!
My brother wears thee not the one half so well
As when thou grew'st thyself.

255 **BELARIUS** O melancholy,
Who ever yet could sound thy bottom? Find
The ooze to show what coast thy sluggish crare
Might easiliest harbour in? Thou blessèd thing,
Jove knows what man thou mightst have made:
      but, ay,
260   Thou died'st a most rare boy, of melancholy.
How found you him?

ARVIRAGUS Stark, as you see:
Thus smiling, as some fly had tickled slumber,
Not as death's dart being laughed at: his right cheek
265   Reposing on a cushion.

GUIDERIUS Where?

239 speak emit sound   **240 answer** correspond to   **accidents** events   **241 Triumphs** public
celebrations   **lamenting toys** lamentation over trivial, inconsequential things   **242 jollity for apes** i.e.
only an imitation of jollity   **grief for boys** considered emotionally fickle   **248 on** of   **250 turned . . .
crutch** i.e. turned my youth into old age   **253 the . . . well** half as well   **256 sound thy bottom** measure
your depths   **Find . . . in** the experience of melancholy is likened to being in a small boat sailing sluggishly
through a muddy river of unknowable depth, with no way of knowing the easiest route to harbour   **Find**
explore   **257 ooze** i.e. the wet mud and slime at the bottom of a river   **sluggish** slow-moving   **crare**
small trading boat   **258 easiliest** most easily   **260 rare** exceptional   **262 Stark** stiff   **263 as . . . slumber**
as though some fly had tickled him while he was sleeping   **264 Not . . . at** not as though he was laughing at
death's arrow

ARVIRAGUS O'th'floor:
His arms thus leagued, I thought he slept, and put
My clouted brogues from off my feet, whose rudeness
270   Answered my steps too loud.
GUIDERIUS Why, he but sleeps:
If he be gone, he'll make his grave a bed:
With female fairies will his tomb be haunted,
And worms will not come to thee.
275 **ARVIRAGUS** With fairest flowers
Whilst summer lasts and I live here, Fidele,
I'll sweeten thy sad grave: thou shalt not lack
The flower that's like thy face, pale primrose, nor
The azured harebell, like thy veins: no, nor
280   The leaf of eglantine, whom not to slander,
Out-sweetened not thy breath: the ruddock would
With charitable bill — O bill sore shaming
Those rich-left heirs that let their fathers lie
Without a monument! — bring thee all this,
285   Yea, and furred moss besides, when flowers are none,
To winter-ground thy corpse—
GUIDERIUS Prithee, have done,
And do not play in wench-like words with that
Which is so serious. Let us bury him,
290   And not protract with admiration what
Is now due debt. To th'grave.
ARVIRAGUS Say, where shall's lay him?
GUIDERIUS By good Euriphile, our mother.
ARVIRAGUS Be't so:
295   And let us, Polydore, though now our voices
Have got the mannish crack, sing him to th'ground
As once our mother: use like note and words,
Save that Euriphile must be Fidele.
GUIDERIUS Cadwal,
300   I cannot sing: I'll weep, and word it with thee,
For notes of sorrow out of tune are worse
Than priests and fanes that lie.

---

268 **leagued** folded   269 **clouted brogues** hobnailed boots   **rudeness** roughness   270 **Answered**...
loud i.e. made his steps echo too loudly   271 **but** only, merely   272 **he'll**...**bed** i.e. because he looks more
like someone asleep   279 **azured** bright blue-coloured   **harebell** a native plant with delicate blue flowers
on slender stems, often called 'bluebell' but actually a distinct species   280 **eglantine** sweet-brier (wild
rose)   281 **ruddock** robin (in folklore believed to cover the dead by strewing them with leaves and flowers,
hence **charitable bill**)   286 **winter-ground** cover and protect in winter   288 **wench-like** womanish
290 **admiration** i.e. of Innogen/amazement, wonder   291 **due debt** the debt that needs to be paid, i.e.
burial   292 **shall's** shall us (i.e. shall we)   296 **Have**...**crack** i.e. have broken   297 **once** we once did
for   **like** the same   298 **Save** except   300 **word** speak   302 **fanes** temples

ARVIRAGUS We'll speak it, then.

BELARIUS Great griefs, I see, med'cine the less, for Cloten
305   Is quite forgot. He was a queen's son, boys,
And though he came our enemy, remember
He was paid for that: though mean and mighty
    rotting
Together have one dust, yet reverence,
That angel of the world, doth make distinction
310   Of place 'tween high and low. Our foe was princely,
And though you took his life as being our foe,
Yet bury him as a prince.

GUIDERIUS Pray you fetch him hither.
Thersites' body is as good as Ajax'
315   When neither are alive.

ARVIRAGUS If you'll go fetch him,
We'll 'say our song the whilst. Brother, begin.
                            [Exit Belarius]

GUIDERIUS Nay, Cadwal, we must lay his head to th'east.
My father hath a reason for't.

320 ARVIRAGUS 'Tis true.

GUIDERIUS Come on then, and remove him.

ARVIRAGUS So. Begin.

                   Song   *Spoken or chanted, not sung?*

GUIDERIUS   Fear no more the heat o'th'sun,
                Nor the furious winter's rages,
325   Thou thy worldly task hast done,
                Home art gone, and ta'en thy wages.
                Golden lads and girls all must,
                As chimney-sweepers, come to dust.

ARVIRAGUS   Fear no more the frown o'th'great,
330   Thou art past the tyrant's stroke,
                Care no more to clothe and eat,
                To thee the reed is as the oak.
                The sceptre, learning, physic, must
                All follow this and come to dust.

335 GUIDERIUS   Fear no more the lightning flash,
     ARVIRAGUS   Nor th'all-dreaded thunder-stone.

---

304 **med'cine the less** cure lesser ones   **306 came** came here as   **307 paid** given his payment, i.e.
death   **mean...dust** i.e. both high and low come to the same end   **308 reverence** respect, deference
314 Thersites in Homer's *Iliad*, the most scurrilous and cowardly of all the Greek warriors at the siege of
Troy   **Ajax** heroic Greek warrior in the *Iliad*   **317 the whilst** in the meanwhile   **318 to th'east**
emphasizing the pagan setting since it is the opposite in Christian practice   **321 remove** move   **326 Home**
i.e. heaven   **ta'en thy wages** payment for the **worldly task**   **327 Golden...dust** i.e. the rich must die as
surely as the poor; dandelions were known as **chimney-sweepers** in Warwickshire   **328 As** like
333 sceptre, learning, physic i.e. kings, scholars, doctors   **336 thunder-stone** thunderbolt

GUIDERIUS	Fear not slander, censure rash.
ARVIRAGUS	Thou hast finished joy and moan.
BOTH	All lovers young, all lovers must
340	Consign to thee and come to dust.
GUIDERIUS	No exorcizer harm thee,
ARVIRAGUS	Nor no witchcraft charm thee.
GUIDERIUS	Ghost unlaid forbear thee.
ARVIRAGUS	Nothing ill come near thee.
345 BOTH	Quiet consummation have,
	And renownèd be thy grave.

Enter Belarius with the body of Cloten

GUIDERIUS We have done our obsequies: come, lay him
    down.

BELARIUS Here's a few flowers, but 'bout midnight more:
    The herbs that have on them cold dew o'th'night
350 Are strewings fitt'st for graves: upon their faces.
    You were as flowers, now withered: even so
    These herblets shall, which we upon you strew.
    Come on, away, apart upon our knees:
    The ground that gave them first has them again:
355 Their pleasures here are past, so is their pain.

                    Exeunt [all but Innogen]

INNOGEN Yes, sir, to Milford Haven, which is the way?

                    Awakes

    I thank you: by yond bush? Pray how far thither?
    'Od's pittikins: can it be six mile yet?
    I have gone all night: faith, I'll lie down and sleep.   *Sees Cloten's*
360 But soft, no bedfellow! O gods and goddesses!   *body*
    These flowers are like the pleasures of the world,
    This bloody man the care on't. I hope I dream:
    For so I thought I was a cave-keeper,
    And cook to honest creatures. But 'tis not so:
365 'Twas but a bolt of nothing, shot at nothing,
    Which the brain makes of fumes. Our very eyes
    Are sometimes like our judgements, blind. Good faith,

---

340 **Consign to thee** seal the same contract with/entrust to your charge   341 **exorcizer** one who conjures or raises spirits   342 **charm** cast a spell on   343 **Ghost . . . thee** let any ghost which has not been laid to rest stay away from you   345 **consummation** end, fulfilment   347 **obsequies** funeral rites   350 **upon their faces** meaning is unclear; possibly 'strew the flowers on the front of their bodies'/'turn the bodies face down'/'strew the flowers on their faces'   352 **herblets shall** small herbs will also (wither)   353 **apart . . . knees** let us go and pray   354 **gave them first** i.e. bore them   358 **'Od's pittikins** a diminutive of 'God's pity', reduced to its mildest form   359 **gone** journeyed   360 **But . . . bedfellow!** But wait, I don't remember any bedfellow!   362 **care on't** its (the world's) grief   363 **so** in the same way, i.e. dreaming   365 **bolt** arrow   366 **fumes** bodily vapours, thought to rise from the body to the brain, thus causing dreams

I tremble still with fear: but if there be
Yet left in heaven as small a drop of pity
370 As a wren's eye, feared gods, a part of it!
The dream's here still: even when I wake it is
Without me, as within me: not imagined, felt.
A headless man? The garments of Posthumus?
I know the shape of's leg: this is his hand:
375 His foot mercurial: his martial thigh:
The brawns of Hercules: but his jovial face—
Murder in heaven! How? 'Tis gone. Pisanio,
All curses madded Hecuba gave the Greeks,
And mine to boot, be darted on thee! Thou,
380 Conspired with that irregulous devil, Cloten,
Hath here cut off my lord. To write and read
Be henceforth treacherous! Damned Pisanio
Hath with his forgèd letters — damned Pisanio —
From this most bravest vessel of the world
385 Struck the main-top! O Posthumus, alas,
Where is thy head? Where's that? Ay me! Where's
      that?
Pisanio might have killed thee at the heart,
And left this head on. How should this be, Pisanio?
'Tis he and Cloten: malice and lucre in them
390 Have laid this woe here. O, 'tis pregnant, pregnant!
The drug he gave me, which he said was precious
And cordial to me, have I not found it
Murd'rous to th'senses? That confirms it home:
This is Pisanio's deed, and Cloten: O,
395 Give colour to my pale cheek with thy blood,
That we the horrider may seem to those
Which chance to find us! O my lord, my lord!   *Embraces the body*
    Enter Lucius, Captains and a Soothsayer

370 wren's eye i.e. a tiny amount, the wren being regarded as the smallest bird   **a part** give me some of it   **372 Without . . . me** outside me (a physical reality), as it was inside me (in my imagination, dream)   **felt** tangible   **375 His . . . face** Innogen likens bodily attributes to those of gods and heroes; Mercury was the messenger of the gods, Mars the God of war, **Hercules** a hero famed for his strength, and Jove (Jupiter) king of the gods   **376 brawns** muscles   **378 madded** maddened   **Hecuba** wife of Priam, King of Troy; accounts describe her frenzied grief, cursing the Greeks as they sacked Troy and murdered Priam   **379 darted** shot like darts (arrows)   **380 Conspired** i.e. having conspired   **irregulous** lawless   **384 this . . . vessel** i.e. Posthumus, likened to a ship   **bravest** most excellent/handsome/courageous, strong   **of** in   **385 Struck the main-top** chopped off the top part of the ship's mainsail, i.e. his head   **389 lucre** greed for money   **390 laid** inflicted/placed, laid out   **pregnant** obvious, clear   **392 cordial** healthful, restorative   **393 home** i.e. to my heart   **395 Give . . . blood** i.e. she smears his blood on her cheeks   **396 horrider** more ghastly, intimidating   **397 Which chance** who happen   *Soothsayer* one who foretells the future

CAPTAIN To them the legions garrisoned in Gallia
    After your will have crossed the sea, attending
400   You here at Milford Haven with your ships:
    They are in readiness.
LUCIUS But what from Rome?
CAPTAIN The senate hath stirred up the confiners
    And gentlemen of Italy, most willing spirits,
405   That promise noble service: and they come
    Under the conduct of bold Iachimo,
    Siena's brother.
LUCIUS When expect you them?
CAPTAIN With the next benefit o'th'wind.
410 LUCIUS This forwardness
    Makes our hopes fair. Command our present
        numbers
    Be mustered: bid the captains look to't. Now, sir,
    What have you dreamed of late of this war's purpose?
SOOTHSAYER Last night the very gods showed me a
        vision —
415   I fast, and prayed for their intelligence — thus:
    I saw Jove's bird, the Roman eagle, winged
    From the spongy south to this part of the west,
    There vanished in the sunbeams: which portends —
    Unless my sins abuse my divination —
420   Success to th'Roman host.
LUCIUS Dream often so,
    And never false.— Soft ho, what trunk is here?   *Sees Cloten's body*
    Without his top? The ruin speaks that sometime
    It was a worthy building. How, a page?
425   Or dead or sleeping on him? But dead rather:
    For nature doth abhor to make his bed
    With the defunct, or sleep upon the dead.
    Let's see the boy's face.
CAPTAIN He's alive, my lord.
430 LUCIUS He'll then instruct us of this body. Young one,
    Inform us of thy fortunes, for it seems

---

398 Gallia France   399 After in accordance with   attending waiting for   403 confiners those dwelling within the confines, inhabitants (presumably means common men, as opposed to gentlemen)   407 Siena Duke of Siena   409 benefit advantage   410 forwardness diligence, industriousness/promptness 413 purpose outcome   415 fast fasted   intelligence information, message   416 winged flying, on the wing   417 spongy damp   418 portends indicates   419 sins . . . divination earthly sins distort my ability to communicate with the gods   420 host army   422 trunk body   423 his its   speaks suggests, attests 425 Or either   426 nature doth abhor i.e. living creatures naturally detest   427 defunct deceased 430 instruct us of tell us about

They crave to be demanded: who is this
Thou mak'st thy bloody pillow? Or who was he
That, otherwise than noble nature did,
435   Hath altered that good picture? What's thy interest
In this sad wreck? How came't? Who is't?
What art thou?

INNOGEN I am nothing; or if not,
Nothing to be were better. This was my master,
440   A very valiant Briton, and a good,
That here by mountaineers lies slain. Alas,
There is no more such masters: I may wander
From east to occident, cry out for service,
Try many, all good, serve truly, never
445   Find such another master.

LUCIUS 'Lack, good youth,
Thou mov'st no less with thy complaining than
Thy master in bleeding: say his name, good friend.

INNOGEN Richard du Champ.— If I do lie and do   *Aside*
450   No harm by it, though the gods hear, I hope
They'll pardon it.— Say you, sir?

LUCIUS Thy name?

INNOGEN Fidele, sir.

LUCIUS Thou dost approve thyself the very same:
455   Thy name well fits thy faith, thy faith thy name.
Wilt take thy chance with me? I will not say
Thou shalt be so well mastered, but be sure
No less beloved. The Roman emperor's letters,
Sent by a consul to me, should not sooner
460   Than thine own worth prefer thee: go with me.

INNOGEN I'll follow, sir. But first, an't please the gods,
I'll hide my master from the flies, as deep
As these poor pickaxes can dig: and when
With wildwood leaves and weeds I ha' strewed his
       grave,
465   And on it said a century of prayers,
Such as I can, twice o'er, I'll weep and sigh,

---

432 **crave . . . demanded** beg to be asked about   435 **altered . . . picture** i.e. by cutting off the head
436 **wreck** ruin, catastrophe/mutilated person   442 **is** are   443 **occident** west   **service** masters to
serve   446 **'Lack** alas (alack)   447 **complaining** lamenting, mourning   451 **Say you** did you speak
454 **approve . . . same** i.e. prove yourself true to your name (**Fidele** means 'the faithful one' in Latin)
460 **prefer** recommend   461 **an't** if it   463 **poor pickaxes** i.e. her fingers   465 **century of** hundred
466 **can** am able to

And leaving so his service, follow you,
So please you entertain me.

LUCIUS Ay, good youth,
470 And rather father thee than master thee.
My friends,
The boy hath taught us manly duties: let us
Find out the prettiest daisied plot we can,
And make him with our pikes and partisans
475 A grave: come, arm him. Boy, he is preferred
By thee to us, and he shall be interred
As soldiers can. Be cheerful, wipe thine eyes:
Some falls are means the happier to arise.   *Exeunt*

Act 4 Scene 3   *running scene 15*

Enter Cymbeline, Lords and Pisanio [with Attendants]

CYMBELINE Again, and bring me word how 'tis with her.
                                    [Exit an Attendant]
A fever with the absence of her son,
A madness of which her life's in danger: heavens,
How deeply you at once do touch me! Innogen,
5 The great part of my comfort, gone: my queen
Upon a desperate bed, and in a time
When fearful wars point at me: her son gone,
So needful for this present. It strikes me, past
The hope of comfort. But for thee, fellow,
10 Who needs must know of her departure and
Dost seem so ignorant, we'll enforce it from thee
By a sharp torture.

PISANIO Sir, my life is yours,
I humbly set it at your will: but for my mistress,
15 I nothing know where she remains, why gone,
Nor when she purposes return. Beseech your
    highness,
Hold me your loyal servant.

FIRST LORD Good my liege,
The day that she was missing he was here:
20 I dare be bound he's true, and shall perform

---

468 **So . . . me** if it please you to take me into your service   474 **pikes** pointed metal tips of a staff or
spear   **partisans** long-handled spears with broad blades   475 **arm him** take him up in your arms
preferred commended   477 **can** are, have the right to be   4.3 *Location: Britain*   1 **Again** i.e. go back
again   2 **with** due to   3 **of** as a result of   4 **touch** wound, afflict   6 **Upon . . . bed** i.e. she is desperately
ill   8 **present** i.e. present moment   11 **enforce . . . thee** force it out of you   15 **nothing know** know
nothing about   16 **purposes** intends to   17 **Hold** consider

All parts of his subjection loyally. For Cloten,
There wants no diligence in seeking him,
And will no doubt be found.
CYMBELINE The time is troublesome.—
25   We'll slip you for a season, but our jealousy   *To Pisanio*
Does yet depend.
FIRST LORD So please your majesty,
The Roman legions, all from Gallia drawn,
Are landed on your coast with a supply
30   Of Roman gentlemen by the senate sent.
CYMBELINE Now for the counsel of my son and queen!
I am amazed with matter.
FIRST LORD Good my liege,
Your preparation can affront no less
35   Than what you hear of. Come more, for more you're
     ready:
The want is but to put those powers in motion
That long to move.
CYMBELINE I thank you: let's withdraw
And meet the time as it seeks us. We fear not
40   What can from Italy annoy us, but
We grieve at chances here. Away.
                       Exeunt [all but Pisanio]
PISANIO I heard no letter from my master since
I wrote him Innogen was slain. 'Tis strange:
Nor hear I from my mistress, who did promise
45   To yield me often tidings. Neither know I
What is betid to Cloten, but remain
Perplexed in all. The heavens still must work.
Wherein I am false I am honest: not true, to be true.
These present wars shall find I love my country,
50   Even to the note o'th'king, or I'll fall in them.
All other doubts, by time let them be cleared:
Fortune brings in some boats that are not steered.
                                 Exit

---

21 **subjection** duty as a subject   22 **wants** lacks   23 **will** he will   25 **slip**...**season** let you be for a while   **jealousy** suspicion   26 **Does yet depend** still hangs in the balance/remains   30 **gentlemen** i.e. officers   31 **Now for** if only I now had   32 **amazed with matter** overwhelmed by all these matters   34 **affront** confront, face   35 **Come more** if more come   36 **The**...**but** the only thing now needed is   40 **annoy** harm   41 **chances** events   42 **no letter** i.e. no news   46 **is betid** has happened   49 **find** reveal, prove   50 **Even**...**o'th'king** even to the point where the king takes note   **fall** die, perish   52 **Fortune**...**steered** i.e. even some boats that are cast adrift are brought safely back to harbour by good fortune

Act 4 Scene 4

running scene 16

Enter Belarius, Guiderius and Arviragus

GUIDERIUS The noise is round about us.

BELARIUS Let us from it.

ARVIRAGUS What pleasure, sir, find we in life, to lock it
From action and adventure?

5 **GUIDERIUS** Nay, what hope
Have we in hiding us? This way the Romans
Must or for Britons slay us or receive us
For barbarous and unnatural revolts
During their use, and slay us after.

10 **BELARIUS** Sons,
We'll higher to the mountains, there secure us.
To the king's party there's no going: newness
Of Cloten's death — we being not known, not
mustered
Among the bands — may drive us to a render

15 Where we have lived, and so extort from's that
Which we have done, whose answer would be death
Drawn on with torture.

GUIDERIUS This is, sir, a doubt
In such a time nothing becoming you,

20 Nor satisfying us.

ARVIRAGUS It is not likely
That when they hear the Roman horses neigh,
Behold their quartered fires, have both their eyes
And ears so cloyed importantly as now,

25 That they will waste their time upon our note,
To know from whence we are.

BELARIUS O, I am known
Of many in the army: many years,
Though Cloten then but young, you see, not wore
him

30 From my remembrance. And besides, the king
Hath not deserved my service nor your loves,

4.4 *Location: Wales, outside Belarius' cave* **1 noise** i.e. of the armies preparing for battle **3 lock it**
lock it away **6 This way** if we do this **7 or for** either as **receive . . . use** recruit us, thinking us rebels to
make use of and then kill us **11 secure us** make ourselves safe, find a stronghold **13 not . . . bands** i.e.
not listed among the forces **mustered** enlisted as soldiers **14 drive . . . render** force us to give an account
of **15 extort from's** extract from us **16 answer** reward, recompense **17 Drawn on with** brought about
by **23 quartered fires** campfires (from their quarters in the field) **24 cloyed importantly** clogged,
filled with important matters **25 upon our note** in taking notice of us **28 Of** by **29 then** was then
wore effaced, removed **30 remembrance** memory

Who find in my exile the want of breeding,
The certainty of this hard life, aye hopeless
To have the courtesy your cradle promised,
35 But to be still hot summer's tanlings and
The shrinking slaves of winter.
GUIDERIUS Than be so,
Better to cease to be. Pray, sir, to th'army:
I and my brother are not known; yourself
40 So out of thought, and thereto so o'ergrown,
Cannot be questioned.
ARVIRAGUS By this sun that shines,
I'll thither: what thing is't that I never
Did see man die, scarce ever looked on blood
45 But that of coward hares, hot goats and venison!
Never bestrid a horse, save one that had
A rider like myself, who ne'er wore rowel
Nor iron on his heel! I am ashamed
To look upon the holy sun, to have
50 The benefit of his blest beams, remaining
So long a poor unknown.
GUIDERIUS By heavens, I'll go:
If you will bless me, sir, and give me leave,
I'll take the better care: but if you will not,
55 The hazard therefore due fall on me by
The hands of Romans.
ARVIRAGUS So say I, amen.
BELARIUS No reason I, since of your lives you set
So slight a valuation, should reserve
60 My cracked one to more care. Have with you, boys!
If in your country wars you chance to die,
That is my bed too, lads, and there I'll lie.
Lead, lead.— The time seems long, their blood thinks   *Aside*
   scorn
Till it fly out and show them princes born.   *Exeunt*

---

32 want of breeding lack of education, cultivation   **33 certainty** inevitability   **aye hopeless** forever
without hope   **34 courtesy** respect/refined manners   **cradle** i.e. your circumstances at birth   **35 still**
forever   **tanlings** i.e. those tanned by constant exposure to the sun   **36 shrinking** as **slaves** will recoil from
and tremble at punishment, so the **winter** cold makes one shiver   **40 out of thought** forgotten about
thereto so o'ergrown in that respect your memory obscured/your face covered with hair   **41 questioned**
suspected   **43 thing is't** ashameful thing it is   **45 hot** lecherous   **venison** deer   **47 rowel Nor iron** i.e.
spurs   **rowel** the rotating blade at the end of the spur   **iron** the framework which attaches it   **54 care**
attention, caution   **55 hazard therefore due** chance, danger coming to me   **60 cracked** i.e. because
old   **61 country** country's   **63 their . . . out** their mettle, noble spirit/royal blood, stock despises everything
until it may break out/be shed in battle

Act 5 Scene 1

running scene 17

Enter Posthumus alone **With a bloody handkerchief**

POSTHUMUS Yea, bloody cloth, I'll keep thee: for I
   wished
   Thou shouldst be coloured thus. You married ones,
   If each of you should take this course, how many
   Must murder wives much better than themselves
5   For wrying but a little? O Pisanio,
   Every good servant does not all commands:
   No bond but to do just ones. Gods, if you
   Should have ta'en vengeance on my faults, I never
   Had lived to put on this: so had you saved
10   The noble Innogen to repent, and struck
   Me, wretch, more worth your vengeance. But alack,
   You snatch some hence for little faults; that's love,
   To have them fall no more: you some permit
   To second ills with ills, each elder worse,
15   And make them dread it, to the doer's thrift.
   But Innogen is your own: do your best wills,
   And make me blest to obey. I am brought hither
   Among th'Italian gentry, and to fight
   Against my lady's kingdom: 'tis enough
20   That, Britain, I have killed thy mistress: peace,
   I'll give no wound to thee. Therefore, good heavens,
   Hear patiently my purpose: I'll disrobe me
   Of these Italian weeds and suit myself
   As does a Briton peasant: so I'll fight
25   Against the part I come with: so I'll die
   For thee, O Innogen, even for whom my life
   Is every breath a death: and thus, unknown,
   Pitied nor hated, to the face of peril
   Myself I'll dedicate. Let me make men know
30   More valour in me than my habits show.

5.1 *Location: Wales* **1 bloody cloth** sent by Pisanio to Posthumus as proof that he had murdered Innogen **3 course** i.e. of action **5 wrying** erring, going astray **6 does not** does not carry out **7 No bond but** there is no obligation except **8 Should have** had **9 put on this** instigate Innogen's murder/ take such a fault upon myself/wear these clothes **10 repent** i.e. her supposed unfaithfulness **11 worth** deserving **13 fall** i.e. sin **14 second** support/follow up **elder** later, next (with the implication that evils mature with time)/earlier, with the more recent evils diminishing in severity until finally repentance sets in **15 make ... it** i.e. make the perpetrators fearful and repentant **thrift** gain, advantage (by becoming saved through repentance) **23 weeds** clothes **suit** dress **25 part** side **28 Pitied** neither pitied **30 habits** peasant's clothes/customary behaviour

Gods, put the strength o'th'Leonati in me!
To shame the guise o'th'world, I will begin
The fashion, less without and more within.   *Exit*

Act 5 Scene 2   *running scene 18*

*Enter Lucius, Iachimo and the Roman army at one door: and
the Briton army at another: Leonatus Posthumus following
like a poor soldier. They march over and go out. Then enter
again, in skirmish, Iachimo and Posthumus: he vanquisheth
and disarmeth Iachimo, and then leaves him*

IACHIMO The heaviness and guilt within my bosom
    Takes off my manhood: I have belied a lady,
    The princess of this country, and the air on't
    Revengingly enfeebles me; or could this carl,
5   A very drudge of nature's, have subdued me
    In my profession? Knighthoods and honours, borne
    As I wear mine, are titles but of scorn.
    If that thy gentry, Britain, go before
    This lout as he exceeds our lords, the odds
10 Is that we scarce are men and you are gods.   *Exit*
*The battle continues, the Britons fly, Cymbeline is taken: then
enter, to his rescue, Belarius, Guiderius and Arviragus*
BELARIUS Stand, stand, we have th'advantage of the
        ground.
    The lane is guarded: nothing routs us but
    The villainy of our fears.
GUIDERIUS *and* ARVIRAGUS Stand, stand and fight.
*Enter Posthumus and seconds the Britons. They rescue
Cymbeline, and exeunt. Then enter Lucius, Iachimo and
Innogen*
15 LUCIUS Away, boy, from the troops, and save thyself:
    For friends kill friends, and the disorder's such
    As war were hoodwinked.
IACHIMO 'Tis their fresh supplies.
LUCIUS It is a day turned strangely: or betimes
20   Let's reinforce, or fly.   *Exeunt*

32 **guise** custom, practice 33 **less . . . within** i.e. to privilege inner qualities over outward finery
5.2 1 **bosom** heart 2 **off** away **belied** slandered, lied about 3 **on't** of it 4 **or could** or else could
carl bondman, peasant 5 **very . . . nature's** natural-born slave 6 **profession** i.e. as a soldier 7 **but of
scorn** only a mockery 8 **go before** outgo, excel 9 **odds** likelihood 12 **routs** defeats *seconds* gives
aid to 17 **As** as though **hoodwinked** blindfolded 19 **or . . . fly** let's either reinforce our numbers or flee
before it's too late

Act 5 Scene 3

Enter Posthumus and a Briton Lord

LORD Cam'st thou from where they made the stand?
POSTHUMUS I did.

Though you, it seems, come from the fliers.
LORD I did.

5   **POSTHUMUS** No blame be to you, sir, for all was lost,
But that the heavens fought: the king himself
Of his wings destitute, the army broken,
And but the backs of Britons seen, all flying
Through a strait lane: the enemy full-hearted,
10   Lolling the tongue with slaught'ring, having work
More plentiful than tools to do't, struck down
Some mortally, some slightly touched, some falling
Merely through fear, that the strait pass was dammed
With dead men hurt behind, and cowards living
15   To die with lengthened shame.
    LORD Where was this lane?
  POSTHUMUS Close by the battle, ditched and walled with
      turf,
Which gave advantage to an ancient soldier,
An honest one, I warrant, who deserved
20   So long a breeding as his white beard came to
In doing this for's country. Athwart the lane,
He, with two striplings — lads more like to run
The country base than to commit such slaughter,
With faces fit for masks, or rather fairer
25   Than those for preservation cased, or shame —
Made good the passage, cried to those that fled,
'Our Britain's harts die flying, not our men:
To darkness fleet souls that fly backwards. Stand,
Or we are Romans, and will give you that
30   Like beasts which you shun beastly, and may save

5.3 **3 fliers** i.e. those who fled   **6 But** had it not been   **7 wings** flank of the army   **8 but** only   **9 strait** narrow **full-hearted** full of confidence   **10 Lolling the tongue** i.e. slavering like dogs, their tongues hanging out   **12 mortally** fatally **touched** wounded   **13 dammed** blocked up, like a dam **15 lengthened** i.e. after spending the rest of their lives in shame   **18 ancient** old/noble   **19 who . . . to** who deserved to have lived as long a life as his white beard showed he had   **22 striplings** young men **run . . . base** play the rural children's game of 'prisoner's base', where players run between two opposing camps or bases and try to capture players on the other team   **24 masks** worn by women to protect their delicate complexions from the sun (**preservation**), or for modesty's sake (**shame**)   **26 Made good** defended   **27 harts** male deer, plays on 'hearts'   **28 To . . . backwards** to hell, damnation with those swift (**fleet**) souls who flee   **29 that** i.e. a fight   **30 Like beasts** with beastlike ferocity **beastly** cowardly

But to look back in frown: stand, stand.' These three,
Three thousand confident, in act as many —
For three performers are the file when all
The rest do nothing — with this word 'Stand, stand',
35   Accommodated by the place, more charming
With their own nobleness, which could have turned
A distaff to a lance, gilded pale looks;
Part shame, part spirit renewed, that some, turned coward
But by example — O, a sin in war,
40   Damned in the first beginners! — 'gan to look
The way that they did, and to grin like lions
Upon the pikes o'th'hunters. Then began
A stop i'th'chaser; a retire: anon
A rout, confusion thick: forthwith they fly
45   Chickens the way which they stooped eagles: slaves,
The strides they victors made: and now our cowards,
Like fragments in hard voyages, became
The life o'th'need: having found the back door open
Of the unguarded hearts, heavens, how they wound!
50   Some slain before, some dying, some their friends
O'erborne i'th'former wave, ten chased by one,
Are now each one the slaughter-man of twenty:
Those that would die or ere resist are grown
The mortal bugs o'th'field.
55 LORD   This was strange chance:
A narrow lane, an old man, and two boys.
POSTHUMUS Nay, do not wonder at it: you are made
Rather to wonder at the things you hear

---

31 frown i.e. anger, resolved to fight   **32 Three . . . many** as confident as if they were three thousand, and having the effect in their actions as if they were   **33 file** entire force, (from front file to rear)
35 Accommodated aided   **charming** spellbinding   **37 distaff** spindle used in spinning wool, i.e. a housewife would have turned soldier at their example   **gilded pale looks** restored colour to **pale**, cowardly faces   **38 Part** it was partly through   **39 But by example** only by imitating the **first beginners** (those who first began to flee)   **40 'gan . . . did** began to turn and face the way they (Belarius, Guiderius and Arviragus) did   **41 grin** i.e. bare their teeth, snarl   **lions . . . o'th'hunters** cornered lions, kept at bay with (rather than skewered by) the hunters' spears   **43 stop i'th'chaser** halt on the part of the pursuer   **retire** retreat
anon at once   **45 they . . . eagles** they flee like chickens along the same path they swooped down (**stooped**) as eagles   **slaves . . . made** like slaves along the same path they strode as victors   **47 Like . . . need** like scraps of food, gathered up as a last resort on tough voyages at sea, which become the source of **life** in a time of desperate **need**   **48 having . . . hearts** i.e. the Romans had dropped their guard, making it easy for the British **cowards** to attack them (possibly literally means stab them in the heart through their backs) as they ran away   **50 Some . . . twenty** i.e. Britons who earlier were cut down, dying, trampled, cowardly (ten being chased by one Roman), are now all the killers of twenty Romans each   **some . . . wave** some of their **friends** knocked down in the previous attack/some who their friends knocked down in the previous retreat
53 or ere resist before they would fight back   **are grown** have now become   **54 mortal bugs** deadly terrors   **o'th'field** of the battlefield   **57 wonder at it** be amazed by it

Than to work any. Will you rhyme upon't,
60 And vent it for a mock'ry? Here is one:
'Two boys, an old man — twice a boy — a lane,
Preserved the Britons, was the Romans' bane.'

LORD Nay, be not angry, sir.

POSTHUMUS 'Lack, to what end?
65 Who dares not stand his foe, I'll be his friend:
For if he'll do as he is made to do,
I know he'll quickly fly my friendship too.
You have put me into rhyme.

LORD Farewell, you're angry. *Exit*

70 **POSTHUMUS** Still going? This is a lord! O noble misery,
To be i'th'field and ask 'What news?' of me.
Today how many would have given their honours
To have saved their carcasses? Took heel to do't,
And yet died too. I, in mine own woe charmed,
75 Could not find death where I did hear him groan,
Nor feel him where he struck. Being an ugly monster,
'Tis strange he hides him in fresh cups, soft beds,
Sweet words, or hath more ministers than we
That draw his knives i'th'war. Well, I will find him:
80 For being now a favourer to the Briton,
No more a Briton, I have resumed again
The part I came in. Fight I will no more,
But yield me to the veriest hind that shall
Once touch my shoulder. Great the slaughter is
85 Here made by th'Roman; great the answer be
Britons must take. For me, my ransom's death,
On either side I come to spend my breath,
Which neither here I'll keep nor bear again,
But end it by some means for Innogen.

Enter two Captains and Soldiers

90 **FIRST CAPTAIN** Great Jupiter be praised, Lucius is taken.
'Tis thought the old man and his sons were angels.

---

59 **work any** perform any (wondrous deeds) **upon't** upon the subject, about it 60 **vent** utter, proclaim **for a mock'ry** as a joke 61 **twice a boy** proverbial, 'old men are twice children' 62 **bane** ruin 64 **'Lack ... end?** Alas, why should I get angry? 65 **stand** stand up to, face 66 **made** naturally inclined 67 **fly my friendship** run from my friendship (so I won't have to put up with him anymore) 70 **going** running away **O noble misery** what a miserable specimen of a noble/what a miserable state for one who is supposedly noble 72 **honours** reputations/titles 73 **Took ... do't** ran away to do it 74 **too** anyway **in ... charmed** protected, kept safe (as if by a magical spell) by my own misery 78 **ministers** agents 80 **For ... Briton** Because he (death) now favours the Britons, I'll no longer be a Briton 82 **part** role/side 83 **veriest hind** merest timid creature **hind** female deer 84 **touch my shoulder** i.e. arrest me 85 **made** committed **Roman** Romans **answer** retribution, retaliation **be** will be 87 **either side** i.e. either dying for the Britons or the Romans **spend** use up/waste 88 **keep** preserve **bear again** bear away again

SECOND CAPTAIN There was a fourth man, in a silly
    habit,
    That gave th'affront with them.
FIRST CAPTAIN So 'tis reported:
95   But none of 'em can be found. Stand, who's there?
POSTHUMUS A Roman,
    Who had not now been drooping here, if seconds
    Had answered him.
SECOND CAPTAIN Lay hands on him: a dog,
100   A leg of Rome shall not return to tell
    What crows have pecked them here: he brags his
      service
    As if he were of note: bring him to th'king.
Enter Cymbeline, Belarius, Guiderius, Arviragus, Pisanio and
Roman Captives [with Jailers]. The Captains present
Posthumus to Cymbeline, who delivers him over to a Jailer
                  [Exeunt all but Posthumus and two Jailers]
FIRST JAILER You shall not now be stol'n, you have locks
    upon you;
    So graze as you find pasture.
105 **SECOND JAILER** Ay, or a stomach.   *[Exeunt Jailers]*
POSTHUMUS Most welcome bondage, for thou art a way,
    I think, to liberty: yet am I better
    Than one that's sick o'th'gout, since he had rather
    Groan so in perpetuity than be cured
110   By th'sure physician, death, who is the key
    T'unbar these locks. My conscience, thou art fettered
    More than my shanks and wrists: you good gods
      give me
    The penitent instrument to pick that bolt,
    Then free for ever. Is't enough I am sorry?
115   So children temporal fathers do appease;
    Gods are more full of mercy. Must I repent,
    I cannot do it better than in gyves,
    Desired more than constrained: to satisfy,
    If of my freedom 'tis the main part, take

---

92 silly habit simple rustic clothes (referring to Posthumus)   **93 th'affront** attack   **97 seconds**
reinforcements   **98 answered him** supported him/acted as he did   **100 A . . . return** i.e. not even the
smallest part of Rome shall return there   **102 note** high rank   **103 You . . . pasture** pastured animals had
weights tied to one leg to prevent them escaping or being **stolen**   **105 stomach** appetite   **109 Groan . . .**
perpetuity i.e. put up with the pain for ever   **111 T'unbar** to unlock   **112 shanks** legs   **113 The . . . bolt**
the means of penitence to release my conscience   **114 Then ever** then (I shall be) free for ever, i.e. in
death   **115 temporal** worldly, as opposed to 'heavenly'   **116 Must I** if I must   **117 gyves** fetters, chains
118 constrained forced (on me)   **satisfy** atone for my sins   **119 If . . . part** if it (atonement) is the most
important element in freeing my conscience

120   No stricter render of me than my all.
          I know you are more clement than vile men,
          Who of their broken debtors take a third,
          A sixth, a tenth, letting them thrive again
          On their abatement: that's not my desire.
125   For Innogen's dear life take mine, and though
          'Tis not so dear, yet 'tis a life; you coined it.
          'Tween man and man they weigh not every stamp:
          Though light, take pieces for the figure's sake.
          You rather mine, being yours: and so, great powers,
130   If you will take this audit, take this life,
          And cancel these cold bonds. O Innogen,
          I'll speak to thee in silence.   *Sleeps*

Solemn music. Enter, as in an apparition, Sicilius Leonatus,
father to Posthumus, an old man, attired like a warrior,
leading in his hand an ancient matron, his wife and mother to
Posthumus, with music before them. Then, after other music,
follows the two young Leonati, brothers to Posthumus, with
wounds as they died in the wars. They circle Posthumus
round as he lies sleeping

SICILIUS   No more, thou thunder-master, show
          Thy spite on mortal flies:
135   With Mars fall out, with Juno chide,
          That thy adulteries
          Rates and revenges.
          Hath my poor boy done aught but well,
          Whose face I never saw?
140   I died whilst in the womb he stayed
          Attending nature's law,
          Whose father then — as men report
          Thou orphans' father art —
          Thou shouldst have been, and shielded him
145   From this earth-vexing smart.

---

120 **render** repayment   121 **clement** merciful   **vile men** general humanity, specifically, usurers, moneylenders   122 **of** from   **broken debtors** bankrupts, those who can no longer repay their debts
124 **their abatement** i.e. the little that's left over by the creditors for the debtors to go on living
126 **coined** created, stamping it like a new coin   127 **stamp** coin   128 **light** underweight/morally deficient   **pieces** coins   **figure's sake** the symbolic sake of the figure stamped on the coin
129 **You . . . yours** i.e. you should accept mine since yours is the image stamped onto it   130 **audit** account   131 **bonds** legal/mortal/literal, i.e. his fetters   133 **thou thunder-master** Jupiter, king of the gods, believed to have thunder and lightning at his command   134 **flies** i.e. people, whom the gods squash like flies   136 **That** who   137 **rates** scolds, berates/reckons   138 **aught** anything   141 **Attending nature's law** i.e. staying the full nine months in the womb, according to nature   145 **earth-vexing smart** suffering that afflicts earthly, mortal men

MOTHER Lucina lent not me her aid,
But took me in my throes,
That from me was Posthumus ripped,
Came crying 'mongst his foes,
150   A thing of pity.

SICILIUS Great nature, like his ancestry,
Moulded the stuff so fair,
That he deserved the praise o'th'world,
As great Sicilius' heir.

155 **FIRST BROTHER** When once he was mature for man,
In Britain where was he
That could stand up his parallel,
Or fruitful object be
In eye of Innogen, that best
160   Could deem his dignity?

MOTHER With marriage wherefore was he mocked,
To be exiled, and thrown
From Leonati seat, and cast
From her his dearest one,
165   Sweet Innogen?

SICILIUS Why did you suffer Iachimo,
Slight thing of Italy,
To taint his nobler heart and brain
With needless jealousy,
170   And to become the geck and scorn
O'th'other's villainy?

SECOND BROTHER For this from stiller seats we came,
Our parents and us twain,
That striking in our country's cause
175   Fell bravely and were slain,
Our fealty and Tenantius' right
With honour to maintain.

FIRST BROTHER Like hardiment Posthumus hath
To Cymbeline performed:
180   Then, Jupiter, thou king of gods,
Why hast thou thus adjourned

---

146 Lucina Roman goddess of childbirth   **147 took** i.e. to death   **in my throes** while I was in labour
148 That so that   **ripped** i.e. born by Caesarian section   **152 stuff** substance   **155 When once** when the
time came that   **mature for man** i.e. grown to manhood   **158 fruitful** gifted, promising/producing love's
fruits   **160 deem his dignity** judge his worth   **161 wherefore** why   **163 Leonati seat** ancestral home of
the Leonati (Britain)/family seat of the Leonati (family honour)   **166 suffer** allow   **167 Slight** worthless,
contemptible   **168 taint** infect   **170 geck** dupe   **172 stiller seats** quieter resting places, i.e. the fields of
Elysium (in classical mythology, a paradise inhabited by the good after death)   **176 fealty** loyalty (to a
lord)   **Tenantius' right** duty owed to Tenantius, Cymbeline's father   **178 Like hardiment** similar deeds of
valour   **181 adjourned** deferred, delayed

The graces for his merits due,
Being all to dolours turned?
SICILIUS Thy crystal window ope, look out,
185 No longer exercise
Upon a valiant race thy harsh
And potent injuries.
MOTHER Since, Jupiter, our son is good,
Take off his miseries.
190 **SICILIUS** Peep through thy marble mansion, help,
Or we poor ghosts will cry
To th'shining synod of the rest
Against thy deity.
BROTHERS Help, Jupiter, or we appeal,
195 And from thy justice fly.
Jupiter descends in thunder and lightning, sitting upon an
eagle: he throws a thunderbolt. The Ghosts fall on their knees
JUPITER No more you petty spirits of region low
Offend our hearing: hush! How dare you ghosts
Accuse the thunderer, whose bolt, you know,
Sky-planted, batters all rebelling coasts?
200 Poor shadows of Elysium, hence, and rest
Upon your never-withering banks of flowers.
Be not with mortal accidents oppressed,
No care of yours it is, you know 'tis ours.
Whom best I love, I cross, to make my gift
205 The more delayed, delighted. Be content,
Your low-laid son our godhead will uplift:
His comforts thrive, his trials well are spent.
Our jovial star reigned at his birth, and in
Our temple was he married. Rise, and fade.
210 He shall be lord of Lady Innogen,
And happier much by his affliction made.
This tablet lay upon his breast, wherein
Our pleasure his full fortune doth confine.
And so away: no further with your din

---

182 graces rewards   **183 dolours** sorrows   **184 crystal** transparent, like crystal   **ope** open   **186 race** breed/family   **190 marble mansion** i.e. the heavens   **192 synod ... rest** assembly of the other gods **194 appeal** i.e. to the other assembled gods, as in a tribunal   **196 region low** Elysium, which was below Jupiter's palace on Mount Olympus   **199 Sky-planted** rooted in the heavens   **200 Elysium** classical equivalent of heaven   **202 mortal accidents** human events   **205 delighted** (the more) delighted (in) **207 well are spent** are very nearly over/have been undergone to good effect   **208 jovial star** the planet Jupiter, supposed to bring good fortune, which was in the ascendant when Posthumus was born **212 tablet** a single sheet, richly bound   **213 confine** enclose, contain

215　Express impatience, lest you stir up mine.
　　Mount, eagle, to my palace crystalline.　　*Ascends*
　　SICILIUS He came in thunder, his celestial breath
　　Was sulphurous to smell: the holy eagle
　　Stooped as to foot us: his ascension is
220　More sweet than our blest fields: his royal bird
　　Prunes the immortal wing and claws his beak
　　As when his god is pleased.
　　ALL Thanks, Jupiter.
　　SICILIUS The marble pavement closes, he is entered
225　His radiant roof. Away, and to be blest,
　　Let us with care perform his great behest.
　　　　　　　　　　　　　　　　[The Ghosts] vanish
　　POSTHUMUS Sleep, thou hast been a grandsire, and
　　　　begot　　　　　　　　　　　　　　　　*Wakes*
　　A father to me: and thou hast created
　　A mother and two brothers. But, O scorn,
230　Gone! They went hence so soon as they were born:
　　And so I am awake. Poor wretches that depend
　　On greatness' favour dream as I have done,
　　Wake and find nothing. But, alas, I swerve:
　　Many dream not to find, neither deserve,
235　And yet are steeped in favours; so am I,
　　That have this golden chance and know not why.
　　What fairies haunt this ground? A book? O rare one,
　　Be not, as is our fangled world, a garment
　　Nobler than that it covers. Let thy effects
240　So follow, to be most unlike our courtiers,
　　As good as promise.　　　　　　　　　　*Reads*
　　'Whenas a lion's whelp shall, to himself unknown,
　　without seeking find, and be embraced by a piece of
　　tender air: and when from a stately cedar shall be
245　lopped branches, which being dead many years, shall
　　after revive, be jointed to the old stock, and freshly

---

218 sulphurous it is very likely that small fireworks were used to create lightning effects which would have left a sulphurous smell　**219 Stooped . . . us** swooped down as if to seize us in its talons　**220 sweet** calm/ sweet-smelling　**221 Prunes** preens, uses his beak to trim his feathers　**claws his beak** scratches his beak with his talons　**222 As when** because/whenever　**224 marble pavement** the floor of the heavens **226 behest** command　**229 O scorn** what a bitter joke　**230 so** as　**232 greatness' favour** the favour of powerful men at court　**233 swerve** digress/go astray　**234 dream . . . deserve** don't dream of finding anything, and neither do they deserve to　**237 A book** i.e. the tablet　**rare** exceptional　**238 fangled** foppish, novelty-obsessed　**239 effects** contents　**241 As . . . good** i.e. as they promise to be　**242 Whenas** when　**whelp** cub　**243 piece** creature, individual　**244 tender air** a false etymology for Latin *mulier*, meaning 'woman'　**246 jointed** grafted　**stock** trunk

grow, then shall Posthumus end his miseries, Britain
be fortunate and flourish in peace and plenty.'
'Tis still a dream, or else such stuff as madmen
250   Tongue, and brain not: either both or nothing,
Or senseless speaking, or a speaking such
As sense cannot untie. Be what it is,
The action of my life is like it, which I'll keep,
If but for sympathy.

Enter Jailer

255 **JAILER** Come, sir, are you ready for death?

POSTHUMUS Over-roasted rather: ready long ago.

JAILER Hanging is the word, sir: if you be ready for that,
you are well cooked.

POSTHUMUS So, if I prove a good repast to the spectators,
260   the dish pays the shot.

JAILER A heavy reckoning for you, sir. But the comfort
is you shall be called to no more payments, fear no
more tavern-bills, which are as often the sadness of
parting as the procuring of mirth: you come in faint
265   for want of meat, depart reeling with too much
drink: sorry that you have paid too much, and
sorry that you are paid too much: purse and
brain both empty: the brain the heavier for being
too light, the purse too light, being drawn of
270   heaviness. Of this contradiction you shall now be
quit. O, the charity of a penny cord! It sums up
thousands in a trice: you have no true debitor and
creditor but it: of what's past, is, and to come, the
discharge: your neck, sir, is pen, book and counters;
275   so the acquittance follows.

POSTHUMUS I am merrier to die than thou art to live.

FIRST JAILER Indeed, sir, he that sleeps feels not the
toothache: but a man that were to sleep your sleep,
and a hangman to help him to bed, I think he would

---

249 **stuff** nonsense   250 **Tongue ... not** speak without comprehending the meaning   **both** i.e. a dream
and madness   253 **which** i.e. the tablet   260 **the ... shot** the meal justifies its price   **shot** tavern bill
261 **reckoning** settlement   267 **paid** punished   268 **heavier ... light** duller/sleepier as a result of being
drunk (light-headed)   269 **drawn of heaviness** emptied of that which made it heavy i.e. money
270 **Of** from   **contradiction** being light and heavy i.e. drunk   **you ... quit** you shall from now on be
acquitted, freed   271 **penny cord** i.e. very cheap hangman's rope   **sums up** pays the reckoning for/
disposes of   272 **in a trice** instantly   **debitor and creditor** account book (referring to the headings of the
two columns in a ledger)   274 **discharge** payment   **counters** tokens used for accounting
275 **acquittance** receipt

280   change places with his officer: for look you, sir, you
        know not which way you shall go.
    POSTHUMUS Yes indeed do I, fellow.
    FIRST JAILER Your death has eyes in's head then: I have
        not seen him so pictured: you must either be directed
285   by some that take upon them to know, or to take
        upon yourself that which I am sure you do not know,
        or jump the after-inquiry on your own peril: and how
        you shall speed in your journey's end, I think you'll
        never return to tell on.
290 **POSTHUMUS** I tell thee, fellow, there are none want eyes
        to direct them the way I am going, but such as wink
        and will not use them.
    FIRST JAILER What an infinite mock is this, that a man
        should have the best use of eyes to see the way of
295   blindness! I am sure hanging's the way of winking.
    Enter a Messenger
    MESSENGER Knock off his manacles, bring your prisoner
        to the king.
    POSTHUMUS Thou bring'st good news, I am called to be
        made free.
300 **FIRST JAILER** I'll be hanged then.
    POSTHUMUS Thou shalt be then freer than a jailer: no
        bolts for the dead.
                              [*Exeunt Posthumus and Messenger*]
    FIRST JAILER Unless a man would marry a gallows and
        beget young gibbets, I never saw one so prone: yet on
305   my conscience, there are verier knaves desire to live,
        for all he be a Roman: and there be some of them too
        that die against their wills; so should I, if I were one. I
        would we were all of one mind, and one mind good:
        O, there were desolation of jailers and gallowses! I
310   speak against my present profit, but my wish hath a
        preferment in't.   *Exit*

---

280 **officer** i.e. the hangman   283 **death** death's head – a skull   284 **pictured** depicted; death's heads
usually have empty eye-sockets   285 **take upon them** profess, claim   287 **jump the after-inquiry** hazard
the final judgement   288 **speed** fare   289 **on** of   290 **want** lack   291 **wink** shut their eyes   293 **mock**
jest   295 **winking** i.e. closing the eyes permanently   302 **bolts** manacles   304 **prone** eager (to go to the
gallows)   305 **verier** truer   306 **for all** even though   309 **there were desolation** that would be the
end of   310 **profit** source of income   311 **preferment** promotion, either because a world that didn't need
jailers and executions would afford better jobs, or there would be a reward in the afterlife

Act 5 Scene 4   *running scene 18 continues*

Enter Cymbeline, Belarius, Guiderius, Arviragus, Pisanio and
Lords

CYMBELINE Stand by my side, you whom the gods have
        made
    Preservers of my throne: woe is my heart
    That the poor soldier that so richly fought,
    Whose rags shamed gilded arms, whose naked breast
5   Stepped before targes of proof, cannot be found:
    He shall be happy that can find him, if
    Our grace can make him so.
BELARIUS I never saw
    Such noble fury in so poor a thing,
10 Such precious deeds in one that promised nought
    But beggary and poor looks.
CYMBELINE No tidings of him?
PISANIO He hath been searched among the dead and
        living,
    But no trace of him.
15 **CYMBELINE** To my grief, I am
    The heir of his reward,— which I will add   *To Belarius and his sons*
    To you, the liver, heart and brain of Britain,
    By whom I grant she lives. 'Tis now the time
    To ask of whence you are. Report it.
20 **BELARIUS** Sir,
    In Cambria are we born, and gentlemen:
    Further to boast were neither true nor modest,
    Unless I add we are honest.
    CYMBELINE Bow your knees: *They kneel*
25 Arise my knights o'th'battle, I create you
    Companions to our person, and will fit you
    With dignities becoming your estates.   *They rise*
Enter Cornelius and Ladies
    There's business in these faces: why so sadly
    Greet you our victory? You look like Romans,
30 And not o'th'court of Britain.

5.4   **3 richly** nobly, profitably   **4 naked** unprotected (by armour)   **5 Stepped before** stood at the front of
(the British)/stood in opposition to (the Romans)   **targes of proof** shields of proven strength   **7 grace**
favour   **13 searched** sought   **16 heir . . . reward** inheritor of the reward I should have given to him
17 liver . . . brain believed to control passion, affection and judgement respectively   **18 grant** acknowledge,
affirm   **19 of . . . are** where you are from   **21 Cambria** Wales   **are** were   **25 knights o'th'battle** knights
created on the battlefield (an especial honour)   **26 fit** supply   **27 estates** i.e. new rank as knights
28 business serious concern

CORNELIUS Hail, great king!
To sour your happiness, I must report
The queen is dead.
CYMBELINE Who worse than a physician
35 Would this report become? But I consider
By med'cine life may be prolonged, yet death
Will seize the doctor too. How ended she?
CORNELIUS With horror, madly dying, like her life,
Which, being cruel to the world, concluded
40 Most cruel to herself. What she confessed
I will report, so please you. These her women
Can trip me if I err, who with wet cheeks
Were present when she finished.
CYMBELINE Prithee, say.
45 **CORNELIUS** First, she confessed she never loved you, only
Affected greatness got by you, not you:
Married your royalty, was wife to your place,
Abhorred your person.
CYMBELINE She alone knew this;
50 And, but she spoke it dying, I would not
Believe her lips in opening it. Proceed.
CORNELIUS Your daughter, whom she bore in hand to
love
With such integrity, she did confess
Was as a scorpion to her sight, whose life,
55 But that her flight prevented it, she had
Ta'en off by poison.
CYMBELINE O most delicate fiend!
Who is't can read a woman? Is there more?
CORNELIUS More, sir, and worse. She did confess she had
60 For you a mortal mineral, which being took,
Should by the minute feed on life, and, ling'ring,
By inches waste you. In which time, she purposed
By watching, weeping, tendance, kissing, to
O'ercome you with her show; and in time,
65 When she had fitted you with her craft, to work
Her son into th'adoption of the crown:
But, failing of her end by his strange absence,

---

42 trip me correct me/catch me out   **46 Affected** desired, longed for   **by** through   **50 but** if it weren't for the fact that   **51 opening** revealing, disclosing   **52 bore in hand** pretended, professed   **55 had Ta'en off** would have destroyed   **57 delicate** beautiful/crafty, skilful   **60 mortal mineral** fatal poison   **61 by the minute** minute by minute   **62 By…you** consume you little by little   **purposed** intended   **63 watching** i.e. at your bedside by night   **tendance** attention   **64 show** pretence   **65 fitted** moulded, shaped   **66 th'adoption…crown** i.e. becoming adopted heir to the crown   **67 end** purpose, design

Grew shameless-desperate, opened, in despite
Of heaven and men, her purposes, repented
70   The evils she hatched were not effected: so
Despairing died.
CYMBELINE Heard you all this, her women?
LADY We did, so please your highness.
CYMBELINE Mine eyes
75   Were not in fault, for she was beautiful,
Mine ears, that heard her flattery, nor my heart,
That thought her like her seeming. It had been
      vicious
To have mistrusted her: yet, O my daughter,
That it was folly in me thou mayst say,
80   And prove it in thy feeling. Heaven mend all!
Enter Lucius, Iachimo, [the Soothsayer] and other Roman
prisoners, [Posthumus] Leonatus behind, and Innogen
Thou com'st not, Caius, now for tribute. That
The Britons have razed out, though with the loss
Of many a bold one: whose kinsmen have made suit
That their good souls may be appeased with
      slaughter
85   Of you their captives, which ourself have granted,
So think of your estate.
LUCIUS Consider, sir, the chance of war. The day
Was yours by accident: had it gone with us,
We should not, when the blood was cool, have
      threatened
90   Our prisoners with the sword. But since the gods
Will have it thus, that nothing but our lives
May be called ransom, let it come: sufficeth
A Roman with a Roman's heart can suffer:
Augustus lives to think on't: and so much
95   For my peculiar care. This one thing only
I will entreat: my boy, a Briton born,
Let him be ransomed: never master had
A page so kind, so duteous, diligent,
So tender over his occasions, true,
100 So feat, so nurse-like: let his virtue join

---

68 **opened** revealed   76 **Mine ears** nor were mine ears   77 **seeming** appearance   **had been vicious**
would have been reprehensible   80 **feeling** emotions/experience   82 **razed out** erased   83 **made suit**
appealed   84 **their** i.e. those killed in battle   86 **estate** spiritual state   88 **had ... us** had we been the
victors   92 **called** named as/taken for   **sufficeth** it is enough that   94 **think on't** i.e. consider a strategy
(with the unspoken implication 'and then revenge it')   95 **peculiar care** personal concerns   99 **tender ...**
occasions sensitive to his master's needs   100 **feat** deft, graceful

With my request, which I'll make bold your highness
Cannot deny: he hath done no Briton harm,
Though he have served a Roman. Save him, sir,
And spare no blood beside.

105 CYMBELINE I have surely seen him:
His favour is familiar to me. Boy,
Thou hast looked thyself into my grace,
And art mine own. I know not why, wherefore,
To say 'Live, boy.' Ne'er thank thy master: live,
110 And ask of Cymbeline what boon thou wilt,
Fitting my bounty and thy state, I'll give it,
Yea, though thou do demand a prisoner,
The noblest ta'en.

INNOGEN I humbly thank your highness.

115 LUCIUS I do not bid thee beg my life, good lad,
And yet I know thou wilt.

INNOGEN No, no, alack,
There's other work in hand: I see a thing
Bitter to me as death: your life, good master,
120 Must shuffle for itself.

LUCIUS The boy disdains me,
He leaves me, scorns me: briefly die their joys
That place them on the truth of girls and boys.
Why stands he so perplexed?   *Innogen looks closely at Iachimo*

125 CYMBELINE What wouldst thou, boy?
I love thee more and more: think more and more
What's best to ask. Know'st him thou look'st on?
        Speak,
Wilt have him live? Is he thy kin? Thy friend?

INNOGEN He is a Roman, no more kin to me
130 Than I to your highness, who, being born your
        vassal,
Am something nearer.

CYMBELINE Wherefore ey'st him so?

INNOGEN I'll tell you, sir, in private, if you please
To give me hearing.

135 CYMBELINE Ay, with all my heart,
And lend my best attention. What's thy name?

---

104 And even if you   **106 favour** face, countenance   **107 looked...grace** won my favour by your looks   **109 Ne'er...master** i.e. because I don't even know why I'm sparing you myself, but it's not due to his pleading on your behalf   **110 boon** request   **111 state** rank   **120 shuffle** shift, look out   **122 briefly** quickly   **123 truth** loyalty, fidelity   **124 perplexed** distressed   **130 vassal** subject   **131 Am something nearer** i.e. I am more closely connected to you by being a British subject   **132 Wherefore...so?** Why do you stare at him in that way?

INNOGEN Fidele, sir.

CYMBELINE Thou'rt my good youth, my page:
    I'll be thy master: walk with me, speak freely.   *Cymbeline and*

140 **BELARIUS** Is not this boy revived from death?   *Innogen converse apart*

ARVIRAGUS One sand another
    Not more resembles that sweet rosy lad
    Who died, and was Fidele. What think you?

GUIDERIUS The same dead thing alive.

145 **BELARIUS** Peace, peace, see further: he eyes us not,
      forbear.
    Creatures may be alike: were't he, I am sure
    He would have spoke to us.

GUIDERIUS But we see him dead.

BELARIUS Be silent: let's see further.

150 **PISANIO** It is my mistress: *Aside*
    Since she is living, let the time run on
    To good or bad.   *Cymbeline and Innogen come forward*

CYMBELINE Come, stand thou by our side,
    Make thy demand aloud.— Sir, step you forth,   *To Iachimo*

155   Give answer to this boy, and do it freely
    Or by our greatness and the grace of it,
    Which is our honour, bitter torture shall
    Winnow the truth from falsehood. On, speak to him.

INNOGEN My boon is that this gentleman may render

160   Of whom he had this ring.   *Points to the ring*

POSTHUMUS What's that to him?   *Aside*

CYMBELINE That diamond upon your finger, say,   *To Iachimo*
    How came it yours?

IACHIMO Thou'lt torture me to leave unspoken that

165   Which to be spoke would torture thee.

CYMBELINE How? Me?

IACHIMO I am glad to be constrained to utter that
    Which torments me to conceal. By villainy
    I got this ring: 'twas Leonatus' jewel,

170   Whom thou didst banish: and — which more may
      grieve thee,
    As it doth me — a nobler sir ne'er lived
    'Twixt sky and ground. Wilt thou hear more, my
      lord?

CYMBELINE All that belongs to this.

---

145 **eyes** sees   **forbear** have patience   **148 But…dead** but we see him who we know to be dead
158 **Winnow** separate, like grain from chaff   **159 render** declare, state   **164 Thou'lt torture me** i.e. if you
had any idea what I have to say, you'd torture me   **173 All…this** everything relating to this matter

IACHIMO That paragon, thy daughter,
175   For whom my heart drops blood, and my false spirits
   Quail to remember — give me leave, I faint.
CYMBELINE My daughter? What of her? Renew thy
    strength:
   I had rather thou shouldst live while nature will
   Than die ere I hear more: strive, man, and speak.
180 IACHIMO Upon a time — unhappy was the clock
   That struck the hour! — it was in Rome — accursed
   The mansion where! — 'twas at a feast — O, would
   Our viands had been poisoned, or at least
   Those which I heaved to head! — the good
    Posthumus —
185   What should I say? He was too good to be
   Where ill men were, and was the best of all
   Amongst the rar'st of good ones — sitting sadly,
   Hearing us praise our loves of Italy
   For beauty that made barren the swelled boast
190   Of him that best could speak: for feature, laming
   The shrine of Venus or straight-pight Minerva,
   Postures beyond brief nature: for condition,
   A shop of all the qualities that man
   Loves woman for, besides that hook of wiving,
195   Fairness which strikes the eye—
CYMBELINE I stand on fire.
   Come to the matter.
IACHIMO All too soon I shall,
   Unless thou wouldst grieve quickly. This Posthumus,
200   Most like a noble lord in love and one
   That had a royal lover, took his hint,
   And not dispraising whom we praised — therein
   He was as calm as virtue — he began
   His mistress' picture, which by his tongue being
    made,
205   And then a mind put in't, either our brags

178 while nature will for as long as nature will have it/for the remainder of your natural life   **179 ere** before   **183 viands** food   **184 heaved to head** raised to my mouth   **187 rar'st** most exceptional   **sadly** soberly, reservedly   **189 made barren** rendered impotent   **190 feature** shape/comeliness/form of face   **laming** crippling by comparison   **191 shrine** veneration, idolizing   **Venus** Roman goddess of love   **straight-pight** straight pitched, i.e. erect, upright in bearing   **Minerva** Roman goddess of arts and war   **192 beyond** surpassing   **brief nature** the brevity of mortal life   **condition** character, personality   **193 shop** storehouse   **194 hook of wiving** i.e. beauty which is bait for marriage   **196 I . . . fire** i.e. I am burning with impatience   **197 matter** point   **201 hint** cue/opportunity   **205 mind put in't** described her character

Were cracked of kitchen-trulls, or his description
Proved us unspeaking sots.

CYMBELINE Nay, nay, to th'purpose.

IACHIMO Your daughter's chastity — there it begins.

210   He spake of her as Dian had hot dreams
And she alone were cold: whereat I, wretch,
Made scruple of his praise, and wagered with him
Pieces of gold gainst this, which then he wore
Upon his honoured finger, to attain

215   In suit the place of's bed and win this ring
By hers and mine adultery. He, true knight,
No lesser of her honour confident
Than I did truly find her, stakes this ring,
And would so had it been a carbuncle

220   Of Phoebus' wheel, and might so safely had it
Been all the worth of's car. Away to Britain
Post I in this design: well may you, sir,
Remember me at court, where I was taught
Of your chaste daughter the wide difference

225   'Twixt amorous and villainous. Being thus quenched
Of hope, not longing, mine Italian brain
'Gan in your duller Britain operate
Most vilely: for my vantage, excellent.
And, to be brief, my practice so prevailed

230   That I returned with simular proof enough
To make the noble Leonatus mad
By wounding his belief in her renown
With tokens thus, and thus: averring notes
Of chamber-hanging, pictures, this her bracelet —   *Shows the*

235   O, cunning, how I got it! — nay, some marks   *bracelet*
Of secret on her person, that he could not
But think her bond of chastity quite cracked,
I having ta'en the forfeit. Whereupon —
Methinks I see him now—

---

206 cracked of boastfully uttered about   **kitchen-trulls** kitchen-maids   **trull** wench/trollop
207 unspeaking sots fools/drunkards, incapable of articulate speech   **208 to th'purpose** get to the point
210 as Dian as though Diana (Roman goddess of chastity)   **hot** erotic, lustful   **211 she** i.e. Innogen   **cold**
chaste   **212 scruple** doubt   **215 In suit** by courtship   **219 carbuncle** precious stone, mythical gem said
to emit light in the dark   **220 Of Phoebus' wheel** from the chariot wheel of Phoebus Apollo, the sun
god   **might so** might have done so   **221 of's car** of his chariot   **222 Post** hurry   **224 Of** by   **227 duller**
Britain refers to the idea that cold, northern countries produced slower-witted people than those from the hot
south   **228 vantage** profit, gain   **230 simular** simulated, specious   **232 renown** reputation   **233 thus,
and thus** of this and that kind   **averring** affirming   **237 cracked** broken   **238 forfeit** that which is due
when a contract is breached

240 **POSTHUMUS** Ay, so thou dost,   *Comes forward*
Italian fiend! Ay me, most credulous fool,
Egregious murderer, thief, anything
That's due to all the villains past, in being,
To come! O, give me cord, or knife, or poison,
245 Some upright justicer! Thou, king, send out
For torturers ingenious: it is I
That all th'abhorrèd things o'th'earth amend
By being worse than they. I am Posthumus,
That killed thy daughter — villain-like, I lie —
250 That caused a lesser villain than myself,
A sacrilegious thief, to do't. The temple
Of virtue was she; yea, and she herself.
Spit, and throw stones, cast mire upon me, set
The dogs o'th'street to bay me: every villain
255 Be called Posthumus Leonatus, and
Be villainy less than 'twas! O Innogen!
My queen, my life, my wife: O Innogen,
Innogen, Innogen!
INNOGEN Peace, my lord, hear, hear.   *She runs to him?*
260 **POSTHUMUS** Shall's have a play of this? Thou scornful
    page,
There lie thy part.   *He strikes her and she falls*
PISANIO O, gentlemen, help!
Mine and your mistress: O, my lord Posthumus,
You ne'er killed Innogen till now. Help, help!
265 Mine honoured lady.
CYMBELINE Does the world go round?
POSTHUMUS How comes these staggers on me?
PISANIO Wake, my mistress!
CYMBELINE If this be so, the gods do mean to strike me
270 To death with mortal joy.
PISANIO How fares my mistress?
INNOGEN O, get thee from my sight,
Thou gavest me poison: dangerous fellow, hence!
Breathe not where princes are.
275 **CYMBELINE** The tune of Innogen.

---

242 **anything** any name, title   243 **in being** present   244 **cord** rope   245 **justicer** judge
246 **ingenious** masterly, skilful   247 **th'abhorrèd** the detested   **amend** make seem better
251 **sacrilegious thief** because he sacked the **temple** that was Innogen   252 **she herself** i.e. virtue
254 **bay** bark at   256 **Be … 'twas** i.e. by comparing it with what I have done   260 **Shall's have** shall we
make   261 **There … part** play your part by lying on the ground   267 **staggers** giddiness, dizziness; a
disease in animals which causes them to walk unsteadily   270 **mortal** earthly, human/deadly, fatal
275 **tune** voice

PISANIO Lady, the gods throw stones of sulphur on me if
That box I gave you was not thought by me
A precious thing: I had it from the queen.

CYMBELINE New matter still.

280 **INNOGEN** It poisoned me.

CORNELIUS O gods!
I left out one thing which the queen confessed,
Which must approve thee honest. 'If Pisanio
Have', said she, 'given his mistress that confection

285 Which I gave him for cordial, she is served
As I would serve a rat.'

CYMBELINE What's this, Cornelius?

CORNELIUS The queen, sir, very oft importuned me
To temper poisons for her, still pretending

290 The satisfaction of her knowledge only
In killing creatures vile, as cats and dogs,
Of no esteem. I, dreading that her purpose
Was of more danger, did compound for her
A certain stuff which, being ta'en, would cease

295 The present power of life, but in short time
All offices of nature should again
Do their due functions. Have you ta'en of it?

INNOGEN Most like I did, for I was dead.

BELARIUS My boys,

300 There was our error.

GUIDERIUS This is sure Fidele.

INNOGEN Why did you throw your wedded lady from
you?
Think that you are upon a rock, and now
Throw me again.   *Embraces him*

305 **POSTHUMUS** Hang there like fruit, my soul,
Till the tree die.

CYMBELINE How now, my flesh, my child?
What, mak'st thou me a dullard in this act?
Wilt thou not speak to me?

310 **INNOGEN** Your blessing, sir.   *Kneels*

BELARIUS Though you did love this youth, I blame ye   *To Guiderius*
not.   *and Arviragus*
You had a motive for't.

---

276 **stones of sulphur** thunderbolts   283 **approve** prove   284 **confection** mixture (drug)   285 **for cordial** as a restorative   289 **temper** mix, concoct   **still pretending** always claiming   292 **esteem** value, worth   294 **cease** halt, arrest   296 **offices of nature** natural faculties/bodily parts   298 **Most like** very likely   301 **sure** definitely   306 **the tree** i.e. himself   308 **mak'st...act** do you cast me as an idiot   312 **motive** reason

CYMBELINE My tears that fall
Prove holy water on thee! Innogen,
315 Thy mother's dead.

INNOGEN I am sorry for't, my lord.

CYMBELINE O, she was naught, and long of her it was
That we meet here so strangely: but her son
Is gone, we know not how nor where.

320 **PISANIO** My lord,
Now fear is from me, I'll speak troth. Lord Cloten,
Upon my lady's missing, came to me
With his sword drawn, foamed at the mouth, and
    swore,
If I discovered not which way she was gone,
325 It was my instant death. By accident,
I had a feignèd letter of my master's
Then in my pocket, which directed him
To seek her on the mountains near to Milford,
Where in a frenzy, in my master's garments,
330 Which he enforced from me, away he posts
With unchaste purpose, and with oath to violate
My lady's honour. What became of him
I further know not.

GUIDERIUS Let me end the story:
335 I slew him there.

CYMBELINE Marry, the gods forfend!
I would not thy good deeds should from my lips
Pluck a hard sentence: prithee, valiant youth,
Deny't again.

340 **GUIDERIUS** I have spoke it, and I did it.

CYMBELINE He was a prince.

GUIDERIUS A most incivil one. The wrongs he did me
Were nothing prince-like, for he did provoke me
With language that would make me spurn the sea,
345 If it could so roar to me. I cut off's head,
And am right glad he is not standing here
To tell this tale of mine.

---

315 **mother's** i.e. stepmother is   317 **naught** nothing/wicked   **long of** because of (along of)
318 **strangely** as strangers/in unusual circumstances   322 **missing** absence   324 **discovered** revealed
325 **accident** chance   326 **feignèd letter** i.e. the letter falsely claiming that Posthumus was waiting at
Milford Haven   330 **enforced** took by force   **posts** hurries   336 **forfend** forbid   339 **Deny't again** take
it back again, unsay it   341 **He . . . prince** i.e. killing him is therefore treasonable and merits death
342 **incivil** unmannerly   347 **To . . . mine** i.e. to tell you that he had cut off my head

CYMBELINE I am sorrow for thee:
By thine own tongue thou art condemned, and must
350 Endure our law: thou'rt dead.

INNOGEN That headless man
I thought had been my lord.

CYMBELINE Bind the offender,
And take him from our presence.

355 **BELARIUS** Stay, sir king.
This man is better than the man he slew,
As well descended as thyself, and hath
More of thee merited than a band of Clotens
Had ever scar for.— Let his arms alone,   *To the Guard*
360 They were not born for bondage.

CYMBELINE Why, old soldier,
Wilt thou undo the worth thou art unpaid for
By tasting of our wrath? How of descent
As good as we?

365 **ARVIRAGUS** In that he spake too far.

CYMBELINE And thou shalt die for't.

BELARIUS We will die all three,
But I will prove that two on's are as good
As I have given out him. My sons, I must
370 For mine own part unfold a dangerous speech,
Though haply well for you.

ARVIRAGUS Your danger's ours.

GUIDERIUS And our good his.

BELARIUS Have at it then, by leave.
375 Thou hadst, great king, a subject who
Was called Belarius.

CYMBELINE What of him? He is
A banished traitor.

BELARIUS He it is that hath
380 Assumed this age: indeed, a banished man,
I know not how a traitor.

CYMBELINE Take him hence,
The whole world shall not save him.

BELARIUS Not too hot:
385 First pay me for the nursing of thy sons,

---

348 **sorrow** sorry/filled with sorrow   350 **dead** condemned to die   357 **As well descended** of as good
lineage, family stock   358 **of** from   **merited** deserved   359 **Had ... for** ever deserved for their wounds in
battle   362 **worth ... for** the reward you have not yet been given   363 **tasting of** experiencing, feeling
366 **thou** i.e. Belarius   368 **But I will** unless I   **on's** of us   369 **given out him** declared him (Guiderius) to
be   370 **For ... speech** i.e. what I am about to say will prove dangerous to me   371 **haply** perhaps, with
luck   **well for** beneficial to   374 **by leave** with your permission   380 **Assumed this age** attained this
aged appearance   384 **hot** hasty

And let it be confiscate all so soon
As I have received it.

CYMBELINE Nursing of my sons?

BELARIUS I am too blunt and saucy, here's my knee: *Kneels*
390   Ere I arise I will prefer my sons,
Then spare not the old father. Mighty sir,
These two young gentlemen that call me father,
And think they are my sons, are none of mine.
They are the issue of your loins, my liege,
395   And blood of your begetting.

CYMBELINE How, my issue?

BELARIUS So sure as you your father's. I, old Morgan,
Am that Belarius whom you sometime banished:
Your pleasure was my mere offence, my punishment
400   Itself, and all my treason. That I suffered
Was all the harm I did. These gentle princes —
For such and so they are — these twenty years
Have I trained up: those arts they have as I
Could put into them. My breeding was, sir,
405   As your highness knows. Their nurse, Euriphile,
Whom for the theft I wedded, stole these children
Upon my banishment: I moved her to't,
Having received the punishment before
For that which I did then. Beaten for loyalty
410   Excited me to treason. Their dear loss,
The more of you 'twas felt, the more it shaped
Unto my end of stealing them. But, gracious sir,
Here are your sons again, and I must lose
Two of the sweet'st companions in the world.
415   The benediction of these covering heavens
Fall on their heads like dew, for they are worthy
To inlay heaven with stars.

CYMBELINE Thou weep'st, and speak'st:
The service that you three have done is more
420   Unlike than this thou tell'st. I lost my children:
If these be they, I know not how to wish
A pair of worthier sons.

---

386 it i.e. the payment   **confiscate all** all confiscated   **so** as   **389 saucy** impudent   **390 prefer** raise in
social stature   **395 blood** offspring   **398 sometime** once   **399 mere** whole   **400 That…did** i.e. I did no
harm at all, unless you think my suffering harmful   **404 put into** teach   **407 moved** persuaded
408 Having…then i.e. he had already been unjustly banished for treason, but stealing the children was
actually a treasonable offence   **409 Beaten** being beaten   **410 Excited** provoked, incited   **411 of** by
shaped Unto fitted, suited   **412 end of** purpose in (to make Cymbeline suffer)   **419 service** i.e. in battle
420 Unlike unlikely, amazing

BELARIUS Be pleased awhile.
This gentleman, whom I call Polydore,

425 Most worthy prince, as yours, is true Guiderius:
This gentleman, my Cadwal, Arviragus,
Your younger princely son. He, sir, was lapped
In a most curious mantle, wrought by th'hand
Of his queen mother, which for more probation

430 I can with ease produce.

CYMBELINE Guiderius had
Upon his neck a mole, a sanguine star.
It was a mark of wonder.

BELARIUS This is he,

435 Who hath upon him still that natural stamp:
It was wise nature's end in the donation
To be his evidence now.

CYMBELINE O, what am I?
A mother to the birth of three? Ne'er mother

440 Rejoiced deliverance more: blest pray you be,
That, after this strange starting from your orbs,
You may reign in them now! O Innogen,
Thou hast lost by this a kingdom.

INNOGEN No, my lord:

445 I have got two worlds by't. O my gentle brothers,
Have we thus met? O, never say hereafter
But I am truest speaker. You called me brother
When I was but your sister: I you brothers,
When ye were so indeed.

450 **CYMBELINE** Did you e'er meet?

ARVIRAGUS Ay, my good lord.

GUIDERIUS And at first meeting loved,
Continued so until we thought he died.

CORNELIUS By the queen's dram she swallowed.

455 **CYMBELINE** O rare instinct!
When shall I hear all through? This fierce
      abridgement
Hath to it circumstantial branches, which
Distinction should be rich in. Where? How lived you?

---

423 **Be pleased awhile** permit me to speak for a few more moments   425 **as yours** as your son
427 **lapped** wrapped   428 **curious** exquisite   429 **probation** proof   432 **sanguine** blood-red
435 **natural stamp** birthmark   436 **end . . . donation** purpose in giving it   440 **deliverance** in giving
birth   **pray** I pray   441 **starting . . . orbs** displacement from your spheres   443 **Thou . . . kingdom**
because Guiderius and Arviragus are immediate heirs to the throne   447 **But** anything other than
455 **rare** exceptional   456 **fierce abridgement** drastically compressed account   457 **branches** details
458 **Distinction . . . in** need to be distinguished fully from one another/should prove plentiful once they have
been distinguished from one another

And when came you to serve our Roman captive?
460 How parted with your brothers? How first met them?
Why fled you from the court? And whither? These,
And your three motives to the battle, with
I know not how much more, should be demanded,
And all the other by-dependences,
465 From chance to chance. But nor the time nor place
Will serve our long interrogatories. See,
Posthumus anchors upon Innogen,
And she, like harmless lightning, throws her eye
On him, her brothers, me, her master, hitting
470 Each object with a joy: the counterchange
Is severally in all. Let's quit this ground,
And smoke the temple with our sacrifices.—
Thou art my brother, so we'll hold thee ever. *To Belarius*

INNOGEN You are my father too, and did relieve me
475 To see this gracious season.

CYMBELINE All o'erjoyed,
Save these in bonds: let them be joyful too,
For they shall taste our comfort.

INNOGEN My good master,
480 I will yet do you service.

LUCIUS Happy be you!

CYMBELINE The forlorn soldier, that so nobly fought,
He would have well becomed this place, and graced
The thankings of a king.

485 **POSTHUMUS** I am, sir,
The soldier that did company these three
In poor beseeming: 'twas a fitment for
The purpose I then followed. That I was he,
Speak, Iachimo: I had you down, and might
490 Have made you finish.

IACHIMO I am down again: *Kneels*
But now my heavy conscience sinks my knee,
As then your force did. Take that life, beseech you,

---

462 your . . . to what motives the three of you (Belarius, Guiderius and Arviragus) had for joining
463 demanded asked about   464 by-dependences side issues, related matters   465 chance happening,
occurrence   nor neither   466 Will serve are suited to   interrogatories interrogations   467 anchors
concentrates his looks, attention   468 throws her eye gazes   470 counterchange . . . all each
reciprocates the looks of the others   471 quit this ground leave this place   472 smoke fill with smoke
(from incense or sacrificial fires)   473 hold consider   474 relieve me help/rescue me   475 gracious
season joyous occasion   477 Save except   478 taste our comfort feel, experience our mercy/share in
our happiness   482 forlorn wretched, destitute   483 becomed become, suited   graced done honour to/
made rich   486 company accompany   487 beseeming appearance, i.e. his peasant's garb   fitment
preparation   490 you finish an end of you   492 sinks makes bend, weighs down

Which I so often owe: but your ring first,
And here the bracelet of the truest princess
That ever swore her faith.

POSTHUMUS Kneel not to me:
The power that I have on you is to spare you:
The malice towards you to forgive you. Live,
And deal with others better.

CYMBELINE Nobly doomed!
We'll learn our freeness of a son-in-law:
Pardon's the word to all.

ARVIRAGUS You holp us, sir,
As you did mean indeed to be our brother.
Joyed are we that you are.

POSTHUMUS Your servant, princes. Good my lord of
    Rome,
Call forth your soothsayer: as I slept, methought
Great Jupiter, upon his eagle backed,
Appeared to me, with other spritely shows
Of mine own kindred. When I waked I found
This label on my bosom, whose containing
Is so from sense in hardness that I can
Make no collection of it. Let him show
His skill in the construction.

LUCIUS Philharmonus.

SOOTHSAYER Here, my good lord.

LUCIUS Read, and declare the meaning.

SOOTHSAYER *Reads* 'Whenas a lion's whelp shall, to
himself unknown, without seeking find, and be
embraced by a piece of tender air: and when from
a stately cedar shall be lopped branches, which being
dead many years, shall after revive, be jointed to the
old stock, and freshly grow, then shall Posthumus
end his miseries, Britain be fortunate and flourish in
peace and plenty.'
Thou, Leonatus, art the lion's whelp:
The fit and apt construction of thy name,
Being leo-natus, doth import so much.—
The piece of tender air, thy virtuous daughter,   *To Cymbeline*

495
500
505
510
515
520
525
530

---

494 **often** many times over   501 **doomed** judged, sentenced   502 **freeness** generosity, benevolence
504 **holp** helped   505 **As** as if   506 **Joyed** overjoyed   509 **upon…backed** riding upon his eagle's
back   510 **spritely shows** ghostly visions   512 **label** sheet of paper (the tablet)   **containing** contents
513 **so…hardness** i.e. hard to understand   514 **collection of** deduction, inference from
515 **construction** interpretation   516 **Philharmonus** i.e. lover of harmony   519 **whelp** cub
529 **leo-natus** born of a lion   **import** signify, mean

Which we call *'mollis aer'*; and *'mollis aer'*
We term it *'mulier'*.— Which *'mulier'* I divine
Is this most constant wife, who even now,
Answering the letter of the oracle,
535 Unknown to you, unsought, were clipped about
With this most tender air.

CYMBELINE This hath some seeming.

SOOTHSAYER The lofty cedar, royal Cymbeline,
Personates thee: and thy lopped branches point
540 Thy two sons forth, who by Belarius stol'n,
For many years thought dead, are now revived,
To the majestic cedar joined, whose issue
Promises Britain peace and plenty.

CYMBELINE Well,
545 My peace we will begin.— And, Caius Lucius,
Although the victor, we submit to Caesar
And to the Roman empire, promising
To pay our wonted tribute, from the which
We were dissuaded by our wicked queen,
550 Whom heavens in justice both on her and hers
Have laid most heavy hand.

SOOTHSAYER The fingers of the powers above do tune
The harmony of this peace. The vision
Which I made known to Lucius ere the stroke
555 Of this yet scarce-cold battle, at this instant
Is full accomplished. For the Roman eagle,
From south to west on wing soaring aloft,
Lessened herself, and in the beams o'th'sun
So vanished; which foreshowed our princely eagle,
560 Th'imperial Caesar, should again unite
His favour with the radiant Cymbeline,
Which shines here in the west.

CYMBELINE Laud we the gods,
And let our crookèd smokes climb to their nostrils
565 From our blest altars. Publish we this peace
To all our subjects. Set we forward: let

---

531 mollis aer Latin for 'soft air'; a false etymology of **mulier**, Latin for 'woman'   **532 divine** interpret (by divine inspiration)   **535 clipped about** embraced   **537 seeming** plausibility   **538 cedar** the tree was an emblem of sovereignty, especially in the Bible   **539 Personates** stands for   **point . . . forth** indicate your two sons   **542 issue** offspring, descendants   **548 wonted** usual, accustomed   **550 Whom** on whom **554 stroke** action, onset   **558 Lessened herself** i.e. by disappearing into the distance   **562 west** understood in classical geography as the location of Britain   **563 Laud** praise   **564 crookèd** curling **565 Publish** announce   **566 Set we forward** let's set on, begin marching

A Roman and a British ensign wave
Friendly together: so through Lud's town march,
And in the temple of great Jupiter
570 Our peace we'll ratify, seal it with feasts.
Set on there! Never was a war did cease,
Ere bloody hands were washed, with such a peace.

Exeunt

---

567 **ensign** standard, banner   570 **seal** confirm   571 **Set on there!** Onwards, forward march!

TEXTUAL NOTES

F = First Folio text of 1623
F2 = a correction introduced in the Second Folio text of 1632
F3 = a correction introduced in the Third Folio text of 1663–64
Ed = a correction introduced by a later editor
SD = stage direction
SH = speech heading (i.e. speaker's name)

List of parts = Ed

1.1.1 SH FIRST GENTLEMAN = Ed. F = 1.*Gent, subsequently* 1 **3 king** = Ed. F = Kings
4 SH SECOND GENTLEMAN = Ed. F = 2 *Gent, subsequently* 2 **35 Cassibelan** = F2.
F = *Cassibulan* **65 clothes the other,** = Ed. F = cloathes, the other **78 SD *Exeunt*** = Ed.
F = *Exeunt / Scena Secunda* **SD *Innogen*** = Ed. F = *Imogen (throughout)* **109 Philario's** =
Ed. F = *Filorio's* **131 cere** *spelled* seare *in* F
Act 1 Scene 2 = Ed. F = *Scena Tertia*
1.2.1 SH FIRST LORD = Ed. F = 1 **7 SH SECOND LORD** = Ed. F = 2
9 thoroughfare = F3. F = thorough-fare
Act 1 Scene 3 = Ed. F = *Scena Quarta*
Act 1 Scene 4 = Ed. F = *Scena Quinta*
1.4.29 Briton *spelled* Britaine *in* F **49 not** = Ed. *Not in* F **75 Britain** = Ed. F = Britanie **75–6
others I have** = Ed. F = others. I haue **77 not but** = Ed. F= not **88 purchase** = Ed.
F = purchases **132 thousand** = F3. F = thousands **139 a friend** = F. *Sometimes emended
to* afraid
Act 1 Scene 5 = Ed. F = *Scena Sexta*
1.5.84 SD *Exit Pisanio* *printed one line earlier in* F
Act 1 Scene 6 = Ed. F = *Scena Septima*
1.6.7 desire = F2. F = desires **26 trust** = F. *Sometimes emended to* truest **29 takes** = Ed. F =
take **38 th'unnumbered** = Ed. F = the number'd **67 Briton** *spelled* Britaine *in* F **125
illustrous** = Ed. F = illustrious **169 Solicit'st** = Ed. F = Solicites **190 men's** =
F2. F = men **192 descended** = F2. F = defended
2.1.7 SH FIRST LORD = Ed. F = 1 *(throughout scene)* **14 give** = F2. F = gaue **26 your** =
Ed. F = you **33 tonight** = F2. F = night **60 husband, than** = Ed. F = Husband. Then **61
make! The** = Ed. F = make the
2.2.51 bare *spelled* beare *in* F
2.3.27 SH CLOTEN = Ed. *Not in* F **28 vice** = Ed. F = voyce **30 amend** = F2. F = amed **47
solicits** = F2. F = solicity **110 cure** = Ed. F = are **132 foil** = F. *Sometimes emended to*
soil **150 garment** = F2. F = Garments **172 you** = Ed. F = your
2.4.7 seared hopes = Ed. F = fear'd hope **20 legions** = Ed. F = Legion **26 mingled** = F2.
F = wing-led **39 through** = Ed. F = thorough **42 tenor** = Ed. F = tenure **44 SH
PHILARIO** = Ed. F = *Post.* **51 had** = Ed. F = haue **59 not** = F2. F = note
71 you = F2. F = yon **74 leaves** = Ed. F = leaue **146 one of** = F2. F = one **169 the** =
Ed. F = her **209 German one** = Ed. F = Iarmen on **220 may be named** = F2. F =
name

3.1.23 oaks = F. *Sometimes emended to* rocks **39 more** *spelled* mo *in* F **56 be. We do say** = Ed. F = be, we do. Say

3.2.2 monster's her accuser = Ed. F = Monsters her accuse **21 fedary** = Ed. F = Fœdarie **64 get** = F2. F = ger **67 score** = F2. F = store **ride** = F2. F = rid **80 here, nor** = F2. F = heere, not

3.3.2 Stoop = Ed. F = Sleepe **25 robe** = Ed. F = Babe. *Sometimes emended to* bauble **27 'em** = Ed. F = him **30 know** = F2. F = knowes **33 known, well** = Ed. F = knowne. Well **35 travelling** *spelled* trauailing *in* F **36 for** = Ed. F = or **88 wherein they bow** = Ed. F = whereon the Bowe **91 Polydore** = Ed. F = *Paladour* **108 reft'st** = Ed. F = refts **111 Morgan** = Ed. F = *Mergan*

3.4.83 afore't = Ed. F = a-foot **93 make** = Ed. F = makes **107 out** = Ed. *Not in* F **165 haply** = Ed. F = happily

3.5.22 SD *and others spelled* &c. *in* F **39 looks us** = Ed. F = looke vs **48 strokes** = Ed. F = stroke **54 th'loud'st** = Ed. F = th'lowd **164 insultment** = F2. F = insulment

3.6.27 F *marks a new scene here: Scena Septima* **78 Ay** = Ed. F = I **I'd** = Ed. F = I do

Act 3 Scene 7 = Ed. F = *Scena Octaua*

4.1.14 imperceiverant = Ed. F = imperseuerant **18 thy face** = F. Ed = her face **19 haply** *spelled* happily *in* F

4.2.63 cookery! He = Ed. F = Cookerie? / *Arui.* He (*some editors assign* 'He...dieter' *to Belarius*) **73 him** = Ed. F = them **75 patience** = Ed. F = patient **90 mountaineers** *spelled* Mountainers *in* F **157 thank** = Ed. F = thanks **169 humour** = Ed. F = Honor **233 ingenious** = Ed. F = ingenuous **257 crare** = Ed. F = care **258 Might** = F2. F = Might'st **easiliest** = Ed. F = easilest **259 ay** *spelled* I *in* F **281 ruddock** = Ed. F = Raddocke **297 once** = Ed. F = once to **355 is** = Ed. F = are **401 are** = F2. F = are heere **464 wildwood leaves** = Ed. F = wild wood-leaues **475 he is** = F2. F = hee's

4.3.18 SH FIRST LORD = Ed. F = *Lord.* **46 betid** = Ed. F = betide

4.4.3 find we = F2. F = we finde **11 us** = F2. F = v.. **22 the** = Ed. F = their **33 hard** = Ed. F = heard

5.1.1 wished = Ed. F = am wisht

5.3.27 harts = Ed. F = hearts **45 stooped** = Ed. F = ftopt **46 they** = Ed. F = the **90 SH FIRST CAPTAIN** = Ed. F = 1 **92 SH SECOND CAPTAIN** = Ed. F = 2 **102 SD** *Jailers* = Ed. F = *Gaoler* **SD** *Exeunt...Jailers* = Ed. F = *Enter Posthumus, and Gaoler* (F *begins new scene here, Scena Quarta*) **103 SH FIRST JAILER** = Ed. F = *Gao.* **170 geck** = Ed. F = geeke **184 look** = F2. F = looke, / looke **221 claws** *spelled* cloyes *in* F **263 are as** = Ed. F = are **270 Of this** = Ed. F = Oh, of this **274 sir** = F2. F = Sis **289 on** = Ed. F = one

Act 5 Scene 4 = Ed. F = *Scena Quinta*

5.4.76 heard = Ed. F = heare **158 On** = Ed. F = One **235 got it** = F2. F = got **302 from** = Ed. F = fro **368 on's** = Ed. F = one's **399 mere** = Ed. F = neere **400 treason. That** = Ed. F = Treason that **416 like** = F2. F = liks **449 ye** = Ed. F = we **460 brothers** = Ed. F = Brother **461 whither? These** = Ed. F = whether these? **482 so** = F2. F = no **519 SH SOOTHSAYER** = Ed. *Not in* F **555 this yet** = F3. F = yet this

SCENE-BY-SCENE ANALYSIS

ACT 1 SCENE 1

Lines 1–78: In Roman Britain, two Gentlemen, courtiers of the Briton king, Cymbeline, discuss in secret the scandals within the court. They reveal that Posthumus Leonatus, an orphan of uncertain lineage brought up by Cymbeline, has been banished for marrying the king's daughter, Innogen, who has been imprisoned. Cymbeline and his new Queen wanted to marry Innogen to the Queen's son, Cloten, who is 'Too bad for bad report', though all the courtiers are inwardly glad she was spared such a fate. They also reveal that Posthumus' elder brothers were killed in battle, his father died in grief for them, and his mother died giving birth to him. However, he has grown to be an honourable man, highly regarded by everyone he meets, and all grieve for the separation of the virtuous young lovers. Cymbeline's anguish at Innogen's revolt, they say, is compounded by the fact that she is his only child; his two infant sons were kidnapped without trace twenty years earlier.

Lines 79–213: Posthumus and Innogen enter with the Queen, who condoles with them, saying she will plead with Cymbeline on their behalf; they play along, but reveal knowledge of her wickedness when she leaves. Innogen gives Posthumus a diamond ring which belonged to her mother as a symbol of their fidelity to one another. He swears to keep it safe, and gives her a bracelet in return. Cymbeline enters and orders Posthumus gone, berating Innogen, who is openly unrepentant, for refusing Cloten. Cymbeline leaves and the Queen again professes sympathy. Pisanio, Posthumus' servant, enters to tell them that as his master was leaving the court Cloten drew his sword on him, but that Posthumus 'rather played than fought' and no harm was done. Innogen feignedly praises Cloten for loyalty to the king, but in an aside wishes Posthumus could have fought him to the death. Pisanio reveals that Posthumus has given him letters with commands to serve Innogen, and the Queen says that he will prove a 'faithful servant'. She entreats Innogen to walk with her, and Innogen sends Pisanio to see Posthumus aboard his ship.

ACT 1 SCENE 2

Cloten enters with two Lords, the First of whom politely tries to persuade him to change his shirt as 'the violence of action' in his duel with Posthumus has clearly made him smell. He flatters Cloten for bravery and fighting skill, suggesting Posthumus was lucky to escape, while the Second Lord, in a series of asides, reveals Cloten's cowardice, his inferiority to Posthumus in every way, and his unworthiness of Innogen.

ACT 1 SCENE 3

Innogen questions Pisanio on every detail of Posthumus' leave-taking at the harbour, saying that she would have watched him on his departing ship until he 'had melted from / The smallness of a gnat to air'. She laments the fact that she did not have the chance to say to him everything she had wanted before her father had forced them apart, chiefly to beware temptation from 'the shes of Italy'. A Lady summons Innogen to the Queen, and Pisanio is sent to undertake errands.

ACT 1 SCENE 4

1–28: In Italy, Philario, an old comrade of Posthumus' father who has agreed to host the young Briton, awaits, with Iachimo (an Italian nobleman) and other lords, the arrival of his old friend's son. The play's move from Roman Britain to Renaissance Italy underlines its fairytale, transhistorical setting. All the others remark that they have met Posthumus in the past and that he does not deserve his high reputation, but Philario alone defends him, saying that he has grown much since then. Iachimo suggests that it is Posthumus' marriage to a king's daughter that falsely enhances his reputation.

29–178: Posthumus arrives and exchanges reminiscences with a French lord, thanking him for cooling an argument he was once in about the virtue of Innogen over any 'ladies in France'. Iachimo scoffs, claiming that no such woman exists, and that every woman, including Innogen, can be seduced. He wagers Posthumus ten thousand ducats against the diamond ring Posthumus wears that he could seduce Innogen 'with no more advantage than the opportunity of a second conference'. Philario tries to stop them, but Posthumus consents on the condition that Iachimo must also fight him if he loses for 'th'assault . . . made to her chastity'. The wager is agreed.

ACT 1 SCENE 5

The Queen asks a doctor, Cornelius, to bring her deadly poisons which she claims she will use on 'such creatures as / We count not worth the hanging' to study their 'virtues and effects'. Suspicious of her intents, he instead gives her a restorative potion that produces the temporary appearance of death in those who take it, but does no harm. The Queen asks Pisanio to persuade Innogen to marry Cloten as Posthumus can never return. Knowing he would never really betray his master, and that he secretly champions Posthumus to Innogen, she drops the box containing the potion on the floor, which Pisanio picks up. She tells him it is a powerful cordial, and that he can keep it, revealing when he exits that she hopes he will take it and die so that Innogen will be alone and easier to manipulate. Pisanio re-enters and exchanges ostensible pleasantries with the Queen, though when she leaves he reveals he will 'choke' himself before acting on her behalf.

ACT 1 SCENE 6

Innogen is cursing her situation when Pisanio brings in Iachimo, introducing him as a 'gentleman of Rome' who brings letters from Posthumus. She welcomes him and in an aside he expresses amazement at her beauty, doubting his ability to win the wager if her 'mind' is as 'rare' as her outward form, but resolves to affect 'Boldness'. He begins to speak cryptically about Posthumus' judgement being horribly skewed, and, when pushed on what he means, eventually claims that Posthumus has all but forgotten Innogen, and lives like a libertine in Rome, whoring, drinking, and laughing at the foolishness of staid, faithful men who willingly submit to 'assurèd bondage'. He urges her to take revenge by likewise being unfaithful, offering his own services to that end. Innogen is disgusted, and calls Pisanio to have him thrown out, saying that if he were truly noble he would have 'told this tale for virtue, not / For such an end thou seek'st'. Iachimo, realizing he is beaten, begs forgiveness and claims he did it only to test her honour, acting on behalf of 'the worthiest sir that ever / Country called his'. Innogen accepts his apology, and welcomes him again. He says that he must return to Italy in the morning and will carry letters to Posthumus for her, asking only that she keep a trunk containing a valuable gift for the emperor safely in her chamber for him overnight. She agrees.

ACT 2 SCENE 1

The boorish Cloten bemoans his bad luck in a game of bowls, in which he also struck a bystander on the head who berated him for 'swearing'. The First Lord again flatters Cloten, while the Second mocks him behind his back, and the former tells of 'an Italian' come to court. Cloten resolves to seek the stranger out and 'win' from him the money he has lost at bowls. In a soliloquy the Second Lord questions how such a crafty person as the Queen could have spawned such an 'ass', and prays for Innogen to be reunited with Posthumus and to become queen.

ACT 2 SCENE 2

Innogen goes to sleep in her bedchamber, into which Iachimo's trunk has been moved. As she lies sleeping, Iachimo emerges from the trunk and in a long, sensuous soliloquy he notes the features of her body and of the room as he moves silently about, writing all down in a notebook. An uncomfortable tension is sustained as to whether he will rape her; he delicately kisses her lips at one point, and likens himself to 'Our Tarquin', a famous ravisher from classical antiquity about whom Shakespeare wrote in *The Rape of Lucrece*. He notes 'A mole cinque-spotted' on her left breast, claiming it will act as a 'voucher' of absolute proof when he tells Posthumus that he succeeded in seducing her. For further assurance, he removes from her wrist the bracelet given to her by Posthumus before creeping back into the trunk, acknowledging that she is a 'heavenly angel' and that he brings 'hell' into her presence.

ACT 2 SCENE 3

Cloten arrives at Innogen's window with musicians who sing for her. Cymbeline and the Queen enter and urge him to keep trying to win Innogen's love as she cannot cling to Posthumus' memory forever. A Messenger arrives to inform them that ambassadors from Rome, including Caius Lucius, who Cymbeline describes as a 'worthy fellow', have arrived at court. They leave Cloten to his wooing; he knocks at Innogen's door. One of her ladies-in-waiting answers, and he attempts to bribe her to speak well of him to Innogen, but she refuses. Innogen enters and tells him not to waste his time. He tells her that Posthumus is a low-born peasant who has no business being married to a princess, but she retorts with a string of insults, saying that Posthumus' 'meanest garment' is worth more than him. This cuts him deeply, but Innogen, realizing in panic that she has lost her bracelet, no longer notices him. She sends Pisanio to go and tell Dorothy, her 'woman', to look for it. Cloten vows to be revenged.

ACT 2 SCENE 4

Posthumus tells Philario he has no doubt Iachimo will return a defeated man. He thanks Philario for his generous hospitality, which he cannot at present repay. Philario tells him his 'goodness and . . . company' are payment enough, and notes that the Roman ambassadors have been sent to Britain to demand the payment of a tribute that has been neglected for some time. Posthumus predicts that the Britons will refuse, and that they are ready and able to fight Rome. Iachimo returns, giving Posthumus Innogen's letters, and boasting that he has won the wager. Posthumus remains unconvinced and demands proof. Iachimo describes the tapestries and carvings in her room, which troubles Posthumus, though he still argues that this is information Iachimo could easily have acquired without sleeping with Innogen. Iachimo ups the stakes by producing the bracelet, and Posthumus becomes extremely agitated, though he still asks for some proof that he has seen her body intimately. Iachimo describes the mole on her breast, and Posthumus flies into a rage, gives Iachimo the ring he has falsely won in their wager, and storms out. Philario resolves to follow Posthumus to prevent him harming himself, and implores Iachimo to follow. As they leave, Posthumus re-enters, and in a long, violent soliloquy, he denounces the falsehood of women and swears vengeance on Innogen.

ACT 3 SCENE 1

In Cymbeline's court Caius Lucius is received to deliver his message. He reminds Cymbeline of a tribute from Julius Caesar's time of 'three thousand pounds' that Cymbeline's uncle had agreed to pay yearly to his Roman conquerors, which has been 'lately . . . left untendered'. The Queen and Cloten rudely express defiance and refuse to pay, while Cymbeline more respectfully echoes the sentiment, saying that he holds Augustus Caesar, under whom he gained much tutelage as a young man, in high regard, but that to 'shake off' the yoke Rome has imposed 'Becomes a warlike people'. Lucius pronounces that Rome will attack Britain with 'fury not to be resisted' when he conveys the message back, which Cymbeline accepts, offering Lucius gracious hospitality until his return.

ACT 3 SCENE 2

Pisanio enters reading a letter from Posthumus, which tells of Innogen's 'adultery'. He cannot believe it, and is convinced that some 'false Italian' has corrupted Posthumus' mind with lies. The letter instructs him to murder Innogen. He is to give her another letter urging her to meet Posthumus at Milford Haven, where, far away from the court, Pisanio will have his opportunity. Not knowing what else to do, he begins to carry out Posthumus' command, giving Innogen the letter that falsely tells of Posthumus' arrival. She is overjoyed, and tells Pisanio to get her a 'riding-suit, no costlier than would fit / A franklin's housewife', intending to leave straight away. Pisanio urges caution but she will not be dissuaded.

ACT 3 SCENE 3

In Wales, Belarius, an old shepherd, emerges with his two sons, Polydore and Cadwal, from the cave in which they live and talks to them of the bounty and goodness of nature. They, however, complain that they have never seen anything of the world, and although Belarius warns them of the corruption and crime of the city, they still see their wilderness home as more prison than pleasure garden. Belarius tells them that the world is full of treachery, and that he used to be a noble in Cymbeline's court until he was banished, falsely accused by 'two villains' of being confederate with the Romans. He sends them up to the mountains to hunt for deer, and in a soliloquy reveals that the young men are in fact Cymbeline's sons, whom he kidnapped to 'bar' Cymbeline 'of succession' in revenge for the loss of his own estate. He reveals that their real names are Guiderius and Arviragus, and expresses amazement that their royal natures shine through them, although they know nothing of their birth. He tells us that they know him only as Morgan, and that they took their wet-nurse, Euriphile, whose grave they 'honour' daily, for their mother.

ACT 3 SCENE 4

Innogen and Pisanio arrive at Milford Haven. There is no sign of Posthumus, and Innogen, seeing signs of distress in Pisanio's face, asks him what is going on. Pisanio shows her the letter accusing her of adultery, at which she weeps and expresses great anger at Posthumus for believing her capable of such a thing. She then tells Pisanio to do as he has been instructed, as she no longer wants to live anyway, but he refuses. She asks why he has bothered bringing her all this way if he doesn't intend to fulfil his command, and he tells her he has done it merely 'to win time' in order to devise a plan. He suggests that they send Posthumus 'Some bloody sign' that she is dead – as in fact he was instructed to do – the proof of which will be bolstered by the fact that she is missing from court. She asks him where she will live in the interim, and, refusing his suggestion to return home in secret lest she be found by Cloten, he advises her to disguise herself as a boy using the clothes he has brought with him and offer her service to Caius Lucius who 'comes to Milford Haven / Tomorrow'. That way, she will be able to go with him back to Italy where she will be near Posthumus and able to keep track of his movements. She enthusiastically agrees. Pisanio says he must hurry back to court so that he is not suspected of her disappearance, and gives her the Queen's potion, which he believes is a restorative cordial that she can take if she becomes ill.

ACT 3 SCENE 5

Cymbeline, the Queen and Cloten bid farewell to Caius Lucius, and Cymbeline promises him a safe conduct to Milford Haven. With Lucius gone, Cymbeline advises that the British powers be amassed as Lucius' army in Gaul (France) is growing by the day and will soon attack. He then asks for Innogen, who has not been seen for days, and sends a Messenger to her chamber. The Messenger returns with the news that Innogen cannot be made to answer her door, and the Queen says that she had almost forgotten Innogen's request to be left alone to grieve for Posthumus. Cymbeline and Cloten rush to find her, noting also that Pisanio has not been seen for some time. The Queen in an aside hopes this is due to him having taken her potion. Cloten returns to confirm that Innogen is missing, saying that Cymbeline is in a rage, which the Queen, in another aside, hopes will hasten his death. Pisanio enters and Cloten threateningly questions him over Innogen's disappearance. Assuming that Lucius has enough headway on them and that Innogen will be safely in his service in her disguise by the time Cloten gets there, Pisanio shows Cloten the letter requesting Innogen to meet Posthumus at Milford Haven. Cloten gives Pisanio money and tells him to bring him some of Posthumus' clothes. He decides to follow them to Milford and be revenged on them both by killing Posthumus and raping Innogen while wearing the 'meanest' garments she insultingly compared him with in Act 2 scene 3. Pisanio delivers the clothes, but silently curses Cloten and wishes him to fail.

ACT 3 SCENE 6

Innogen, in her boy's disguise, hungry and weary, arrives at Belarius' cave. She calls aloud, but, receiving no answer, draws her sword and enters. Belarius and the two boys return with their catch from the hunt, and see her inside. She begs them not to harm her, saying her name is Fidele – the faithful one – and that she would have died had she not trespassed on their home to eat and get warm. Belarius welcomes the young boy (as he thinks), and Guiderius and Arviragus (Innogen's brothers, unbeknownst to any of them), immediately feel a strong bond of kinship with her that they are not able to explain, as she does with them. They go in to eat and to hear her story.

ACT 3 SCENE 7

A Roman Senator advises a Tribune that the common soldiery is stretched very thin with other foreign wars, and so hands responsibility for the Briton wars over to the gentry. Lucius, who was due to return, is made general and given command of the regiments in Wales.

ACT 4 SCENE 1

Cloten arrives in Milford Haven, stating himself every bit as good as Posthumus, whose head he swears to cut off 'within this hour'.

He also plans to rape Innogen, confident that his mother will be able to excuse his conduct to Cymbeline.

ACT 4 SCENE 2

Lines 1–228: Innogen complains of feeling ill and decides to stay behind in the cave while Belarius and the boys go out to hunt. She takes Pisanio's potion and goes in to rest. As the others set out for the hunt, Cloten enters. Belarius recognizes him, and, fearing he comes with soldiers to arrest them as outlaws, he takes Arviragus to scout for enemy troops, leaving Cloten to Guiderius. Cloten rudely asks Guiderius who he is, telling him that he is the Queen's son, but Guiderius greets him with contempt, at which Cloten draws his sword. They exit fighting, and Belarius and Arviragus return having found nobody else around. Guiderius re-enters carrying Cloten's head, and Belarius despairs that they will be hunted down for this act of treason. The boys remain unmoved, ready to face any danger that may come. Guiderius goes off to throw Cloten's head in the creek behind their cave, while Arviragus goes to tend to Innogen/Fidele. Belarius comments again in an aside how tenderness and bravery combine in their natures.

Lines 229–396: Arviragus, within, plays upon an instrument last played at Euriphile's funeral, and enters carrying Innogen, who, under the effects of the Queen's potion, they believe dead. They all grieve bitterly for the loss, and resolve to bury her along with Cloten, who, Belarius urges, was still a prince and deserves a proper interment. After they have spoken a moving funeral lament, they strew the bodies with flowers and leave. Innogen awakes, the potion having at last worn off, to find herself next to Cloten's headless body. In a long soliloquy she struggles to reorient herself and ascertain what has happened. Seeing Posthumus' clothes on Cloten's body, she believes she is lying next to her dead husband, and suspects Pisanio of foul play. She embraces the body.

Lines 397–478: Caius Lucius enters with a Soothsayer, who predicts Roman success in the wars. They see Innogen upon the body, and rouse her. She tells them it is the body of her master, Richard du Champ, killed 'by mountaineers'. Lucius, impressed with Innogen/Fidele's loyalty, takes her into his service, ordering his men to bury Cloten's body properly.

ACT 4 SCENE 3

Cymbeline anguishes over Innogen's flight and the dangerous illness of the Queen caused by her son's disappearance. Pisanio comforts Cymbeline and offers to serve him, and though Cymbeline still suspects him, a Lord avouches that Pisanio was at court when Innogen went missing, and must be innocent. The Lord also advises Cymbeline to prepare his armies against the advancing Romans. Pisanio, in an aside, wonders why he has not heard from either Posthumus or Innogen, and vows to fight bravely for Cymbeline in the ensuing wars.

ACT 4 SCENE 4

Belarius sees the Roman armies on the move, and urges Guiderius and Arviragus to run, saying that they have enemies on both sides; they cannot join the Britons as they will be captured and executed for Cloten's death. The boys refuse, however, sensing their time finally to taste battle and prove their valour. Belarius agrees to join them.

ACT 5 SCENE 1

Posthumus enters alone, carrying the bloody cloth sent to him by Pisanio, and in a long, tortured soliloquy, expresses deep repentance for what he has done to Innogen. He has been brought back to Britain to fight with the Romans, but resolves to doff his 'Italian weeds' and dress as a British peasant to fight for his country.

ACT 5 SCENE 2

Iachimo fights Posthumus in his peasant's disguise, and is beaten. Posthumus leaves Iachimo on the ground, who says that guilt at slandering Innogen 'enfeebles' him. In the continuing battle, some Britons beat a retreat and Cymbeline is captured, but Belarius, Guiderius and Arviragus, seconded by Posthumus, come to his rescue. Lucius, with the Romans facing defeat, tells Innogen/Fidele to run.

ACT 5 SCENE 3

Lines 1–102: Posthumus tells a British Lord, one of the deserters from the front line, about the battle. He describes how in a narrow lane, as the Romans chased the fleeing Britons, an old man and his two sons took a stand, fighting so bravely that they restored the British army's courage. He then berates the Lord for cowardice, who leaves him. Posthumus, wanting to be captured, has changed back into his Italian garments. Having partly atoned for Innogen's death by helping Britain win the battle, he now seeks to atone fully through self-destruction. Two British Captains enter and tell of Lucius' capture. Seeing Posthumus, and thinking him a Roman, they take him also.

Lines 103–311: In a British stockade, taunted by his Jailers, Posthumus speaks of his desire for death and falls asleep. While sleeping he is visited by the ghosts of his father, mother and two brothers, who plead with the gods to intercede on the young man's behalf. Jupiter descends amidst thunder and lightning and berates the spirits for their impertinence. Nonetheless, he agrees to help Posthumus, leaving him a tablet inscribed with a prophecy telling of Jupiter's will in the events to come. The spirits thank Jupiter, and all vanish. Posthumus awakes and sees the tablet, but is not able to interpret its meaning. A Jailer comes to fetch Posthumus to the gallows, but a Messenger intervenes, saying the prisoner has been summoned before the king.

ACT 5 SCENE 4

Lines 1–306: Cymbeline knights Belarius, Guiderius and Arviragus for their valour and service in battle, wishing that the 'poor soldier' who helped them (Posthumus) could be found and likewise rewarded. Cornelius, the doctor, enters to tell Cymbeline that the Queen is dead, and that she confessed before dying that she hated Innogen, that she never loved Cymbeline, and was plotting to kill him slowly with poisons so that Cloten could become king. Cymbeline says that he was utterly deceived by her, and that her beauty was the cause. Innogen (as Fidele), Caius Lucius, the Soothsayer, Iachimo and Posthumus (disguised as a Roman) are brought in as prisoners. Lucius begs only that his page (Innogen) be freed, to which Cymbeline agrees, taking the 'boy' into his service, and offering Fidele any 'boon' he can give. Innogen has seen Iachimo wearing her ring, and talks aside with Cymbeline, during which time Belarius and the two boys express amazement to each other that Fidele is alive again. Innogen questions Iachimo about the ring, and he confesses at length everything that he has done. Posthumus, revealing his own identity, comes forward to attack Iachimo, and admits remorsefully to being the cause of Innogen's death. Innogen rushes to him but he spurns her away, thinking her to be an insolent pageboy intruding on his grief. Pisanio then steps forward to tell everyone that the page is in fact Innogen in disguise, and Innogen curses Pisanio for trying to poison her. Cornelius remembers that the Queen had also confessed to giving Pisanio what she thought was poison, hoping to kill him, and that Pisanio was innocent of what the compound really was, thinking it medicinal. Reunited at last, Posthumus and Innogen embrace.

Lines 307–572: Cymbeline and Innogen lovingly reunite, and Cymbeline questions Cloten's disappearance. Pisanio tells of Cloten's leaving for Milford Haven in pursuit of Innogen and Posthumus, and Guiderius finishes the story. Cymbeline, filled with regret because he still admires the young warrior, has no choice but to sentence him to death for killing a prince. Belarius intercedes, telling Cymbeline that the young man is 'better than the man he slew', confessing that he is the banished Belarius, disguised as Morgan, and that the young men with him are Cymbeline's sons, whom he raised these twenty years. Cymbeline is at first incredulous, but upon seeing the star-shaped birthmark he remembers upon Guiderius' neck, all doubt is removed, and, overcome with joy, he pardons Belarius and is tearfully reunited with his sons. The boys and Innogen now realize why they felt such a natural bond with each other. Innogen has Caius Lucius freed, and Posthumus, after forgiving Iachimo, calls upon the Soothsayer to interpret the strange tablet he found in his jail cell. The prophecy relates to what has just taken place; to Posthumus finding Innogen again, and to Cymbeline's sons being 'jointed' back onto the royal family tree, ensuring the continued stability of the realm. 'Pardon's the word to all', Cymbeline declares, and even promises to continue paying the tribute to Rome as a sign of mutual respect. All go in together to celebrate and to make offerings to the gods who have ensured that everything has ended in 'peace'.

CYMBELINE
IN PERFORMANCE:
THE RSC AND BEYOND

The best way to understand a Shakespeare play is to see it or ideally to participate in it. By examining a range of productions, we may gain a sense of the extraordinary variety of approaches and interpretations that are possible – a variety that gives Shakespeare his unique capacity to be reinvented and made 'our contemporary' four centuries after his death.

We begin with a brief overview of the play's theatrical and cinematic life, offering historical perspectives on how it has been performed. We then analyse in more detail a series of productions staged over the last half-century by the Royal Shakespeare Company. The sense of dialogue between productions that can only occur when a company is dedicated to the revival and investigation of the Shakespeare canon over a long period, together with the uniquely comprehensive archival resource of promptbooks, programme notes, reviews and interviews held on behalf of the RSC at the Shakespeare Birthplace Trust in Stratford-upon-Avon, allows an 'RSC stage history' to become a crucible in which the chemistry of the play can be explored.

Finally, we go to the horse's mouth. Modern theatre is dominated by the figure of the director, who must hold together the whole play, whereas the actor must concentrate on his or her part. The director's viewpoint is therefore especially valuable. Shakespeare's plasticity is wonderfully revealed when we hear directors of highly successful productions answering the same questions in very different ways.

FOUR CENTURIES OF *CYMBELINE*: AN OVERVIEW

Shakespeare had dealt with overt fantasy onstage before *Cymbeline*, but with this play he seems to ask a different sort of imaginative engagement from his audiences. Like *Pericles* and *The Winter's Tale* before it, *Cymbeline* has long been seen as what Ben Jonson described as 'some mouldy tale',[24] piling coincidence, misrecognition, revelation and confusion one on top of the other until the effect seems almost farcical, and has thus been largely neglected in the theatre. There has, however, been a long-running parallel tradition of practitioners and audiences deriving bounteous rewards from the play in performance, taking the effort to see past what at first glance seem shortcomings, and to revel both in the comic opportunities the play's structure affords, and in its truly tender emotional core. *Cymbeline* is a virtuoso piece of dramatic management, and while it introduces more plot threads than a five-act narrative seems designed to bear, and while we are openly invited to laugh at the absurdity of so many threads reconvening at the end, we are simultaneously invited to marvel silently at the skill of the authorial puppet-master and to succumb to the unfeigned tenderness of the dramatic conclusion.

The earliest account we have of *Cymbeline* onstage – in fact, the earliest writing we have on the play at all – comes in the form of a private memorandum of 1611 by the astrologer Simon Forman, jotted into one of his eclectic notebooks. Forman died on 8 September that year, and this entry comes after accounts of having seen *Macbeth* and *The Winter's Tale* at the Globe in April and May, making it highly probable that he also saw *Cymbeline* there that summer. He provides little in the way of performance detail, being more concerned with cataloguing the play's plot intrigues one after another:

> Remember also the story of Cymbeline King of England, in Lucius' time, how Lucius came from Octavius Caesar for tribute, and being denied, after sent Lucius with a great army of soldiers who landed at Milford Haven, and after were vanquished by Cymbeline, and Lucius taken prisoner, and all by means of 3 outlaws, of the which 2 of them were the sons of Cymbeline,

stolen from him when they were but 2 years old by an old man whom Cymbeline banished, and he kept them as his own sons 20 years with him in a cave.[25]

Forman jumbles the plot order, mentioning these events before the wager plot, which, some have argued, merely illustrates the play's difficulty, while others have felt he deliberately rearranged things in order to afford a primacy to the Roman and British dynastic plot (the play has often been seen as a Jacobean panegyric). The other significant detail is that Forman calls the heroine Innogen, against the Folio's Imogen, suggesting strongly that this reflects what he heard onstage that day. The rest of the play's early public performance history is obscure, though we do know that it was performed at Whitehall on 1 January 1634 before Charles I, and, according to the Master of the Revels, was 'well liked by the King'.[26]

Shakespeare's plays came to be performed mainly in heavily adapted versions from the Restoration into the eighteenth and nineteenth centuries, and *Cymbeline* was no different, being reworked into Thomas D'Urfey's *The Injured Princess, or The Fatal Wager* in 1682, performed at the Theatre Royal, Drury Lane, and revived in 1720 at Lincoln's Inn Fields. A rare production of Shakespeare's text was undertaken at the Haymarket Theatre in 1744 by Theophilus Cibber, which was revived two years later at Covent Garden, starring Lacy Ryan as Posthumus and the great actor-manager David Garrick's long-time stage partner Hannah Pritchard as Innogen.

Next came William Hawkins' adaptation, which retained the play's title but largely gutted the text to make way for Hawkins' own verse and a cast of renamed characters. Perhaps most significant of all was the rearrangement of the plot to bring it into line with neo-classical sensibilities about dramatic unity, somewhat missing the point of Shakespeare's sophisticated and experimental narrative structuring.

The most significant and influential of the eighteenth-century adaptations, however, was Garrick's. Fittingly, the text Garrick produced for his 1761 production was remarkably actor-friendly, as well as being very faithful to the Shakespearean original. The more substantial alterations he made were to conflate or omit many prose passages, especially in the early Cloten scenes, and to transpose certain scenes for the sake of continuity of action, as well as entirely omitting the scene of Posthumus' imprisonment in Act 4, including the vision episode. Still, critical judgements of the time lasting into the twentieth century commented on the efficacy and stage-worthiness of Garrick's version. Garrick himself took the role of Posthumus to great acclaim alongside Miss Bride as Innogen, Thomas Davies as Cymbeline, and Charles Holland as Iachimo. Contemporary reviews of the production reflect heavily upon the particular aesthetic sensibilities of the age, with one anonymous reviewer sniping at the 'great deal of Shakespear's [sic] irregularity'[27] on display in Cymbeline, choosing to fix on the verse-speaking abilities of the cast rather than anything the production might have yielded as an interpretation of the text. A review from the following year though speaks out in defence of the play, attributing its oddities to Shakespeare's native genius, and praising both Garrick's performance as Posthumus and Shakespeare's writing of the part:

> It is very strange that so admirable a piece as this play should have remained so long unacted; but at least Mr Garrick, to whose taste we owe so many excellent revived pieces, has brought it to the stage. In Shakespeare's plays we are not to look for an observance of the unities, his genius soared above restraint ... Mr Garrick's Posthumus was admirable: he entered into the spirit of that fine-drawn character and displayed great power of acting. It is a character that gives the actor a fine opportunity to express the feelings of his soul; the transmissions of the passions were exquisitely represented by him.[28]

Garrick's revival restored the play's stage fortunes somewhat and his adaptation became the orthodox text over the next forty years for producers at both Covent Garden and Drury Lane. In 1787 the great female tragedian Sarah Siddons gave her Innogen in London with her brother, John Philip Kemble, as Posthumus, a role in which Kemble was to appear twenty-six times between 1785 and 1817.

It was said of Kemble's first Innogen, Mrs Jordan, that 'she could act only the *disguise* of the character',[29] whereas Siddons rose to meet the 'variety of manner and expression'[30] required. However, aspects of Siddons' performance met with critical displeasure; the power and grandeur of her style – cultivated in performances of tragedy – were seen to overbear upon 'the softness, delicacy, affectionate tenderness, and interesting distress'[31] of Innogen. And it was Kemble, as well as the grandiosity of his set designs, that really held the critics' attention: 'Mr Kemble was, by a thousand degrees, the best Posthumus of my time. It was a learned, judicious, and in the fine burst upon Iachimo at the close, a most powerful effort.'[32]

The early nineteenth century saw numerous performances of *Cymbeline*, and laid the foundations for an era of unprecedented appreciation on both stage and page for the story's heroine, Innogen. Arguably it was Helen Faucit who helped establish this image for the theatregoing public with her famous portrayals of the role in 1838 and 1843, in two productions staged by one of the great actors of the day, William Charles Macready. Macready had in fact acted in several productions of the play between 1811 and 1837, usually playing Posthumus, although he did take on the role of Iachimo three times, once in the 1843 revival in a text again heavily excised (the prison scene went, as did many of Cloten's 'indecorous' moments). Commentators at the time noted the surprising levity and recklessness he brought to the part, while James R. Anderson's largely ineffective Posthumus nonetheless made an interesting foil in the wager scene through his stiff conservatism: 'he marked out the growing indignation at the levity of Iachimo, carefully managing the curling lip and darkened brow'.[33] The contrast between the two men and the daring of Macready's performance brought about a vivid reappraisal of the dynamics of the scene for a reporter of the *Spectator*, who noted 'a veil of voluptuous wantonness over the repulsive incident of a man, wagering on the virtue of his wife' and saw Anderson's Posthumus as 'merely a rash boaster, and Iachimo a licentious profligate inflamed with wine, both acting on a hasty impulse'.[34]

Faucit's Innogen, however, captured the public imagination above all other facets of the production, her inherent grace and dignity and physically delicate form lending her a great sympathy in the part with audiences. She even played the role again in 1864 at the age of forty-seven at Drury Lane, and, probably in the same year, at Edinburgh, in a cast that featured an up-and-coming Henry Irving in the role of Pisanio. In a review of the Drury Lane production, one critic recorded how *Cymbeline* was still largely unfamiliar stage fodder, but that Faucit demonstrated the unique depth and beauty of Innogen as an overlooked gem in the pantheon of Shakespeare's great characters:

> But that unconscious propriety of Imogen, that innate virtue which guards her as a shield and enfolds her as a garment, that purity of soul which speaks in her slightest movements . . . There is something so inimitably picturesque in Miss Faucit's acting that one constantly longs to see each successive attitude fixed in a photograph, and bound into a volume to form a psychological illustration to the play . . . To appreciate to its full extent the value of Miss Faucit's triumph it is necessary to recur to the fact that to the multitude *Cymbeline* is not a known play.[35]

The play's nebulous status again led to its decline from the repertoire after the 1860s, the only other major Victorian production being a then-established Henry Irving's at the Lyceum in 1896, starring Ellen Terry as Innogen. It was a portrayal that was to be as significant as Faucit's in cementing the character as one of the greats. A surviving private correspondence between Terry and Shakespeare's most notorious antagonist, George Bernard Shaw, allows unique insights into her preparation for, and his opinions on, the role and the play:

> Imogen is an impulsive person, with quick transitions, absolutely frank self-expression, and no half affections or half forgivenesses. The moment you abuse anyone she loves, she is in a rage; the moment you praise them she is delighted.[36]

Shaw's influence on Terry's interpretation seems to have been active and strong, though it is difficult to gauge the tone. Shaw is fastidiously precise about the way moments 'ought' to be played in the sheaves of advice he sent to her, while Terry's responses are often brief and apparently deferential. We cannot know, however, how much she actually took on board and how much is intended to placate an eccentric, overbearing and probably somewhat intimidating friend:

> Yes, yes, yes, I see what you mean about the 'headless man' bit; and the '5 bars rest' in the Cave Scene is of course all wrong. I see it now, and will try and try at it. Delightful. Difficult to undo all the wrong things which have been practised quite carefully, but I shall delight to try at it.[37]

Shaw wrote a now infamous review of the production which he used as a springboard to attack Shakespeare's artistry in general, the character of Innogen, and Henry Irving's inability to play anything other than himself (even though, oddly, he praised his Iachimo in this production). Shaw, ever the contrarian, was impressed with Terry's rejection of the sentimental Innogen whose 'virtuous indignation is chronic' in favour of a more naturalised 'innocent rapture and frank gladness'.[38] He also blasted Irving for 'disembowel[ing]'[39] the text, though arguably showed far greater presumptuousness in his rewrite of the play's final act in 1937, which was performed in place of Shakespeare's in a staging that year at London's Embassy Theatre. In 1945 Shaw revisited Irving's production – which, he claimed, did much to ruin his view of *Cymbeline* as a piece of drama – to justify dispensing with the original ending:

> Irving, as Iachimo, a statue of romantic melancholy, stood dumb on the stage for hours (as it seemed) whilst the others toiled through a series of denouements of crushing tedium, in which the characters lost all their vitality and individuality, and had nothing to do but identify themselves by moles on their necks, or explain why they were not dead.[40]

The play was certainly among the least performed in the canon during the twentieth century, although there were several other notable productions in the fifty years following Irving's, usually emphasizing the play's folk-tale, mythical dimensions, its niche

1. Ellen Terry, 1896, Lyceum. Her performance as Innogen was a portrayal that was to be as significant as Faucit's in cementing the character as one of the greats.

popularity lying in its perceived escapism from any weighty human realities. Frank Benson staged three productions at the Shakespeare Memorial Theatre in Stratford in 1909, 1920 and 1922, and Sybil Thorndike played Innogen in Ben Greet's 1918 production at the Old Vic. Iden Payne's production in Stratford featuring Joyce Bland, Godfrey Kenton and Donald Wolfit as Innogen, Posthumus and Iachimo, respectively, ran concurrently with the Shavian version at the Embassy in 1937, and Michael Benthall produced the play at the Old Vic in 1956 – with greater critical success than his Stratford production seven years earlier – in a very stripped-down setting, with a young Barbara Jefford as Innogen. Benthall continued the long stage tradition of cutting the vision scene in the prison, and excising many of the lines in the denouement reiterative of plot and smacking too heavily of absurd coincidence. Jefford was universally praised for her Innogen, and Mary Clarke noted how well her youthful vigour served the part.[41]

Peggy Ashcroft first undertook the role in a 1932 production, again at the Old Vic, and reprised it to great acclaim in 1957 in Peter Hall's Stratford production. Strangely – and in contrast to critical responses to Jefford's youth – Faucit, Terry, and now Ashcroft had all enjoyed tremendous success in a part scarcely associated with mature actresses. Hall emphasized fairytale elements, uniting critics in praise of what they saw as a directorial strategy to knock the play into some kind of definite shape and measure up to the interest generated by Innogen, a sentiment that continued to dog criticism, as W. A. Darlington illustrated:

> Imogen stands alone among Shakespeare's heroines because the play in which she appears gives her hardly any support. It is a ramshackle, slung-together piece, a wild mixture of ancient Rome, prehistoric Britain and Renaissance Italy – a real director's headache.[42]

Kenneth Tynan praised Hall's

> throwing over the whole production a sinister veil of faery, so that it resembles a Grimm fable transmuted by the Cocteau of

La Belle et la Bête. He creates, in short, an ambience in which the ludicrous anomalies of the plot are believable and even loveable.[43]

2. Peter Hall's production, Stratford, 1957. Kenneth Tynan praised Hall's 'throwing over the whole production a sinister veil of faery, so that it resembles a Grimm fable transmuted by the Cocteau of *La Belle et la Bête*'. Photo shows the Queen (Joan Miller) giving poison to Pisanio (Mark Dignam), Act 1 scene 5.

The early 1970s saw two major North American stagings of the play, at the Shakespeare Festival at Stratford, Ontario, in 1970, and at the New York Shakespeare Festival the following year. Barry Kyle and John Barton's 1974 RSC Stratford production (discussed in more detail below) revisited the fairytale vision of the play, while a more modern, self-conscious theatricality dominated Braham Murray's 1984 outing of the play for the Royal Exchange, Manchester, starring Janet McTeer as Innogen and Hugh Quarshie in a rare but thoughtful doubling of parts:

> while the viciousness of Cloten is quite beyond [Quarshie], the bemused nobility of Posthumus is not . . . Art Malik's Iachimo is, like [Avril] Elgar's Queen, disarmingly casual in villainy.[44]

Peter Hall bade farewell to his directorship of the National in 1988 with productions of three of Shakespeare's late plays, *Cymbeline*, *The Winter's Tale* and *The Tempest*, with the former coming in for the loftiest praise of the three. His relationship with the play had clearly changed in the thirty years since he had last staged it:

> Hall discovers in the play much more than the sumptuous romantic fairy-tale he directed in 1957. Instead it becomes a complex confrontation of virtue and vice, civility and degradation always shadowed by mortality: it is the *Into the Woods* of its day with everyone put on trial.[45]

Hall and his designer, Alison Chitty, felt the plays owed much of their atmospheres to the indoor Blackfriars theatre for which he believed they were written, and adopted a broad Renaissance aesthetic, not 'aimed at a historical reconstruction',[46] but rather 'a boldly emblematic, self-contained universe'[47] in which the imaginative dimensions of the three plays could be explored for possible consistencies and interrelationships. Geraldine James played Innogen, and the production tried hard to force audiences to rethink the entrenched image of the character as a saintly vision of feminine perfection in an otherwise slight or unworthy play:

> although she did not disguise the fact that Innogen, in Hall's phrase, is 'a difficult girl' when she defies her father, bawls out

Cloten, and does not conceal her impatience with Pisanio. With the experience of repeated performances, Geraldine James insisted further upon the 'difficult' aspects of the part as well as the attractive ones, even to the point of risking alienating the audience in the first half.[48]

Michael Billington felt James 'emerge[d] superbly as a tough, strong-jawed woman full of irony and anger',[49] also seeing the production's more nuanced and mature vision of character in Basil Hendon's Belarius, who Billington praised for making the character 'not some wayside preacher but a figure of golden-voiced stoicism'.[50] This led, naturally, to an increased sense of the real dangers of the fragile psyches now seen behind what had for so long seemed cardboard cut-out characters:

> Ken Stott's Cloten is not simply comic but a dangerous regal thug. Peter Woodward discovers in Posthumus an insecure neurotic who lapses into Leontes-like madness when he believes Innogen has betrayed him.[51]

In 2001 the play was staged at Shakespeare's Globe in an experimental six-man version, with Mark Rylance playing both Cloten and Posthumus and Jane Arnfield as Innogen. Arnfield was noted to move 'with a stylised grace: at one point she cartwheels with joy',[52] while Rylance brought superb comedy to his Cloten, playing it 'like an early version of Caliban – or a Grizzly baby walking bandy-legged in uncomfortable nappies'.[53] The complexity and psychological danger of both Cloten and Posthumus, so evident in Hall's production, were here jettisoned in favour of a more straightforward hero/villain dichotomy, with Susannah Clapp actually referring to 'the hero Posthumus', played by Rylance as 'Cloten's graceful, muted counter-part, making you feel he's whispering secrets in your ear'.[54] Charles Spencer also noted of the design:

> Simplicity rules. The cast all wear the same pyjama-like white costumes, there is no scenery, and much of the Globe's gilded decoration has been covered. The cast also occasionally act as narrators, briefly setting the scene and describing who they are,

so that the complex narrative is developed with satisfying clarity.[55]

That same year saw New York company Theatre for a New Audience bring the play to Stratford in a magnificent reimagining of the play, characterized by a 'disciplined and generous-spirited eclecticism' which took in cowboys and kabuki.[56] Rachel Kavanaugh staged a modern-dress, open-air version at Regent's Park in 2005, the reviews somewhat reflective of a play that had been welcomed into the repertory now that critics had accepted its playful vacillation between reality and self-conscious fantasy:

The play's politics and its fraught romantic entanglements are deftly caught, and Kavanaugh is responsive too to the changes of mood in a work that constantly juxtaposes the beautiful and the ugly, the real and the mythic.[57]

The play returned to the stage in 2007 in Declan Donnellan's acclaimed Cheek by Jowl production, starring Tom Hiddleston, again doubling the roles of Posthumus and Cloten, and Jodie McNee as Innogen. It was another minimalist, modern-dress affair, though the company's trademark conspicuous theatricality and informal relationship with the audience brought the play's imaginative excesses vividly to life, with the production achieving 'a spell-binding imaginative unity'[58] that made perfect sense of a play too long marginalized by critics unsure what to do with it:

The handling of the potentially ridiculous crescendo of coincidences and reunions in the final scene is quite masterly. At each turn, we see people struggling to adjust to bewildering new realities and the mood at the end is expertly mixed, allowing a sense that some things cannot be resolved to complicate the atmosphere of wonder and spiritual transcendence.[59]

Cymbeline has been filmed a handful of times, firstly as an illustrated sequence of seven slides in the 1890s, followed by a twenty-two-minute silent film version of 1913 produced by the Thanhouser film company. It starred Florence La Badie as Innogen and James Cruze as Posthumus, and relied heavily on wordy exposition and 'a striking number of screened letters in an attempt to clarify and explain the action'.[60] A German film version followed in 1925, directed by Ludwig Berger, and the play was filmed again in Germany in 2000 as *Cymbelin*, directed by Dieter Dorn. But its major outing on celluloid in the twentieth century was in Elijah Moshinsky's star-studded BBC version, with Helen Mirren as Innogen, Michael Pennington as Posthumus, Claire Bloom as the Queen, Robert Lindsay as Iachimo, and Richard Johnson as Cymbeline. It was in the main a low-budget, studio-bound affair, as was the rest of the BBC series, but Moshinsky attempted to overcome these constraints by claustro-phobically containing most of the action within windowless interior sets, in part a pragmatic decision because exteriors 'look dreadful in the studio, so phoney',[61] though partly to suggest a stifling isolation within the court. Moshinsky also felt there was a tension between the domestic and the political within the play and wanted to emphasize the former, as well as engaging the audience visually with 'Shakespeare's world'. The sets were in fact high Renaissance in the style of interiors found in the works of the Dutch masters, which 'not only look authentic on television but suit television's conventional pressure towards domestication'.[62] The production was well received, and Mirren's performance was praised as being 'as good as anything she has done on television':[63]

> The trouble with Imogen . . . is that she normally seems too good to be true in a world where nothing is what it seems, where the outward impression never matches the inner nature. [Mirren] overcomes this with what Moshinsky calls her 'sexual voltage' and by showing her discovery, invisible even to her tempter Iachimo, that she is corruptible, open to seduction. She is far from the usual idea of a porcelain idol on a pedestal.[64]

Cymbeline is unlike any other play in the canon in that its many lives onstage, and the many critical responses these lives have engendered, have been as focused on justifying engagement with what seems like a baffling, inconsequential narrative as on the desire simply to reinterpret a complex artwork. Productions of the play – far less frequent than with the more central of Shakespeare's works – have almost all been labours of love, while responses have often been characterized by trepidation on the part of critics perennially unsure how to approach it as a piece of drama. It is either a tangled mess of inconsequentiality; a fairytale world inhabited by unreal and unconvincing characters; or an ethereal and haunting masterwork played out by some of the most complex creations of Shakespeare's career. What is certain is that this too-neglected masterpiece has, justly, enjoyed something of a renaissance in recent decades by directors willing to accept that the play needs no apology. Neither have the best productions striven to take the play 'on its own terms', as no healthy interpretation would presume to know what they are. Rather, acceptance of *Cymbeline* as a worthy and rewarding stage vehicle has ensured that directors, performers, reviewers and audiences will keep returning to it with a sense of expectancy and wonder.

AT THE RSC

Cymbeline is commonly regarded as the strangest of Shakespeare's plays. It reworks the themes of the other late romances, or lyrical dramas – loss and trial, recovery and reunion, forgiveness and redemption – with an extraordinary freedom, drawing eclectically on elements of myth, legend and folk-tale and clothing them in some of his most highly-developed verse. Set in ancient Britain during the early Roman Empire, it also wanders unashamedly into Renaissance Europe; categorized as a romance, it recklessly juxtaposes the tragic, the comic and the grotesque; above all, it employs almost every plot device available to the dramatist. Its cast includes kidnapped infants, star-crossed lovers, a wicked stepmother, a deceived king, an oafish villain and a smooth one, ghosts and gods, while its plot involves attempted poisonings, plots against a princess's honour and life, revenges, murders, battles, disguises, wild coincidences and multiple reunions. To some it is a 'glorious mishmash',[65] while others join Dr Johnson in deploring its 'unresisting imbecility'. What is certain is that it is an enticing play for a director, offering challenge and opportunity. There is no such thing as a 'standard' production of *Cymbeline*; each director comes to the play afresh, to find a consistency in its diverse elements and to negotiate the minefield of its booby-trapped plot. There have been seven productions of the play for the RSC since 1961: four at the Royal Shakespeare Theatre, two at the Swan and one at The Other Place.

Finding a Theme

1962, 1974, 1987, 1997 – telling a story

When William Gaskill directed the play in 1962, he came fresh from directing Brecht's *The Caucasian Chalk Circle* and the Brechtian influence was clear. The theatricality of the performance was made overt, the play's story being performed to a group of scene shifters, who carried on appropriate scenery as required, with the stage lights up. Although quite unremarkable now, for audiences used to scene changes performed behind closed curtains or in a stage blackout, this was a radical departure, consistent with the extremes and improbabilities of the play's plot. Don Chapman of the *Oxford Mail* noted, 'the scene shifters very gently attempt to prepare us for the excesses of theatrical contrivance which are to come'.[66] There was no Brechtian alienation in the actors' performances, however, which were naturalistic and whole-hearted.

Several subsequent productions adopted the story-telling approach: in the 1974 production, on an almost bare stage, John Barton, working with Barry Kyle and Clifford Williams, turned the play even more overtly into a piece of story-telling. Barton cut 820 lines from the text and developed the minor character of Cornelius into a narrator. Jeffery Dench in the role read out stage directions from the First Folio text and guided the audience through the story, much as Gower does in *Pericles*, preparing them for the abrupt shifts from horror to pathos to comedy. It was an approach welcomed by the critics: '[they] turned the unwieldy fable into moving and even magical theatrical experience';[67] 'swift, romantic. Poetic and dashing';[68] 'a production full of colour, fantasy and magic'.[69]

In 1987, Bill Alexander took the pared-down story-telling approach a step further in his studio production at The Other Place. Here, the actors gave a fireside telling of the tale within a circle of audience, and often engaged with the audience, sitting in spare seats among them. Andrew Rissik, in the *Independent*, eloquently described the mood of the production:

> At The Other Place is a joyous and deeply affecting production. Bill Alexander has directed it as a glowing yeoman fairy-tale where the gracious dignity of historical legend gets an added lustre from homespun country wisdom and down-to-earth folklore ... The lighting, done in burnished golds and autumnal reds, leaves the stage basking in sunny magic. Although the action darts with deft complexity between Machiavelli's Italy, Celtic Britain and the Roman Empire, we are plainly somewhere in Warwickshire, in the bright, wooded landscape which always haunted Shakespeare's imagination.[70]

In place of conventional sound effects, Ilona Sekacz wrote a vivid score, performed by the actors on instruments ranging from steel drums and wind chimes to the bared wires of an old piano.

In 1997, Adrian Noble followed John Barton in cutting a thousand lines of text and replacing the scene-setting dialogue between two Gentlemen in the first scene with a prologue which more clearly established the characters and situation. The prologue was spoken by the Soothsayer to the cast, again as a fireside tale. Noble sidestepped the mix of historical periods in the play by transferring the story to samurai Japan, finding a unifying setting which emphasized the play's celebration of aristocratic and martial values, of blood and birth, as well as finding a new context for its magical qualities. Charles Spencer found this 'the most rewarding production on the RSC's main stage since the 1993 *King Lear* with Robert Stephens'.[71]

1979 – splintered reality

David Jones' production, rather than seeking to knit up the disparate strands of the play, allowed it to unravel with the disjointed realism of a dream. Rather than striving to smooth out the absurdities of plot, he allowed the comedy to become overt and run alongside the pathos. Critics tended to find his approach too anarchic: 'I do not sense the imaginative unity that can hold the play together.'[72]

2001 – 'generous-spirited eclecticism' or wilful zaniness?

The New York-based company, Theater for a New Audience, brought a production to The Other Place that sharply divided both audiences and critics. Director Bartlett Sher made no attempt to find unity in the play's disparate elements but rather revelled in its discontinuities, offering a 'gorgeously multicultural' experience[73] or, alternatively, one which was 'mischievously weird'.[74] In Sher's hands, Britain was Japan as depicted by Hokusai, a stiffly formal world in which the action was played out on a black and scarlet platform, but when Innogen and her attendant had battled their way through a swirling snowstorm with only their black parasols as weapons, they found that Milford Haven was not just in the west but in the Wild West, complete with Stetsons, drawls and plaintive, plunking country music, which included a touching country version of 'Fear no more the heat o'th'sun'.

At least two critics celebrated the chutzpah of the production's irreverence: 'winning chutzpah'[75] wrote Paul Taylor, and 'endearing chutzpah' Rachel Halliburton, who commented too that 'there is something both wonderful and terrible about its bouncily irreverent way with one of Shakespeare's lesser dramas'.[76] 'Kitsch' was a word critics reached for too, but while Dominic Cavendish complained that 'it brings occidental and oriental influences into kitsch collision',[77] Paul Taylor declared that the move to the guitar-plunking West at the end of the first half, marked by a full company song, 'Love is Everywhere', 'joyfully transcends the kitsch with which it knowingly toys'. 'This isn't merely cheap stylistic promiscuity', he argued, 'but a disciplined and generous-hearted eclecticism. The company really understands what is at issue, morally and aesthetically, in the play.'[78]

While audiences and many critics appreciated the production's irreverence, energy, humour and sheer zest, some missed the play's finer lyrical and emotional moments. Many felt that it failed to respond to the play's dreamlike quality and that the actors were not

3. Bartlett Sher production, Theatre for a New Audience, The Other Place, 2001. Cloten (Andrew Weems) with prop horse.

vocally equipped for the open-hearted, high-flying lyricism which should surprise and delight us at times. They were 'cruelly exposed and emotionally underpowered',[79] wrote Dominic Cavendish, and Benedict Nightingale, 'Sher's approach doesn't call for finesse and doesn't get it.'[80] For Paul Taylor, however, there was 'a delightful blend of robust jokiness and dreamy delicacy'.[81]

2003 – redemption through suffering

At the Swan, Dominic Cooke gave the audience a version of the play which was bound together by the characters' emotional truth. Michael Billington, commenting first on the impossibility of finding a realistic setting for the play, said of this production, 'Cooke gives us an alternative *Magic Flute*-style universe in which pain and suffering lead to understanding.'[82] Emma Fielding as Innogen, Daniel Evans as Posthumus and Anton Lesser as a wicked but anguished Iachimo all used the intimacy of the Swan stage to draw the audience into their emotional worlds. The production played extravagantly, lifting an ironic eyebrow at the plot's wilder excesses, while relishing them at the same time.

2006 – a fairytale world

In 2006, for the Complete Works Festival, the RSC commissioned the small Cornwall-based Kneehigh company to perform their version of the play. Kneehigh is known for its radical updating of classic stories and for its use of music and physical theatre. As adapted and directed by Emma Rice (who also played the Queen) the play lost most of the original language, which was replaced with consciously banal soap opera speech. Susanna Clapp commented, 'It squeaks into the RSC's year of Complete Works not as a performance of a written play but as a response to it.'[83] While following the plot's twists and turns, it offered 'a pared-down, revved-up look at fractured families and forbidden love'.[84] Emma Rice, writing in the programme, said:

> But for me *Cymbeline* is a fairytale. It is about where we come from, who we are and how we find our way home. It is about family, but not a sentimental notion of family, no. This story tackles stepfamilies and dead parents, abduction and surrogate care. This is about families as we know them, damaged, secretive, surprising and frustrating.

She went on to say, 'I want this production to celebrate the child in all of us' (this was signalled in the programme by photos of the actors as children). The production ended with Innogen, Posthumus and Cymbeline's sons climbing into single beds to be read a bedtime story.

Like the 2001 production, this one polarized critics and audiences. Some welcomed it whole-heartedly: 'Kneehigh has laid hands on [the play's] unruly heart';[85] 'a jubilantly free-wheeling re-write';[86] '*Cymbeline* is a mad play and Kneehigh is a mad company. Plainly they were made for one another...[they] revel in the blackly comic clash of tones and anarchic knowingness.'[87] Others felt that the losses from the rewriting were too great. Michael Billington found it 'coarsely reductive', disliked its 'relentless jokiness' and felt that 'Rice substitutes sentimentality for real sentiment';[88] Fiona Mountford argued that 'the humour sits uneasily with the strong surges of emotion and the real anguish of the separated lovers';[89] Sam Marlowe concluded that, 'While the production has abundant appeal, it lacks emotional weight.'[90] Both Susannah Clapp of the *Observer* and Michael Billington of the *Guardian* found the abandoning of Shakespeare's language a step too far: '"Fear no more the heat of the sun", the only Shakespeare passage of any length that is retained, makes you feel that the decision to slip away from Shakespeare's verse was misguided';[91] 'It ducks the real challenge of making Shakespeare live through his language.'[92]

The Design Challenge

For a designer, the play is wide open. The very contradictions which make it seem impossible on the page offer endless design possibilities.

1962 – a white box

For Gaskill's Brechtian production, René Allio designed a white-carpeted stage, with the back wall and wings draped with white netting. Onto this, stagehands brought symbolic pieces of scenery, while the actors were very simply dressed with only a minimum of indicative elements, such as cloaks, headdresses, beards and wigs. When the characters reached Wales, a cluster of rocks on a swivel was introduced, which could be angled as cave, camp or battlefield.

1974 and 1987 – fairytale country

For John Barton's production, with its introduction of a story-teller, designers John Napier, Martyn Bainbridge and Sue Jenkinson designed 'a Britain which has all the appearance of a Hans Andersen fairytale and costumes that would not have disgraced Titania's glade'.[93] As in the 1962 production, the set was, in fact, very simple – a sloping, carpeted stage onto which emblematic images were introduced. As in 1962, rocks were brought on for the Wales scenes, but Billington complained that Milford Haven 'looked to me like an *avant garde* sculpture exhibition at the Hayward Gallery'.[94] The costumes, too, were simple and emblematic: Sebastian Shaw's 'almost unreachably senile'[95] Cymbeline carried the symbol of his entrapment by the Queen in the form of a cloak that was 'like a gilded cobweb'.[96]

In 1987, at The Other Place, the action was played on a bare arena stage, but one bathed in warm light to create a place at once homely and magical. Harriet Walter describes how the actors were given a range of costumes from stock to choose from.[97] (This unusual approach to costume design was also adopted in the 2003 production – a sign of the anarchic power wielded by this play.) The result was largely a mix of Jacobean jerkins with medieval robes, enhancing the nostalgic Englishness of the production.

1979 – 'not so much of no time as of every time'

Christopher Morley's costume designs supported the anarchic quality of David Jones' production. Where earlier designers had gone for a timeless quality to match the play's shifting time zones, Morley designed a kaleidoscope, ranging from a trailing robe for Cymbeline to Roman soldiers in something very like SS uniforms. The stage, as in previous productions, was bare until the introduction of 'a couple of crags like giants' teeth'[98] when the action moved to Wales. Symbolic backdrops indicated Britain with a golden sun against a dark portcullis and Rome with fascistic black and silver.

1997 – the Japanese influence

For Adrian Noble's production, Anthony Ward designed a kabuki-style staging: the forestage at the RST was extended into the auditorium and entrances were made along walkways running from the stalls. The stage was a cerulean blue cube with a vast white cloth that could act as groundsheet, backdrop or canopy. The actors wore high ponytails and stiffly pleated robes. The effect was one of 'economy and grace'.[99]

4. Adrian Noble's production, 1997. Image highlights the Japanese-influenced, kabuki-style staging. Photo shows Iachimo (Paul Freeman, right) making a wager with Posthumus (Damian Lewis) about Innogen's virtue whilst the Spaniard (Rex Obano), Philario (David Glover), the Dutchman (Vincent Leigh), and the Frenchman (Rod Arthur) look on, Act 1 scene 4.

2003 – Britons as barbarians

At the Swan, Rae Smith designed a production in which the costumes were eclectic and symbolic. Not everyone was happy with them: Rhoda Koenig, in the *Independent*, complained that the design 'piled artifice upon confusion'[100] and the *Sunday Times* reviewer remarked that it was 'as if Stella McCartney had tried to do a send-up of Vivienne Westwood and made a hash of it'.[101] Although there was an overall design concept, the actors (as in the 1987 production) were given some choice in their costumes: during rehearsals, racks of costumes from stock were brought in for the actors to try out, and the costumes became symbolic of character. So, for example, Emma Fielding, as Innogen the rebel princess, wore a silky golden gown with heavy, scuffed walking boots (Fielding has said that she remembered, as a teenager, annoying her mother by accessorizing the pretty dresses she bought her with Doc Martens boots);[102] Iachimo and the other Italians wore designer suits, ironically in pure white; the Britons all wore feathers; the more feathers, the higher their rank, so Cymbeline himself was elaborately feathered and the Queen wore a trailing cloak of peacock feathers, 'a frightening and appropriately unlucky garment'.[103] The feathers gave the Britons a barbaric air which was heightened by their stamping, chanting rituals. The audience was invited to see them as the Romans saw them – an uncivilized people ripe for colonization.

2006 – an urban wasteland

For Kneehigh's production at the Swan, Michael Vale designed a stark, cage-like design, with clanging doors and an enclosed stage area above, which housed the band, and on which some interior scenes were played. At the opening of the play, hooded figures appeared in the half-light, fixing flowers, teddy bears and messages to the cage bars – tokens of remembrance, we realized, for the little lost princes, kidnapped years before, establishing the brooding sense of loss which hovered over this production.

Innogen's Journey

The role of Innogen lies at the heart of the play. It is with her separation, rejection, betrayal, loss, danger, recovery and restoration that the audience must engage. Harriet Walter, who played the role in the 1987 production, says of her:

> Imogen is a coveted role. It is her range that chiefly appeals. In one evening an actress can play a bit of Desdemona, Juliet, Cordelia, Lady Anne, Rosalind, Cleopatra. In reading up about Imogen, I came across many descriptive adjectives: 'divine', 'enchanting', 'virtuous' ... To play a heroine one must look for her faults, her human weaknesses. If a flawed and vulnerable person is seen to be tested, to learn, to change, to make brave choices and to overcome the odds, this puts heroic achievement within our reach and gives us hope or humankind.[104]

The most successful Innogens have found the character's flaws as well as her heroism.

1962 – golden girl

The young Vanessa Redgrave, fresh from a triumphant run as Rosalind in *As You Like It*, played Innogen and sent the (male) critics into poetic flourishes. Her performance was not universally admired: Charles Graves of the *Scotsman* felt that she was affected by playing Katherine in *The Taming of the Shrew* in the same season, and the reviewer in *The Stage* wrote, 'I do not care greatly for Vanessa Redgrave's Imogen. The gentle, tender, womanly yet firm-willed young wife demands greater maturity than she seems yet to possess . . . There is a touch of schoolgirlishness in her intensities and

5. William Gaskill's production, 1962. Vanessa Redgrave as Innogen gave the character 'such a heartfelt honesty and beauty that I swear that every man in the audience must have felt the urge to jump onto the stage to her rescue'.

her agonies leave one unmoved.'[105] These critics were, however, very much in the minority; the majority reached for golden images: 'delightful, glowing, tender and despairing, crazed, angry and joyous by turns, every mood convincing';[106] 'Miss Redgrave's flaxen beauty';[107] 'She gave Imogen such a heartfelt honesty and beauty that I swear that every man in the audience must have felt the urge to jump onto the stage to her rescue';[108] 'Miss Redgrave, in aspect and tone, will be the Imogen-Fidele of her generation – the season's daffodil';[109] 'Vanessa Redgrave's Imogen has a golden lustre';[110] 'Vanessa Redgrave strode through the nightmare wonderland like a noble-voiced goddess';[111] 'Her ardour, here in full billow, is now a ready gift for parodists, but as she ranges the peaks of love, joy, shock and anguish, the spectator is shaken into a recognition of true beauty and greatness.'[112]

1974 – bold adventurer

Susan Fleetwood was an Amazonian Innogen, less obviously vulnerable than some others, but more convincing than most in boy's clothes. B. A. Young found her 'a rather unromantic Imogen, square and undemonstrative',[113] but Irving Wardle wrote that she was 'not obvious casting physically but utterly consistent to the limpid openness of the role, and superbly in control of its broken elegiac verse'.[114] She also managed the difficult blend of pathos and comedy in Innogen's role: 'Her height and her bold, incisive style, ensure that the girl's innocence is not maudlin . . . She is, at once, a creature lit from within by the lamp of her own integrity and, in her naivety, rather funny.'[115]

1979 – 'mercurial humour'

Judi Dench won critics' and audiences' hearts: 'Judi Dench's beautiful performance as the adorable Imogen, pure but passionate, sensitive but spirited, is reason enough for this year's RSC production';[116] 'Blonde, impassioned and comely, Miss Dench is a divine Imogen.'[117] She dealt with the difficulty of the play's potential for unintended comedy by investing her role with 'a constant mercurial humour',[118] as though

Imogen herself was aware of the absurdities in her situation. Billington commented, too, on a quality which has become a quintessential part of the Dench armoury – the sudden switch to cutting coolness, 'particularly fine is her treatment of Iachimo's attempted seduction, regarding his recantation with the studied coolness of a hostess who has found a house guest walking off with the cutlery'.[119]

1987 – 'fanatical ardour'

Irving Wardle described Harriet Walter as 'the RSC's reigning specialist in fanatical ardour',[120] while Andrew Rissik encapsulated the general critical acclaim for her performance when he wrote, 'Harriet Walter's grave, passionate wide-eyed Imogen is an auburn-haired pre-Raphaelite princess, setting out with unswerving, head-strong ardour on the troublous adventure of love.'[121] She herself says that she wanted to challenge the idealization of Imogen, describing her thus: 'My image of Imogen was something of Boudicca and something of Fuchsia in Mervyn Peake's *Gormenghast* – the smutty rebel child grown to wilful adult with Amazon potential.'[122] She was defiantly independent and rebellious and her explosive relationship with her father was emphasized by the (genuine) slap on the jaw that David Bradley, as Cymbeline, gave her every night.

1997 – verbal musicality

In the Japanese-inspired setting of Adrian Noble's 1997 production, Joanne Pearce played a softer Innogen, a woman of deep sweetness with a seemingly limitless capacity for suffering. Using her considerable vocal range, she explored and exploited the possibilities offered by the language of the play. Charles Spencer commented, 'Joanne Pearce plays her with a mixture of sense and sensuality that left the viewer besotted.'[123]

2003 – rebel princess

Emma Fielding's performance was universally praised. She played a strong, tough young woman: 'Her Imogen may lack vulnerability

6. Bill Alexander's production, 1987. Harriet Walter describes her characterization of Innogen as 'the smutty rebel child grown to wilful adult with Amazon potential'. She was also 'defiantly independent and rebellious' and had an 'explosive relationship with her father'. David Bradley as Cymbeline.

but she radiantly personifies virtue without being merely lady-like.'[124] She had 'emotional candour, charm and courage'.[125] Physically slight and fragile, she was all determination and will, and whether in her self-chosen costume of golden gown and boots or dressed as a boy, she had 'a look a accidental glamour – an intense waif'.[126]

2006 – rejected child

In Kneehigh's updated production, Hayley Carmichael, in sandals and plaits, played Innogen, in Susanna Clapp's words, 'like a radiant seven-year-old'.[127] Tiny and bewildered, '[her] beautifully impulsive Imogen feels the pain of rejection like a child does, without limit'.[128]

Pure Malice: Iachimo

Iachimo and the Queen are the drivers of the plot through their self-centred malice, but the most successful Iachimos have been those who suffered from the consciousness of their guilt. In 1962, Eric Porter's Iachimo 'insisted on being a richly rounded, living character'[129] and 'his treachery was undertaken with such grace that we almost forgave him';[130] in 1974, Ian Richardson, often the epitome of cold detachment, played Iachimo as a 'bored Italian aristocrat who has no sooner slandered Imogen but he is stricken by grave remorse'.[131] In 2003, Anton Lesser, in white designer suit, played 'chilly arrogance' and 'vicious lasciviousness': his emergence from the trunk in Innogen's bedroom – first a hand and then the rest of him – was performed with agonizing slowness in a scarcely breathing theatre. However, his repentance was moving – in his appearance in the final scene he appeared to have shrunk physically with his loss of *brio*. Ben Kingsley, in 1979, was 'gleefully villainous',[132] a suave renaissance villain who committed to memory the details of Innogen's bedroom 'with the manic zeal of a private eye cracking a particularly difficult case',[133] while Donald Sumpter, in 1987, in the close intimacy of The Other Place, scrutinized the sleeping Innogen 'with the cool fascination of a surgeon'.[134] In 1997, Paul Freeman was a wolfishly-grinning Iago-like villain, who invested the bedroom scene with 'an amazing erotic charge'.[135]

The Queen

The Queen is given no name – like a fairytale wicked queen. She is pure malice. Patience Collier, in 1962, though 'as tart as a basket of sloes', was felt to be a little underpowered vocally but, in 1974, Sheila Allen was 'like a psychedelic superstar who shops at Biba',[136] 'a queen of night, whirling in multi-coloured plumage, reserving her most honeyed manner for those she plans to destroy';[137] in the 1997 kabuki-style production, Joanna McCallum, in ferocious conical hair, reminded Charles Spencer of Disney's wicked queen in *Snow White*, and in Dominic Cooke's 2003 production Ishia Bennison stalked the stage on stiletto heels, trailing her cloak of peacock feathers with its hundred spying eyes like a great, predatory bird. Heather Canning, in 1979, offered 'only the fair face of this dissembling schemer'[138] and, in keeping with the production's willingness to embrace the play's humorous elements, her evil was 'cunningly transmuted into mischief', so that, B. A. Young wrote, 'I almost expected her to wink at me as she handed over the poison to Pisanio.'[139] In 2006, Emma Rice, also adapter and director of Kneehigh's production, played her as a fantasy nurse, raunchy and lethal, in black stockings and latex gloves. The Queen's deadly potions became prescription drugs, administered with a syringe big enough to treat a horse, by means of which she kept Cymbeline in a zombie-like state of dependence.

Difficult Moments

The headless corpse

When Imogen wakes up from a drug-induced coma to find, as she thinks, the headless corpse of Posthumus beside her, she is given a hand grenade of a line: 'O Posthumus, alas, / Where is thy head?' The dilemma for director and actress is whether to suppress the line's potential for comedy or submit to it. Of Vanessa Redgrave, the

Birmingham Mail critic wrote, 'She goes full out for the horror . . . She might perhaps have brought this off completely had the corpse not been so gruesomely thrust at us – but how cleverly she buries the most embarrassing line in the folds of its tunic';[140] Milton Shulman commented that she 'not only beautifully portrayed unsullied innocence but managed to make believable her affection for a headless corpse';[141] and *The Times* critic, 'Her uncompromising playing . . . was utterly satisfying in its truthfulness.'[142] Susan Fleetwood 'surmounted' the moment, while Judi Dench was presented with a horrifically realistic blood-soaked corpse, which defied laughter. Of Harriet Walter, Michael Billington wrote, 'she conquers the appallingly difficult moment when she awakes next to a headless corpse and proceeds to daub her face with its blood'.[143] Emma Fielding deftly combined horror and comedy and Cloten's head appeared on a pole later, swung round by its bearer so that he appeared to be following the conversation. In 2006, Hayley Carmichael exploited the comic, as the production did in general.

The battle

The lengthy, messy battle between the Britons and the Romans in Act 5, in which several characters change sides, is almost impossible to make dramatic and even more impossible to follow. Directors have to find a strategy to manage these scenes and most eschew realism for symbolism. In William Gaskill's 1962 production, the British and Roman forces performed a balletic fight, and in John Barton's 1974 story-telling production in which Jeffery Dench, as Cornelius, became a narrator figure, he read out the account of the battle while it was acted in dumb-show behind him. In David Jones' 1979 production, three figures whirling huge flags represented the action, while Bill Alexander's 1987 studio production simply used strobe lighting, with painfully loud metallic drumming and in 1997, Japanese staves and banners were used, while Cymbeline sat enthroned above the action. In 2006, in the Kneehigh production which emphasized the child inside the adult, the battle was played out on a giant games board.

7. David Jones' production, 1979. Judi Dench as Innogen was presented with a horrifically realistic blood-soaked corpse, which defied laughter.

The descent of Jupiter

When Shakespeare wrote the descent of Jupiter as *deus ex machina* in Act 5, he was exploiting, as he did in writing the descending goddesses in *The Tempest*, the technical possibilities of his company's new theatre, the Blackfriars, to which they moved in 1608. For his contemporary audiences, the ability to fly a deity from the heavens was impressive enough, but for blasé modern audiences directors and designers have to look further for the magical *coup de théâtre* that the moment requires. In 1962, Jupiter descended on a golden eagle; in 1974, he was inside a great golden shell, which split open to

8. John Barton's production, 1974. The descent of Jupiter in this production was inside a great golden shell, which split open to reveal him.

reveal him; in 1979, he was represented by a golden globe mounted on an eagle. At The Other Place, in 1987, Irving Wardle complained, 'we get all the build-up for a masque, only to be fobbed off with the voice of Jupiter instead of the god's descent on an eagle.'[144] Michael Billington had complained about the 1997 production, where the kabuki model was abandoned at this point, and Jupiter descended on a hydraulic platform.[145] In 2003, the descent of Jupiter was highly extravagant in sight and sound, accompanied by a barrage of lighting effects and music almost painfully loud. By contrast, in 2001 one of the two bow-tied 'observers' who had wandered through Theatre for a New Audience's production spoke Jupiter's lines, while in 2006 Kneehigh portrayed Jupiter as a military general.

THE DIRECTORS CUT: INTERVIEWS WITH DOMINIC COOKE AND EMMA RICE

Dominic Cooke was born in London in 1966, and studied at Warwick University, taking up his first job in television as a runner shortly after graduating. He founded his own theatre company, Pan Optic, which he ran for two years before starting work as an assistant director for the RSC, as well as freelance director, in the early 1990s. In 1996 he joined the Royal Court as an assistant director under Stephen Daldry, returning to the RSC in 2003 to direct the production of *Cymbeline* he discusses here. Other successes with the company include *Macbeth* (2004), *As You Like It* (2005), promenade productions of *The Winter's Tale* and *Pericles* for the RSC's Complete Works season in 2006, and, the same year, a production of *The Crucible*, for which he won the Olivier Award for Best Director. He has been the artistic director of the Royal Court theatre since 2006.

Emma Rice was born in Nottingham in 1968 and studied drama at London's Guildhall and then at the Gardzienice Theatre Association, Poland. She joined Kneehigh, directing her first show for the company, *The Red Shoes*, in 2002, for which she won the TMA Theatre Award for Best Director. She has been artistic director at Kneehigh, who are based in Cornwall, since 2005. Her other directorial successes include *The Wooden Frock* (2004) and *The Bacchae* (2005), both of which won the TMA Award for Best Touring Production; *Tristan and Yseult* (2006); *Cymbeline*, which she brought to Stratford as part of the RSC's Complete Works season, also in 2006; Don John, also performed at the RSC in 2008; and *Brief Encounter*, for which she was nominated for the Olivier Award for Best Director in 2009.

Why do you think the play's called *Cymbeline*?

DC: Innogen and Posthumus are the central roles, but the play tells the story of how Cymbeline becomes legitimately restored to power. I think that's the reason for its title.

ER: I'm always looking for clues in the source material I choose, and the title is one of them. The fact that Shakespeare called the play *Cymbeline* means that it was Cymbeline that he wanted to cast as the main character. In fact Cymbeline is quite a minor character in simple text and action terms, but what's really interesting is his narrative curve. It's an unusual story structure as we meet Cymbeline when he has lost almost all of his power – he is spiritually at rock bottom. He flounders and sinks further into confusion but then finds the strength to ascend and find dignity, empathy and forgiveness by the end of the play. The title is always a clue.

Cymbeline has caused much critical consternation arising from an inability to decide what kind of play it is – fairytale, tragicomedy, etc. What kind of play is it to you, or does such categorization not really matter?

DC: Critics, especially literary critics, are very fond of fitting things into pre-existing genres, but there are some plays or works of art that defy existing categories or create their own. The style of *Cymbeline* is drawn from the different styles that Shakespeare has used throughout his career. You get elements of the classic Shakespearean comedy, with girls dressed as boys, mistaken identity and romance; you get the military conflict of the Roman plays; you get the political intrigue of a history play; you get some of the horror of a play like *Titus Andronicus*; and you get the sense of loss of tragedy. So, in our production we created a patchwork visual style that reflected this.

ER: Those categorizations don't matter in the slightest. It's simply a story. Agreed, it is a very peculiar story, but it is a story nonetheless. I think it has a fairytale structure: the going into the woods, getting lost in the wilderness and finally finding a way through to hope. It has a male fairytale structure of going to war and surviving conflict, woven with a female fairytale structure of finding your identity having been outcast. In many ways, it's about lots of people finding their way home, which is a recurrent fairytale theme.

Traditionally, the play's three main plots have been identified as the marriage/wager plot (Innogen/Posthumus/Iachimo/ Cloten), the dynastic plot (Guiderius and Arviragus, the future rulers of Britain), and the nations plot (involving the Roman invasion of Britain). What was your approach to marrying all these elements, and did you see one as being more significant or appealing than the others?

DC: The idea of death, or grief, as a transformative force is a feature of all of Shakespeare's late plays and it is, for me, the central idea of *Cymbeline.* By experiencing loss and grief all the characters learn the true value of relationships they previously took for granted. In the play, grief becomes a potential gateway to a form of spiritual rebirth. At the beginning of the play Innogen and Posthumus are out of balance. They are headstrong, hyperbolic and trapped in a rigid sense of youthful certainty. In many ways their decision to marry is an act of rebellion – they have little sense of what the commitment of marriage really means. By the end of the play you feel that they are at the start of a marriage that could last and grow, that their love has depth and maturity. I think this sense of evolution through loss is also true of Cymbeline himself, who loses his daughter, and of Guiderius and Arviragus. They are exposed to loss through the 'death' of Fidele and experience profound new feelings, expressed in some of the most beautiful language Shakespeare ever wrote. This is the gateway to a new maturity and on some psychic level prepares them to be restored back to the Royal Family.

ER: Without a doubt some are easier to do. The Posthumus story is an easy plot for us to enjoy and get to grips with as it's the simplest. We all understand jealousy and idiocy! The boys in the woods is a challenging story line and, at times, hard to get your head around because it can feel unbelievable. In fact it's a very powerful motor in the play, challenging the nature of family, friendship and society. Certainly the hardest storyline for a modern audience is what is going on with Rome. It's not a well-known part of our history and, to be honest, it's not that interesting. It's the hardest plot to reveal, and in my production and adaptation we used it primarily as a metaphor for war. We didn't try to explain the conflict, which is such ancient history that it's very hard to connect to. It really became about what happens to our characters if they go through something as major, and non-domestic, as war. The trick to making all these narrative strands weave together is to find a way of them all inhabiting the same world. We created a world that was brutal and full of conflict, one in which women were treated as objects and possessions and where friends turned against each other in war and peace. It was a fearful and barren world which ultimately presented a place for hope, truth and reconciliation to bloom.

Although we know Iachimo is lying about sleeping with Innogen, critics have argued for a kind of sexual conquest in the 'trunk' scene, which many also consider the finest in the play. What are your memories about that scene in your productions and how did you want it to read to your audiences?

DC: It's clear from the text that Iachimo kisses Innogen and we didn't feel the need to take it any further than that. The kiss, and his presence in her bedroom as she sleeps, is uninvited, and this seems like a violation in itself. We staged the scene with Innogen asleep on cushions on the floor which represented her bed, with her head facing downstage. The trunk was upstage of her, and when Iachimo came out of the trunk, which he did very slowly, he stood upstage looking down at her. This enhanced the sense of her vulnerability in the face of his predatory sexual desire.

ER: I often find Shakespeare very difficult, and I found *Cymbeline* a particularly dense and confusing play. And yet, in the middle of it is this brilliant scene – 'man wrestles with unconscious girl'. It's bloody interesting and very entertaining. It's a little bit sinister, a little bit funny, a little bit titillating and very visual. There's everything from *Carry On* to *Footballers' Wives* in there. It's brilliant. My memory is of relief when we came to work on that scene because we had such great fun with it. We used no words at all because the actions spoke quite loudly enough. Hayley Carmichael, who created the role of Innogen, marvellously went for a wee half-way through it and then came back in and went back to sleep, and all the while there was Iachimo trying to get hold of the bracelet. That's what I call a scene!

Do I think there was any sort of sexual conquest? Absolutely not! That's the male fantasy talking. Innogen had nothing to do with it. What's interesting is whether men see consent as part of the conquest, or whether it is just the act itself that counts. There is a

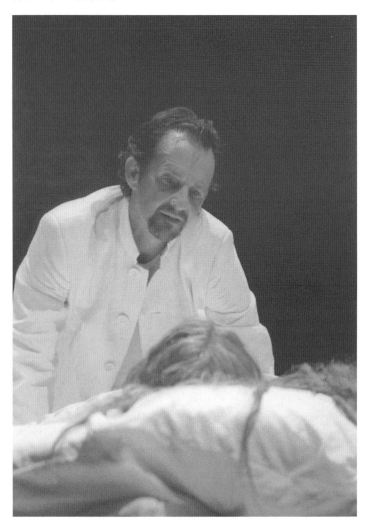

9. Dominic Cooke's production, 2003. Anton Lesser as Iachimo. 'We staged the scene with Innogen asleep on cushions on the floor which represented her bed, with her head facing downstage . . . [Iachimo] stood upstage looking down at her. This enhanced the sense of her vulnerability in the face of his predatory sexual desire.'

strong theme throughout the play about consciousness and consent, with Innogen being drugged by Cloten later in the narrative. So I'm fairly dismissive of the question in terms of the critics, but in terms of the play it's a brilliant scene and a very contemporary issue. I referred to Rohypnol directly in the script to highlight the relevance and reality of this behaviour.

How did you depict the relationship – and reconciliation – between Posthumus and Innogen?

DC: There's a complexity to Innogen and Posthumus' reconciliation at the end of the play. We played it as a hard-won moment. They approached each other tentatively and made slow physical contact as if neither assumed that they would be accepted by the other. They eventually held each other, but it felt like the beginning of something new and uncharted and therefore slightly scary. It felt like they were meeting each other for the first time as adults, rather than as headstrong teenagers, and negotiating a new relationship together which is exciting but frightening. We made the final image of the play a wedding witnessed by Jupiter, a genuine commitment rather than the hurried, clandestine union that precedes the play.

ER: The whole fifth act I did as a dreamscape. It was the characters emerging after war, but as a metaphor, not as a reality. It was as if the world had exploded and they all had to re-find themselves and each other. There is a line in the play – 'he lives'. I really felt that this encapsulated what they all felt; they were still alive and they were noticing the life in others. So I saw the reconciliation as the very peaceful coming together of two people who had journeyed from childhood into adulthood and survived. But, significantly, they made this journey separately. This is not a romantic story; Innogen and Posthumus spend so little time together in the play that we don't invest in their relationship like we would in Romeo and Juliet. We're told they love each other, and we're told they are married. However, I cut the marriage in this production because I wanted them to have not quite made that commitment. I wanted them to think they were ready to make that decision, and then in true fairytale form, to only really discover the reality of a lifelong love after passing the tests that life threw at them. I wanted it to be like the coming together of two freshly born adults, who may or may not make it as a couple. There was a very gentle, dreamlike quality, but not sentimental at all.

Some have argued that the Wales scenes are chiefly of the domain of the 'wild man' rather than the shepherd, and therefore they are not of the pastoral mode in the same way as *As You Like It* or *A Midsummer Night's Dream*. How did you envisage and stage them?

DC: The world of Wales in the play has an innocence and connects with a sense of escape from the falseness and sophistication of city life. In this way it reflects plays like *As You Like It*, although Shakespeare's treatment of the pastoral is never sentimental. He frequently presents nature as cruel. The Forest of Arden in *As You Like It*, for example, is partly a place of recuperation and escape, but Orlando escapes being bitten by a snake there only to be attacked by a lion. The Wales of *Cymbeline* is equally a dangerous place, hostile to outsiders – Guiderius kills Cloten virtually on sight. In our design we created a contrast between the three worlds of the play through costume and props – the set stayed the same throughout. It was a spare, stripped back stage with the usual floor of the Swan Theatre stacked up against the back wall. There was a trapdoor in the stage that Guiderius and Arviragus crawled out of. But within that theatrical setting there was also a sense of realism in the way that the characters lived in the wild – realistic hunting knives and bows and arrows were used.

ER: These scenes were the hardest in the whole show. The reason for this was not necessarily Shakespeare. I think, in the UK, that theatre tends to be a very middle-class pursuit, and middle-class people trying to look rough and wild can just look ridiculous. We laughed more than is possible trying to make these scenes real. In spite of this, I think the concept for them was very strong. I wanted the two lost children to live on the streets and to be the human fallout of conflict. I didn't want these scenes to be in a cave, I didn't feel that had any resonance for us. I wanted to create a world that was challenging and recognizable. We got there in the end, but it was hard to marry the epic language with such a social realism. We wrestled with these ideas and managed to create an edgy environment, with old mattresses and spray cans. We struggled to make it believable and often lost confidence, but then a really magic thing happened. When we took the show to Colombia, the audience had an amazing reaction. They completely understood the story we were trying to tell and had a genuine reference to it. That really inspired us to believe in that choice. It was going to Colombia that made us believe that this was not only strong, but very important.

How did you represent Rome and the Roman gods in your productions?

DC: We went with the idea that the gods were real to the characters in the play. So we created a shrine to Jupiter, with an eagle's head, above the audience. Whenever someone spoke to the gods, which they did frequently, they addressed the shrine. This made the characters' relationship to the gods a concrete one. In the play, Rome is characterized as a hybrid of the machiavellian intrigue of the Italian Renaissance and the efficiency of the Roman army. So we created a world which was part Ancient Rome – Roman armour and sandals in the military sections – with contemporary Rome, very fashion conscious and with a strong sense of display. Iachimo and most of the men wore white suits.

ER: I had Jupiter as a god of war, which of course he is. We had him in an army uniform. I don't think we have any connection to the Roman gods any more, and only very faint ones to Greek gods. However, I love the notion of gods with a small 'g'. In many ways theatre is all about three levels of communication. There's one's relationship with oneself, one's relationship to the people on stage with you and the audience, and the relationship to the 'super-structure' of life. That's where the gods come in. You have those times in life where you just wish somebody would come and help. It's like looking for a fantasy dad. It's not even your own dad you want, you need a Superdad to come and tell you it's all right and

10. Emma Rice's production, 2006. Image shows Hayley Carmichael, Carl Grose and Craig Johnson. The Welsh scenes 'were the hardest in the whole show . . . I didn't want these scenes to be in a cave, I didn't feel that had any resonance for us. I wanted to create a world that was challenging and recognizable . . . [we] managed to create an edgy environment, with old mattresses and spray cans.'

what to do. That's how I wanted Jupiter to be, although he is a little harsh and judgemental! As I said earlier, in some ways war can be a positive force in fairy tales, in that it makes people grow up and see the world in a broader picture. What I wanted to do with the gods was to say, look, this destroys lives on every level. He looked magnificent, my god/dad, and I had him flying, so used quite old-fashioned god-like imagery.

Many critics have remarked on the difficulty of Shakespeare's late style in general, and on *Cymbeline* in particular. How did you and your actors find the language of the play? Is it more difficult than that of earlier Shakespeare plays, and could this be a reason for its relative unpopularity?

DC: Much of the play's language is convoluted and we did edit some of the sub-clauses from the lengthy sentences of the opening scene where the characters are speaking in a courtly code. It's as if everyone is nervous about being overheard and potentially incriminated. The Queen is at the height of her corrupt power as the play opens, so there is a strong dramatic reason for the courtiers to be speaking in such an indirect way. However, given how much exposition there is as the play opens, the indirect language felt like a significant obstacle for the audience which we dealt with by making a few small cuts. With the rest of the play, we spent a lot of time making sure that all the actors knew exactly what every word meant. Then we worked on inhabiting each word and getting the flow and forward thinking of the very long sentences. The language in the play is self-feeding and hyperbolic. An idea can be set up at the start of the speech and can snowball through many lines and many, seemingly diversionary sub-clauses. However, by and large, when you commit to the sub-clauses, as with many of the idiosyncrasies of the play, it works.

ER: I've said this before, and I'm not ashamed about it, but I find some Shakespeare almost impossible to understand. Obviously some plays are easier than others, but they're all really difficult. *Cymbeline* is almost impenetrable at times. When we first tried to read it at Kneehigh, we felt the terrible weight of the text and it almost destroyed our process. So I did what I always do, which is to push through until I can tell the story. Then I leave the text behind for as long as possible. By really understanding what the story is and what it means to me, and then making that structure work, then, and only then, do I feed the text back in. At that point I use only what we need to make the story work. I was fairly irreverent with the text, because I didn't think it stood up in the modern world. I don't mean as a play, because I'm not an expert, I mean as a story. I'm a story-teller and the story structure of *Cymbeline* is very complicated. I always try and retain a childlike state when making work. That doesn't mean that the work becomes simplified – it absolutely shouldn't – but it should be simple. I think Einstein said 'work should be as simple as possible and no simpler', and that's a really good mantra for Shakespeare. People should be able to understand it, otherwise what are we saying?

Famously people say that the first scene in *Cymbeline* is one of the worst scenes in Shakespeare, and yet I bloody love it! It's a fairly ropey piece of work: he doesn't even give them names, it's just Gentleman 1 and Gentleman 2 and then we never see them again. They come on and one says 'You'll never guess what' and the other says 'What?' and then they basically give us the plot up to that point. It's really crude, but it is such a relief! In this production I wanted to give that person a name and a character, so I created a woman called Joan who was returning home (another home-coming!) after being in the Costa del Sol for 30 years. We did this because we had to work out why this character didn't have a clue what was going on! I had the idea of somebody returning, full of life, and realizing what an awful state the nation was in. The critics found that very challenging, but I know that any young people who came to see that show were relieved that they were helped to know what was going on.

Critics have been divided over the last act; some have been troubled by the way it re-narrates plot at great length, and at times evinces – horror of horrors – laughter from its audience, while others have conversely described the virtuosity of Shakespeare's dramatic management in *Cymbeline*, and the skill with which the plot threads reconvene at the end. Do you see Shakespearean senility or Shakespearean magic at work in this play?

DC: I think it's magic. All of the late plays, and *Cymbeline* is the most extreme example, have moments of self-conscious theatricality. If you think of the bear in *The Winter's Tale*, or Thaisa coming back to life in *Pericles*, it's as if Shakespeare is daring the audience not to accept what's being presented. That playful quality of testing theatricality is a feature of the final scene of *Cymbeline* and, by contrast, it deepens the authentic emotion of the discoveries and reunions. The contradiction in the play between truth and artificiality is part of its pleasure and it's why the play frequently works very well in performance, even if it seems improbable on the page. The golden rule of performing this play is to commit one

the lighted stage. Shakespeare, by contrast, wrote for a bare platform stage with a standing audience gathered around it in a courtyard in full daylight. The audience were always conscious of themselves and their fellow-spectators, and they shared the same 'room' as the actors. A sense of immediate presence and the creation of rapport with the audience were all-important. The actor could not afford to imagine he was in a closed world, with silent witnesses dutifully observing him from the darkness.

Shakespeare's theatrical career began at the Rose Theatre in Southwark. The stage was wide and shallow, trapezoid in shape, like a lozenge. This design had a great deal of potential for the theatrical equivalent of cinematic split-screen effects, whereby one group of characters would enter at the door at one end of the tiring-house wall at the back of the stage and another group through the door at the other end, thus creating two rival tableaux. Many of the battle-heavy and faction-filled plays that premiered at the Rose have scenes of just this sort.

At the rear of the Rose stage, there were three capacious exits, each over ten feet wide. Unfortunately, the very limited excavation of a fragmentary portion of the original Globe site, in 1989, revealed nothing about the stage. The first Globe was built in 1599 with similar proportions to those of another theatre, the Fortune, albeit that the former was polygonal and looked circular, whereas the latter was rectangular. The building contract for the Fortune survives and allows us to infer that the stage of the Globe was probably substantially wider than it was deep (perhaps forty-three feet wide and twenty-seven feet deep). It may well have been tapered at the front, like that of the Rose.

The capacity of the Globe was said to have been enormous, perhaps in excess of three thousand. It has been conjectured that about eight hundred people may have stood in the yard, with two thousand or more in the three layers of covered galleries. The other 'public' playhouses were also of large capacity, whereas the indoor Blackfriars theatre that Shakespeare's company began using in 1608 – the former refectory of a monastery – had overall internal dimensions of a mere forty-six by sixty feet. It would have made for a much more intimate theatrical experience and had a much smaller capacity, probably of about six hundred people. Since they paid at least sixpence a head, the Blackfriars attracted a more select or 'private' audience. The atmosphere would have been closer to that of an indoor performance before the court in the Whitehall Palace or at Richmond. That Shakespeare always wrote for indoor production at court as well as outdoor performance in the public theatre should make us cautious about inferring, as some scholars have, that the opportunity provided by the intimacy of the Blackfriars led to a significant change towards a 'chamber' style in his last plays – which, besides, were performed at both the Globe and the Blackfriars. After the occupation of the Blackfriars a five-act structure seems to have become more important to Shakespeare. That was because of artificial lighting: there were musical interludes between the acts, while the candles were trimmed and replaced. Again, though, something similar must have been necessary for indoor court performances throughout his career.

Front of house there were the 'gatherers' who collected the money from audience members: a penny to stand in the open-air yard, another penny for a place in the covered galleries, sixpence for the prominent 'lord's rooms' to the side of the stage. In the indoor 'private' theatres, gallants from the audience who fancied making themselves part of the spectacle sat on stools on the edge of the stage itself. Scholars debate as to how widespread this practice was in the public theatres such as the Globe. Once the audience were in place and the money counted, the gatherers were available to be extras on stage. That is one reason why battles and crowd scenes often come later rather than early in Shakespeare's plays. There was no formal prohibition upon performance by women, and there certainly were women among the gatherers, so it is not beyond the bounds of possibility that female crowd members were played by females.

The play began at two o'clock in the afternoon and the theatre had to be cleared by five. After the main show, there would be a jig – which consisted not only of dancing, but also of knockabout comedy (it is the origin of the farcical 'afterpiece' in the eighteenth-century theatre). So the time available for a Shakespeare play was about two and a half hours, somewhere between the 'two hours' traffic' mentioned in the prologue to *Romeo and Juliet* and the 'three hours' spectacle' referred to in the preface to the 1647 Folio of Beaumont and Fletcher's plays. The prologue to a play by Thomas Middleton refers to a thousand lines as 'one hour's words', so the likelihood is that about two and a half thousand, or a maximum of three thousand lines made up the performed text. This is indeed the length of most of Shakespeare's comedies, whereas many of his tragedies and histories are much longer, raising the possibility that he wrote full scripts, possibly with eventual publication in mind, in the full knowledge that the stage version would be heavily cut. The short Quarto texts published in his lifetime – they used to be called 'Bad' Quartos – provide fascinating evidence as to the kind of cutting that probably took place. So, for instance, the First Quarto of *Hamlet* neatly merges two occasions when Hamlet is overheard, the 'Fishmonger' and the 'nunnery' scenes.

The social composition of the audience was mixed. The poet Sir John Davies wrote of 'A thousand townsmen, gentlemen and whores, / Porters and servingmen' who would 'together throng' at the public playhouses. Though moralists associated female play-going with adultery and the sex trade, many perfectly respectable citizens' wives were regular attendees. Some, no doubt, resembled the modern groupie: a story attested in two different sources has one citizen's wife making a post-show assignation with Richard Burbage and ending up in bed with Shakespeare – supposedly eliciting from the latter the quip that William the Conqueror was before Richard III. Defenders of theatre liked to say that by witnessing the comeuppance of villains on the stage, audience members would repent of their own wrongdoings, but the reality is that most people went to the theatre then, as they do now, for entertainment more than moral edification. Besides, it would be foolish to suppose that audiences behaved in a homogeneous way: a pamphlet of the 1630s tells of how two men went to see *Pericles* and one of them laughed while the other wept. Bishop John Hall complained that people went to church for the same reasons that they went to the theatre: 'for company, for custom, for recreation . . . to feed his eyes or his ears . . . or perhaps for sleep'.

Men-about-town and clever young lawyers went to be seen as much as to see. In the modern popular imagination, shaped not least by *Shakespeare in Love* and the opening sequence of Laurence Olivier's

Henry V film, the penny-paying groundlings stand in the yard hurling abuse or encouragement and hazelnuts or orange peel at the actors, while the sophisticates in the covered galleries appreciate Shakespeare's soaring poetry. The reality was probably the other way round. A 'groundling' was a kind of fish, so the nickname suggests the penny audience standing below the level of the stage and gazing in silent open-mouthed wonder at the spectacle unfolding above them. The more difficult audience members, who kept up a running commentary of clever remarks on the performance and who occasionally got into quarrels with players, were the gallants. Like Hollywood movies in modern times, Elizabethan and Jacobean plays exercised a powerful influence on the fashion and behaviour of the young. John Marston mocks the lawyers who would open their lips, perhaps to court a girl, and out would 'flow / Naught but pure Juliet and Romeo'.

THE ENSEMBLE AT WORK

In the absence of typewriters and photocopying machines, reading aloud would have been the means by which the company got to know a new play. The tradition of the playwright reading his complete script to the assembled company endured for generations. A copy would then have been taken to the Master of the Revels for licensing. The theatre book-holder or prompter would then have copied the parts for distribution to the actors. A partbook consisted of the character's lines, with each speech preceded by the last three or four words of the speech before, the so-called 'cue'. These would have been taken away and studied or 'conned'. During this period of learning the parts, an actor might have had some one-to-one instruction, perhaps from the dramatist, perhaps from a senior actor who had played the same part before, and, in the case of an apprentice, from his master. A high percentage of Desdemona's lines occur in dialogue with Othello, of Lady Macbeth's with Macbeth, Cleopatra's with Antony and Volumnia's with Coriolanus. The roles would almost certainly have been taken by the apprentice of the lead actor, usually Burbage, who delivers the majority of the cues. Given that apprentices lodged with their masters, there would have been

11. Hypothetical reconstruction of the interior of an Elizabethan playhouse during a performance.

ample opportunity for personal instruction, which may be what made it possible for young men to play such demanding parts.

After the parts were learned, there may have been no more than a single rehearsal before the first performance. With six different plays to be put on every week, there was no time for more. Actors, then, would go into a show with a very limited sense of the whole. The notion of a collective rehearsal process that is itself a process of discovery for the actors is wholly modern and would have been incomprehensible to Shakespeare and his original ensemble. Given the number of parts an actor had to hold in his memory, the forgetting of lines was probably more frequent than in the modern theatre. The book-holder was on hand to prompt.

Backstage personnel included the property man, the tire-man who oversaw the costumes, call-boys, attendants and the musicians, who might play at various times from the main stage, the rooms above and within the tiring-house. Scriptwriters sometimes made a nuisance of themselves backstage. There was often tension between the acting companies and the freelance playwrights from whom they purchased scripts: it was a smart move on the part of Shakespeare and the Lord Chamberlain's Men to bring the writing process in-house.

Scenery was limited, though sometimes set-pieces were brought on (a bank of flowers, a bed, the mouth of hell). The trapdoor from below, the gallery stage above and the curtained discovery-space at the back allowed for an array of special effects: the rising of ghosts and apparitions, the descent of gods, dialogue between a character at a window and another at ground level, the revelation of a statue or a pair of lovers playing at chess. Ingenious use could be made of props, as with the ass's head in *A Midsummer Night's Dream*. In a theatre that does not clutter the stage with the material paraphernalia of everyday life, those objects that are deployed may take on powerful symbolic weight, as when Shylock bears his weighing scales in one hand and knife in the other, thus becoming a parody of the figure of Justice who traditionally bears a sword and a balance. Among the more significant items in the property cupboard of Shakespeare's company, there would have been a throne (the 'chair of state'), joint stools, books, bottles, coins, purses, letters (which are brought on stage, read or referred to on about eighty occasions in the complete works), maps, gloves, a set of stocks (in which Kent is put in *King Lear*), rings, rapiers, daggers, broadswords, staves, pistols, masks and vizards, heads and skulls, torches and tapers and lanterns which served to signal night scenes on the daylit stage, a buck's head, an ass's head, animal costumes. Live animals also put in appearances, most notably the dog Crab in *The Two Gentlemen of Verona* and possibly a young polar bear in *The Winter's Tale*.

The costumes were the most important visual dimension of the play. Playwrights were paid between £2 and £6 per script, whereas Alleyn was not averse to paying £20 for 'a black velvet cloak with sleeves embroidered all with silver and gold'. No matter the period of the play, actors always wore contemporary costume. The excitement for the audience came not from any impression of historical accuracy, but from the richness of the attire and perhaps the transgressive thrill of the knowledge that here were commoners like themselves strutting in the costumes of courtiers in effective defiance of the strict sumptuary laws whereby in real life people had to wear the clothes that befitted their social station.

To an even greater degree than props, costumes could carry symbolic importance. Racial characteristics could be suggested: a breastplate and helmet for a Roman soldier, a turban for a Turk, long robes for exotic characters such as Moors, a gabardine for a Jew. The figure of Time, as in *The Winter's Tale*, would be equipped with hourglass, scythe and wings; Rumour, who speaks the prologue of *2 Henry IV*, wore a costume adorned with a thousand tongues. The wardrobe in the tiring-house of the Globe would have contained much of the same stock as that of rival manager Philip Henslowe at the Rose: green gowns for outlaws and foresters, black for melancholy men such as Jaques and people in mourning such as the Countess in *All's Well that Ends Well* (at the beginning of *Hamlet*, the prince is still in mourning black when everyone else is in festive garb for the wedding of the new king), a gown and hood for a friar (or a feigned friar like the duke in *Measure for Measure*), blue coats and tawny to distinguish the followers of rival factions, a leather apron and ruler for a carpenter (as in the opening scene of *Julius Caesar* – and in *A Midsummer Night's Dream*, where this is the only sign that Peter Quince is a carpenter), a cockle hat with staff and a pair of sandals for a pilgrim or palmer (the disguise assumed by Helen in *All's Well*), bodices and kirtles with farthingales beneath for the boys who are to be dressed as girls. A gender switch such as that of Rosalind or Jessica seems to have taken between fifty and eighty lines of dialogue – Viola does not resume her 'maiden weeds', but remains in her boy's costume to the end of *Twelfth Night* because a change would have slowed down the action at just the moment it was speeding to a climax. Henslowe's inventory also included 'a robe for to go invisible': Oberon, Puck and Ariel must have had something similar.

As the costumes appealed to the eyes, so there was music for the ears. Comedies included many songs. Desdemona's willow song, perhaps a late addition to the text, is a rare and thus exceptionally poignant example from tragedy. Trumpets and tuckets sounded for ceremonial entrances, drums denoted an army on the march. Background music could create atmosphere, as at the beginning of *Twelfth Night*, during the lovers' dialogue near the end of

The Merchant of Venice, when the statue seemingly comes to life in *The Winter's Tale*, and for the revival of Pericles and of Lear (in the Quarto text, but not the Folio). The haunting sound of the hautboy suggested a realm beyond the human, as when the god Hercules is imagined deserting Mark Antony. Dances symbolized the harmony of the end of a comedy – though in Shakespeare's world of mingled joy and sorrow, someone is usually left out of the circle.

The most important resource was, of course, the actors themselves. They needed many skills: in the words of one contemporary commentator, 'dancing, activity, music, song, elocution, ability of body, memory, skill of weapon, pregnancy of wit'. Their bodies were as significant as their voices. Hamlet tells the player to 'suit the action to the word, the word to the action': moments of strong emotion, known as 'passions', relied on a repertoire of dramatic gestures as well as a modulation of the voice. When Titus Andronicus has had his hand chopped off, he asks 'How can I grace my talk, / Wanting a hand to give it action?' A pen portrait of 'The Character of an Excellent Actor' by the dramatist John Webster is almost certainly based on his impression of Shakespeare's leading man, Richard Burbage: 'By a full and significant action of body, he charms our attention: sit in a full theatre, and you will think you see so many lines drawn from the circumference of so many ears, whiles the actor is the centre . . . .'

Though Burbage was admired above all others, praise was also heaped upon the apprentice players whose alto voices fitted them for the parts of women. A spectator at Oxford in 1610 records how the audience were reduced to tears by the pathos of Desdemona's death. The puritans who fumed about the biblical prohibition upon cross-dressing and the encouragement to sodomy constituted by the sight of an adult male kissing a teenage boy on stage were a small minority. Little is known, however, about the characteristics of the leading apprentices in Shakespeare's company. It may perhaps be inferred that one was a lot taller than the other, since Shakespeare often wrote for a pair of female friends, one tall and fair, the other short and dark (Helena and Hermia, Rosalind and Celia, Beatrice and Hero).

We know little about Shakespeare's own acting roles – an early allusion indicates that he often took royal parts, and a venerable tradition gives him old Adam in *As You Like It* and the ghost of old King Hamlet. Save for Burbage's lead roles and the generic part of the clown, all such castings are mere speculation. We do not even know for sure whether the original Falstaff was Will Kempe or another actor who specialized in comic roles, Thomas Pope.

Kempe left the company in early 1599. Tradition has it that he fell out with Shakespeare over the matter of excessive improvisation. He was replaced by Robert Armin, who was less of a clown and more of a cerebral wit: this explains the difference between such parts as Lancelet Gobbo and Dogberry, which were written for Kempe, and the more verbally sophisticated Feste and Lear's Fool, which were written for Armin.

One thing that is clear from surviving 'plots' or story-boards of plays from the period is that a degree of doubling was necessary. *2 Henry VI* has over sixty speaking parts, but more than half of the characters only appear in a single scene and most scenes have only six to eight speakers. At a stretch, the play could be performed by thirteen actors. When Thomas Platter saw *Julius Caesar* at the Globe in 1599, he noted that there were about fifteen. Why doesn't Paris go to the Capulet ball in *Romeo and Juliet?* Perhaps because he was doubled with Mercutio, who does. In *The Winter's Tale*, Mamillius might have come back as Perdita and Antigonus been doubled by Camillo, making the partnership with Paulina at the end a very neat touch. Titania and Oberon are often played by the same pair as Hippolyta and Theseus, suggesting a symbolic matching of the rulers of the worlds of night and day, but it is questionable whether there would have been time for the necessary costume changes. As so often, one is left in a realm of tantalizing speculation.

THE KING'S MAN

On Queen Elizabeth's death in 1603, the new king, James I, who had held the Scottish throne as James VI since he had been an infant, immediately took the Lord Chamberlain's Men under his direct patronage. Henceforth they would be the King's Men, and for the rest of Shakespeare's career they were favoured with far more court performances than any of their rivals. There even seem to have been rumours early in the reign that Shakespeare and Burbage were being considered for knighthoods, an unprecedented honour for mere actors – and one that in the event was not accorded to a member of the profession for nearly three hundred years, when the title was bestowed upon Henry Irving, the leading Shakespearean actor of Queen Victoria's reign.

Shakespeare's productivity rate slowed in the Jacobean years, not because of age or some personal trauma, but because there were frequent outbreaks of plague, causing the theatres to be closed for long periods. The King's Men were forced to spend many months on the road. Between November 1603 and 1608, they were to be found at various towns in the south and Midlands, though Shakespeare probably did not tour with them by this time. He had bought a large house back home in Stratford and was accumulating other property. He may indeed have stopped acting soon after the new king took the throne. With the London theatres closed so much of the time and a large repertoire on the stocks, Shakespeare seems to have focused his energies on writing a few long and complex tragedies that could have been played on demand at court: *Othello*, *King Lear*, *Antony and Cleopatra*, *Coriolanus* and *Cymbeline* are among his longest and poetically grandest plays. *Macbeth* only survives in a shorter text, which shows signs of adaptation after Shakespeare's death. The bitterly satirical *Timon of Athens*, apparently a collaboration with Thomas Middleton that may have failed on the stage, also belongs to this period. In comedy, too, he wrote longer and morally darker works than in the Elizabethan period, pushing at the very bounds of the form in *Measure for Measure* and *All's Well that Ends Well*.

From 1608 onwards, when the King's Men began occupying the indoor Blackfriars playhouse (as a winter house, meaning that they only used the outdoor Globe in summer?), Shakespeare turned to a more romantic style. His company had a great success with a revived and altered version of an old pastoral play called *Mucedorus*. It even featured a bear. The younger dramatist John Fletcher, meanwhile, sometimes working in collaboration with Francis Beaumont, was pioneering a new style of tragicomedy, a mix of romance and royalism laced with intrigue and pastoral excursions. Shakespeare experimented with this idiom in *Cymbeline* and it was presumably with his blessing that Fletcher eventually took over as the King's Men's company dramatist. The two writers apparently collaborated on three plays in the years 1612–14: a lost romance called *Cardenio* (based on the love-madness of a character in Cervantes' *Don Quixote*), *Henry VIII* (originally staged with the title 'All is True'), and *The Two Noble Kinsmen*, a dramatization of Chaucer's 'Knight's Tale'. These were written after Shakespeare's two final solo-authored plays, *The Winter's Tale*, a self-consciously old-fashioned work dramatizing the pastoral romance of his old enemy Robert Greene, and *The Tempest*, which at one and the same time drew together multiple theatrical traditions, diverse reading and contemporary interest in the fate of a ship that had been wrecked on the way to the New World.

The collaborations with Fletcher suggest that Shakespeare's career ended with a slow fade rather than the sudden retirement supposed by the nineteenth-century Romantic critics who read Prospero's epilogue to *The Tempest* as Shakespeare's personal farewell to his art. In the last few years of his life Shakespeare certainly spent more of his time in Stratford-upon-Avon, where he became further involved in property dealing and litigation. But his London life also continued. In 1613 he made his first major London property purchase: a freehold house in the Blackfriars district, close to his company's indoor theatre. *The Two Noble Kinsmen* may have been written as late as 1614, and Shakespeare was in London on business a little over a year before he died of an unknown cause at home in Stratford-upon-Avon in 1616, probably on his fifty-second birthday.

About half the sum of his works were published in his lifetime, in texts of variable quality. A few years after his death, his fellow-actors began putting together an authorized edition of his complete *Comedies, Histories and Tragedies*. It appeared in 1623, in large 'Folio' format. This collection of thirty-six plays gave Shakespeare his immortality. In the words of his fellow-dramatist Ben Jonson, who contributed two poems of praise at the start of the Folio, the body of his work made him 'a monument without a tomb':

And art alive still while thy book doth live
And we have wits to read and praise to give ...
He was not of an age, but for all time!

SHAKESPEARE'S WORKS:
A Chronology

1589–91	*? Arden of Faversham* (possible part authorship)
1589–92	*The Taming of the Shrew*
1589–92	*? Edward the Third* (possible part authorship)
1591	*The Second Part of Henry the Sixth*, originally called *The First Part of the Contention betwixt the Two Famous Houses of York and Lancaster* (element of co-authorship possible)
1591	*The Third Part of Henry the Sixth*, originally called *The True Tragedy of Richard Duke of York* (element of co-authorship probable)
1591–92	*The Two Gentlemen of Verona*
1591–92 perhaps revised 1594	*The Lamentable Tragedy of Titus Andronicus* (probably co-written with, or revising an earlier version by, George Peele)
1592	*The First Part of Henry the Sixth*, probably with Thomas Nashe and others
1592/94	*King Richard the Third*
1593	*Venus and Adonis* (poem)
1593–94	*The Rape of Lucrece* (poem)
1593–1608	*Sonnets* (154 poems, published 1609 with *A Lover's Complaint*, a poem of disputed authorship)
1592–94/ 1600–03	*Sir Thomas More* (a single scene for a play originally by Anthony Munday, with other revisions by Henry Chettle, Thomas Dekker and Thomas Heywood)
1594	*The Comedy of Errors*
1595	*Love's Labour's Lost*

1608	*Pericles, Prince of Tyre*, with George Wilkins
1610	*The Tragedy of Cymbeline*
1611	*The Winter's Tale*
1611	*The Tempest*
1612–13	*Cardenio*, with John Fletcher (survives only in later adaptation called *Double Falsehood* by Lewis Theobald)
1613	*Henry VIII (All is True)*, with John Fletcher
1613–14	*The Two Noble Kinsmen*, with John Fletcher

THE HISTORY BEHIND THE TRAGEDIES: A Chronology

Era/Date	Event	Location	Play
Greek myth	Trojan war	Troy	*Troilus and Cressida*
Greek myth	Theseus King of Athens	Athens	*The Two Noble Kinsmen*
c.tenth–ninth century BC?	Leir King of Britain (legendary)	Britain	*King Lear*
535–510 BC	Tarquin II King of Rome	Rome	*The Rape of Lucrece*
493 BC	Caius Martius captures Corioli	Italy	*Coriolanus*
431–404 BC	Peloponnesian war	Greece	*Timon of Athens*
17 Mar 45 BC	Battle of Munda: Caesar's victory over Pompey's sons	Munda, Spain	*Julius Caesar*
Oct 45 BC	Caesar returns to Rome for triumph	Rome	*Julius Caesar*
15 Mar 44 BC	Assassination of Caesar	Rome	*Julius Caesar*
27 Nov 43 BC	Formation of Second Triumvirate	Rome	*Julius Caesar*
Oct 42 BC	Battle of Philippi	Philippi, Macedonia	*Julius Caesar*
Winter 41–40 BC	Antony visits Cleopatra	Egypt	*Antony and Cleopatra*
Oct 40 BC	Pact of Brundisium; marriage of Antony and Octavia	Italy	*Antony and Cleopatra*
39 BC	Pact of Misenum between Pompey and the triumvirs	Campania, Italy	*Antony and Cleopatra*
39–38 BC	Ventidius defeats the Parthians in a series of engagements	Syria	*Antony and Cleopatra*

Era/Date	Event	Location	Play
34 BC	Cleopatra and her children proclaimed rulers of the eastern Mediterranean	Alexandria	*Antony and Cleopatra*
2 Sep 31 BC	Battle of Actium	On the coast of western Greece	*Antony and Cleopatra*
Aug 30 BC	Death of Antony	Alexandria	*Antony and Cleopatra*
12 Aug 30 BC	Death of Cleopatra	Alexandria	*Antony and Cleopatra*
Early first century AD	Cunobelinus/ Cymbeline rules Britain (and dies before AD 43)	Britain	*Cymbeline*
During the reign of a fictional (late?) Roman emperor		Rome	*Titus Andronicus*
c.ninth–tenth century AD	Existence of legendary Amleth?	Denmark	*Hamlet*
15 Aug 1040	Death of Duncan I of Scotland	Bothnguane, Scotland	*Macbeth*
1053	Malcolm invades Scotland	Scotland	*Macbeth*
15 Aug 1057	Death of Macbeth	Lumphanan, Scotland	*Macbeth*
7 Oct 1571	Naval battle of Lepanto between Christians and Turks	The Mediterranean, off the coast of Greece	A context for *Othello*

FURTHER READING AND VIEWING

CRITICAL APPROACHES

Adelman, Janet, 'Masculine Authority and the Maternal Body: The Return to Origins in the Romances', *in Suffocating Mothers: Fantasies of Maternal Origin in Shakespeare's Plays, Hamlet to The Tempest* (1992). Influential psychoanalytical reading: chapter 8 deals with *Cymbeline* and the other romances.

Brockbank, J. P., 'History and Histrionics in Cymbeline (1958)', in *Shakespeare's Later Comedies*, ed. D. J. Palmer (1971). Looks at Shakespeare's use of both Holinshed and Geoffrey of Monmouth's tales of Brute, arguing that Shakespeare's dovetailing of sources creates a magical, principally theatrical, yet brilliantly researched historical narrative.

Bullough, Geoffrey, *Narrative and Dramatic Sources of Shakespeare: Volume 8* (1975). In-depth analysis of Shakespeare's source material for *Cymbeline* and his dramatic accomplishment in its reworking.

Hawkes, Terence, *Shakespeare in the Present* (2002). Focuses on the significance of Wales in the play's various articulations of nationhood.

Jones, Emrys, 'Stuart Cymbeline (1961)', in *Shakespeare's Later Comedies*, ed. D. J. Palmer (1971). Excellent discussion of the play as a Jacobean panegyric.

King, Ros, Cymbeline: *Constructions of Britain* (2005). In-depth re-evaluation of many aspects of the play, including language, reception, literary and historical contexts, and stageworthiness.

McDonald, Russ, *Shakespeare's Late Style* (2006). Invaluable close study of Shakespeare's somewhat strange and experimental language use throughout the late plays in general.

Miola, Robert S., *Shakespeare's Rome* (1983). Discusses Shakespeare's changing visions of Rome across his drama: chapter 7 deals with *Cymbeline*.

Simonds, Peggy Muñoz, *Myth, Emblem, and Music in Shakespeare's Cymbeline* (1992). Examines the play specifically as a product of the Renaissance, exploring such themes as Renaissance symbology, myth, art, theology and craftsmanship, and how they are used by Shakespeare.

Thompson, Ann, 'Cymbeline's Other Endings', in *The Appropriation of Shakespeare*, ed. Jean I. Marsden (1991). Looks at the dramaturgy of the play's often baffling final scene.

Traversi, Derek, *Shakespeare: The Last Phase* (1954). Examines the poetic and formal characteristics of Shakespeare's later work.

Wilson Knight, G., *The Crown of Life* (1947). Classic study of Shakespeare's late plays: chapter 4 deals with *Cymbeline*.

THE PLAY IN PERFORMANCE

Jackson, R., and R. Smallwood, eds, *Players of Shakespeare* 3 (1993). Featuring Harriet Walter on playing the role of Innogen.

Shaw, George Bernard, 'Blaming the Bard', in *Shaw on Shakespeare*, ed. Edwin Wilson (1961). Full text of Shaw's vitriolic Lyceum review.

Warren, Roger, *Shakespeare in Performance: Cymbeline* (1990). Introductory volume devoted exclusively to the play.

Warren, Roger, *Staging Shakespeare's Late Plays* (1990). Excellent analysis of the staging considerations of Shakespeare's late plays, using Peter Hall's productions of *Cymbeline*, *The Winter's Tale* and *The Tempest* at the National in 1988 as a central case study.

AVAILABLE ON DVD

Cymbeline, directed by Elijah Moshinsky for the BBC Shakespeare series (1982, DVD 2005). One of the better entries in the BBC series, and somewhat star-studded, with a vivacious Helen Mirren as Innogen, Michael Pennington as Posthumus, Robert Lindsay as Iachimo and Claire Bloom as the Queen.

REFERENCES

1 Samuel Johnson, Footnote to *Cymbeline* in *Samuel Johnson on Shakespeare*, ed. H. R. Woudhuysen (1989), p. 235.
2 George Bernard Shaw, 'Blaming the Bard', in *Shaw on Shakespeare*, ed. Edwin Wilson (1961), p. 72.
3 William Hazlitt, *Characters of Shakespeare's Plays* (1817), p. 1.
4 Alexander Leggatt, *Shakespeare's Comedy of Love* (1974), p. 260.
5 Geoffrey Bullough, *Narrative and Dramatic Sources of Shakespeare: Volume 8* (1975), pp. 13–14.
6 Georg Brandes, *William Shakespeare. A Critical Study*, Volume 2 (1898), p. 321.
7 R. G. Moulton, *The Moral System of Shakespeare* (1903), p. 79.
8 Janet Adelman, 'Masculine Authority and the Maternal Body: The Return to Origins in the Romances', in *Suffocating Mothers: Fantasies of Maternal Origin in Shakespeare's Plays, Hamlet to The Tempest* (1992), p. 210.
9 Adelman, 'Masculine Authority and the Maternal Body', p. 211.
10 Terence Hawkes, *Shakespeare in the Present* (2002) p. 53.
11 Ros King, *Cymbeline: Constructions of Britain* (2005), p. 120.
12 Rosalie Colie, '"Nature's Above Art In That Respect": Limits of the Pastoral Pattern', in *Shakespeare's Living Art* (1974), pp. 297–8.
13 King, *Cymbeline*, p. 120.
14 Robert Henke, *Pastoral Transformations: Italian Tragicomedy and Shakespeare's Late Plays* (1997), pp. 100–1.
15 Northrop Frye, *A Natural Perspective* (1965), p. 67.
16 J. P. Brockbank, 'History and Histrionics in *Cymbeline* (1958)', in *Shakespeare's Later Comedies*, ed. D. J. Palmer (1971), pp. 238–9.
17 G. Wilson Knight, *The Crown of Life* (1947), p. 129.
18 Philip Edwards, *Threshold of a Nation* (1979), p. 93.
19 Jodi Mikalachki, 'The Masculine Romance of Roman Britain: *Cymbeline* and Early Modern English Nationalism', *Shakespeare Quarterly* 46 (1995), p. 303.
20 Adelman, 'Masculine Authority and the Maternal Body: The Return to Origins in the Romances', in *Suffocating Mothers: Fantasies of Maternal Origin in Shakespeare's Plays, Hamlet to The Tempest* (1992), p. 201.
21 Robert S. Miola, *Shakespeare's Rome* (1983), p. 237.
22 Hawkes, *Shakespeare in the Present*, p. 58.
23 Emrys Jones, 'Stuart *Cymbeline* (1961)', in *Shakespeare's Later Comedies*, ed. D. J. Palmer (1971), pp. 259–60.
24 Ben Jonson, *The New Inn*, Ode l. 22.
25 E. K. Chambers, *William Shakespeare: A Study of Facts and Problems*, Volume 2 (1930), pp. 338–9.
26 Chambers, *William Shakespeare*, p. 352.
27 *The Court Magazine*, December 1761.
28 Universal Museum, March 1762.

29 James Boaden, *J. P. Kemble*, Volume 1 (1825), p. 300.

30 Boaden, *J. P. Kemble*, p. 343.

31 Boaden, *J. P. Kemble*, p. 343.

32 Boaden, *J. P. Kemble*, p. 343.

33 *The Times* (London), 23 January 1843.

34 *Spectator*, 28 January 1843.

35 *Saturday Review*, 22 October 1864.

36 Private letter from Shaw to Terry, 8 September 1896.

37 Private letter from Terry to Shaw, 24 September 1896.

38 *Saturday Review*, 26 September 1896.

39 *Saturday Review*, 26 September 1896.

40 Shaw, *Shaw on Shakespeare*, p. 80.

41 Mary Clarke, *Shakespeare at the Old Vic* (1957).

42 *New York Times*, 25 August 1957.

43 Kenneth Tynan, *A View of the English Stage* (1975), p. 267.

44 *Observer*, 23 September 1984.

45 Michael Billington, *Guardian*, 23 May 1988.

46 Roger Warren, *Staging Shakespeare's Late Plays* (1990), p. 23.

47 Warren, *Staging Shakespeare's Late Plays*, p. 24.

48 Warren, *Staging Shakespeare's Late Plays*, p. 60.

49 Billington, *Guardian*, 23 May 1988.

50 Billington, *Guardian*, 23 May 1988.

51 Billington, *Guardian*, 23 May 1988.

52 Susannah Clapp, *Observer*, 15 July 2001.

53 Clapp, *Observer*, 15 July 2001.

54 Clapp, *Observer*, 15 July 2001.

55 Charles Spencer, *Daily Telegraph*, 12 July 2001.

56 Paul Taylor, *Independent*, 28 November 2001.

57 Charles Spencer, *Daily Telegraph*, 13 May 2005.

58 Paul Taylor, *Independent*, 31 May 2007.

59 Taylor, *Independent*, 31 May 2007.

60 Judith Buchanan, *Shakespeare on Film* (2005), p. 43.

61 David Myerscough Jones quoted in Henry Fenwick, 'The Production', *All's Well That Ends Well*, The BBC TV Shakespeare (1980), p. 25. Moshinsky had directed *All's Well* and followed his designer Jones's maxim into his work on *Cymbeline*.

62 Neil Taylor, 'Two Types of Television Shakespeare', in *Shakespeare and the Moving Image*, ed. Anthony Davies and Stanley Wells (1994), p. 93.

63 Sean Day-Lewis, *Daily Telegraph*, 11 July 1983.

64 Day-Lewis, *Daily Telegraph*, 11 July 1983.

65 Michael Billington, *Guardian*, 8 August 2003.

66 Don Chapman, *Oxford Mail*, 18 July 1962.

67 Michael Billington, *Guardian*, 5 June 1974.

68 John Barber, *Daily Telegraph*, 5 June 1974.

69 Herbert Kretzmer, *Daily Express*, 5 June 1974.

70 Andrew Rissik, *Independent*, 14 November 1987.

71 Charles Spencer, *Daily Telegraph*, 27 February 1979.

72 Michael Billington, *Guardian*, 18 April 1979.

73 Alastair Macaulay, *Financial Times*, 26 November 2001

74 Benedict Nightingale, *The Times* (London), 26 November 2001.

75 Taylor, *Independent*, 28 November 2001.

76 Rachel Halliburton, *Evening Standard*, 23 November 2001.

77 Dominic Cavendish, Daily Telegraph, 24 November 2001.
78 Taylor, *Independent*, 28 November 2001.
79 Cavendish, *Daily Telegraph*, 24 November 2001.
80 Nightingale, *The Times*, 26 November 2001.
81 Taylor, *Independent*, 28 November 2001.
82 Michael Billington, *Guardian*, 8 August 2003.
83 Susanna Clapp, *Observer*, 24 September 2006.
84 Fiona Mountford, *Evening Standard*, 26 September 2006.
85 Dominic Cavendish, *Daily Telegraph*, 26 September 2006.
86 Kate Bassett, *Independent on Sunday*, 1 October 2006.
87 Paul Taylor, *Independent*, 27 September 2006.
88 Michael Billington, *Guardian*, 22 September 2006.
89 Mountford, *Evening Standard*, 26 September 2006.
90 Sam Marlowe, *The Times* (London), 25 September 2006.
91 Clapp, *Observer*, 24 September 2006.
92 Billington, *Guardian*, 22 September 2006.
93 Jack Tinker, *Daily Mail*, 5 June 1974.
94 Billington, *Guardian*, 5 June 1974.
95 Irving Wardle, *The Times* (London), 5 June 1974.
96 Wardle, *The Times*, 5 June 1974.
97 Harriet Walter in *Players of Shakespeare* 3, ed. Russell Jackson and Robert Smallwood (1993).
98 Billington, *Guardian*, 18 April 1979.
99 Charles Spencer, *Daily Telegraph*, 27 February 1997.
100 Rhoda Koenig, *Independent*, 8 August 2003.
101 *Sunday Times* (London), 17 August 2003.
102 Emma Fielding in a question and answer session at the Shakespeare Institute in 2003.
103 Kate Kellaway, *Observer*, 10 August 2003.
104 Harriet Walter in *Players of Shakespeare* 3, pp. 202–3.
105 *The Stage*, 18 July 1962.
106 *Daily Worker*, 17 July 1962.
107 *Birmingham Mail*, 18 July 1962.
108 Clive Barnes, *Daily Express*, 18 July 1962.
109 J. C. Trewin, *Birmingham Post*, 18 July 1962.
110 Dennis Barker, *Express and Star*, 18 July 1962.
111 Colin Frame, *Evening News*, 18 July 1962.
112 Robert Muller, *Daily Mail*, 18 July 1962.
113 B. A. Young, *Financial Times*, 5 June 1974.
114 Wardle, *The Times*, 5 June 1974.
115 Barber, *Daily Telegraph*, 5 June 1974.
116 Norah Lewis, *Birmingham Evening Mail*, 18 April 1979.
117 Billington, *Guardian*, 18 April 1979.
118 Billington, *Guardian*, 18 April 1979.
119 Billington, *Guardian*, 18 April 1979.
120 Irving Wardle, *The Times* (London), 14 November 1987.
121 Rissik, *Independent*, 14 November 1987.
122 Harriet Walter in *Players of Shakespeare* 3.
123 Spencer, *Daily Telegraph*, 27 February 1997.
124 Charles Spencer, *Daily Telegraph*, 8 August 2003.
125 Spencer, *Daily Telegraph*, 8 August 2003.
126 Kellaway, *Observer*, 10 August 2003.

127 Clapp, *Observer*, 24 September 2006.
128 Dominic Cavendish, *Daily Telegraph*, 29 September 2006.
129 *The Stage*, 18 July 1962.
130 *Daily Worker*, 17 July 1962.
131 Billington, *Guardian*, 5 June 1974.
132 *Morning Star*, 18 April 1979.
133 Billington, *Guardian*, 18 April 1979.
134 Rissik, *Independent*, 14 November 1987.
135 Spencer, *Daily Telegraph*, 27 February 1997.
136 Kretzmer, *Daily Express*, 5 June 1974.
137 Irving Wardle, *The Times* (London), 5 June 1974.
138 Billington, *Guardian*, 18 April 1979.
139 B. A. Young, *Financial Times*, 18 April 1979.
140 *Birmingham Mail*, 18 July 1962.
141 Milton Shulman, *Evening Standard*, 17 July 1962.
142 *The Times* (London), 17 July 1962.
143 Michael Billington, *Guardian*, 14 November 1987.
144 Wardle, *The Times*, 14 November 1987.
145 Michael Billington, *Guardian*, 27 February 1997.

ACKNOWLEDGEMENTS AND PICTURE CREDITS

Preparation of '*Cymbeline* in Performance' was assisted by a generous grant from the CAPITAL Centre (Creativity and Performance in Teaching and Learning) of the University of Warwick for research in the RSC archive at the Shakespeare Birthplace Trust.

Thanks as always to our indefatigable and eagle-eyed copy-editor Tracey Day and to Ray Addicott for overseeing the production process with rigour and calmness.

Picture research by Michelle Morton. Grateful acknowledgement is made to the Shakespeare Birthplace Trust for assistance with picture research (special thanks to Helen Hargest) and reproduction fees.

Images of RSC productions are supplied by the Shakespeare Centre Library and Archive, Stratford-upon-Avon. This Library, maintained by the Shakespeare Birthplace Trust, holds the most important collection of Shakespeare material in the UK, including the Royal Shakespeare Company's official archive. It is open to the public free of charge.

For more information see www.shakespeare.org.uk.

1. Ellen Terry (1896) Reproduced by permission of the Shakespeare Birthplace Trust.
2. Directed by Peter Hall (1957) Angus McBean © Royal Shakespeare Company
3. Directed by Bartlett Sher (2001) Malcolm Davies © Shakespeare Birthplace Trust
4. Directed by Adrian Noble (1997) Malcolm Davies © Shakespeare Birthplace Trust

FROM THE ROYAL SHAKESPEARE COMPANY
AND MACMILLAN

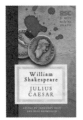

William Shakespeare
JULIUS CAESAR

William Shakespeare
THE MERRY WIVES OF WINDSOR

William Shakespeare
THE COMEDY OF ERRORS

William Shakespeare
CORIOLANUS

MORE HIGHLIGHTS IN THE RSC SHAKESPEARE SERIES

William Shakespeare
MEASURE FOR MEASURE

William Shakespeare
THE TAMING OF THE SHREW

William Shakespeare
RICHARD II

William Shakespeare
TROILUS & CRESSIDA

William Shakespeare
AS YOU LIKE IT

William Shakespeare
HENRY V

William Shakespeare
TWELFTH NIGHT

William Shakespeare
THE MERCHANT OF VENICE

William Shakespeare
THE TEMPEST

William Shakespeare
HAMLET

William Shakespeare
A MIDSUMMER NIGHT'S DREAM

William Shakespeare
LOVE'S LABOUR'S LOST

William Shakespeare
RICHARD III

William Shakespeare
ROMEO AND JULIET

William Shakespeare
THE WINTER'S TALE

William Shakespeare
MACBETH

William Shakespeare
OTHELLO

William Shakespeare
ANTONY AND CLEOPATRA

William Shakespeare
MUCH ADO ABOUT NOTHING

AVAILABLE IN ALL GOOD BOOKSHOPS OR TO ORDER ONLINE
VISIT:
www.rscshakespeare.co.uk